OLD
STONE
PRESS

DAVID A. JONES Always Moving Forward
By David A. Jones
with Bob Hill

Editors: David A. Jones, Jr. and Jill Johnson Keeney
Book design: Julia Comer

For information about special discounts for bulk purchases
or autographed copies of this book, please contact
John Clark, Old Stone Press at john@oldstonepress.com

Library of Congress Control Number: 2023902439
ISBN: 978-1-938462-63-4 (hardcover with dustjacket)
ISBN: 978-1-938462-64-1 (eBook)

Published by
Old Stone Press,
an imprint of J. H. Clark & Associates, Inc.
Louisville, Kentucky 40207
www.oldstonepress.com

Printed in U.S.A.

*For the friends, colleagues, and family
without whom none of the accomplishments described in this book
would have occurred—or been any fun.*

"It is common sense to take a method and try it. If it fails, admit it frankly and try another. But above all, try something."

FRANKLIN DELANO ROOSEVELT, May 1932

"Look out! Here comes T-Model Tommy!"

T-Model Tommy
by STEPHEN MEADER, 1938

DAVID A. JONES

Always
Moving Forward

with

Bob Hill

OLD
STONE
PRESS

TABLE OF CONTENTS

Foreword

NEVER FAR FROM HOME

by Bob Hill

"As a creature of American fiction, the successful business executive is often not a pleasant person. Sacrificing friends, family, love, and principles in his lust for success, he is depicted as outwardly brutal, inwardly empty, having killed off even his capacity for joy. Rich, powerful, alone at the top.

"On the other hand, there is David Jones."

Courier Journal columnist JOHN ED PEARCE, 1980

Humana co-founder David Allen Jones is wearing casual black shoes and slacks, a slightly wrinkled Parklands of Floyds Fork shirt, and his ever-present confident smile. He is standing on an empty lot, once the site of his small, crowded boyhood home at 1737 Garland Avenue in Louisville, Kentucky.

We had come to visit and talk about a place—even a time—that he had never really left: this neighborhood, this home site, who he was, who he became. His roots were here in blue-collar West Louisville, where his dreams began in the 1930s. The many neighborhood problems that needed changing then are still here now.

The stories of home included his part-time jobs: pumping gas at all-night stations, handing out hundreds of flyers door-to-door, and repairing and replacing windows with his father. He told of the old-world grocery stores whose owners gave the needy neighborhood credit, the local saloons serving take-home beer in a bucket, the poker games in back rooms.

His life's memories are vivid, heartfelt, and picture-perfect. He can just as easily tell of his father's backyard vegetable garden on Garland Avenue as his later experience walking the debris-littered streets of New York on 9/11 as the city crashed down around him.

He can repeat these stories almost word-for-word: his grandmother's big house and ready kitchen; a favorite schoolteacher; his Golden Gloves career; moving on to college and the Navy; becoming a millionaire in one day on Wall Street; his phone call from President George H. W. Bush asking if he could do something about the entire failed Romanian medical system.

On this day, standing on green grass that fronts a cyclone fence and what's now a Louisville distillery parking lot, he begins with tales of the old neighborhood.

It was from here that his mother, Elsie Thurman Jones, would begin raising six children. The daughter of an Irish immigrant, Elsie worked nights in a downtown Louisville laundry to help support her family.

Elsie would pull a wagon along the 1.5 miles of city sidewalks to Parkland Library, returning with books for her children, who were never allowed to miss a day of school or church on Sunday.

On some trips, four-year-old David would join her, helping to pull the wagon, a living metaphor that would identify him for the next eighty-four years.

David's father, Evan Logan Jones—a carpenter and handyman—was unemployed for years during the Depression, a common reality in their blue-collar world of narrow, boxy homes, small yards, and cheap front porches, with many of those houses rented. Their neighborhood commonality was that if everyone is poor, no one really feels poor.

It was from here that David, along with his much-admired older brother, Evan Logan Jones, Jr., would walk the several miles to downtown Louisville, hiding from the railroad cops as they crossed the nearby train yards, passing without incident through the nearby black neighborhoods of a very segregated city, but always taking notice of its limits and boundaries—and the very separate lives of people on each side of those boundaries.

It was from this neighborhood that David spent days in nearby city parks. He played basketball and football in public schools and still lived at home while attending the University of Louisville on a Navy ROTC scholarship. After graduation in 1954, David proudly served three years, often at sea, while bringing his natural leadership to the fore. He called it the best experience of his life.

It was from this neighborhood that he met and married Betty Lee Ashbury, a pharmacist's daughter and a fellow U of L student who became his lifelong supporter and equal partner.

David and Betty were both excellent students. They married in July 1954, soon after his college graduation. They were married for sixty-five years. While David was earning a law degree at Yale University, they lived three years in a metal coal-heated Quonset hut in New Haven, Connecticut. They returned to Louisville with two small children, a law firm job, and no money.

David supplemented his first-year law firm wages working nights teaching business and accounting courses. He and Betty, later a French teacher at U of L and Jefferson Community College, would raise five very successful children with old-school values demonstrated daily. Family always came first.

It was in 1961, when he was barely thirty, that he and fellow lawyer Wendell Cherry, himself only twenty-six, each borrowed $1,000 to build a nursing home.

That led to the pair forming what became Extendicare, Inc., the nation's largest nursing home chain, then Humana Inc., the world's biggest hospital chain and, later, an insurance giant. A great American success story.

It was Jones who decided to move from hospitals to insurance at a time when hospitals were much more profitable. Humana's insurance revenues were $21.4 billion in 2006, the year after he retired, up from $2.9 billion just before the hospital and insurance businesses split in 1993. When

3

he died in 2019, consolidated revenues were $64.9 billion, with 46,000 employees and nearly seventeen million insurance members. In 2023, the company was ranked fortieth in the Fortune 500.

Along the way, he also created Main Street Realty, a Louisville real estate development company. Main Street's talented team supported his civic work in affordable housing, adaptive reuse of historic buildings, advocacy around government and private projects, land acquisition, and the creation of public parks. This while quietly developing industrial, commercial, and residential real estate projects of great quality and value, including the warehouse out of which UPS delivered Covid-19 vaccines worldwide during the pandemic.

With Humana, each early growth step was carefully measured. Everything they were doing was new and required a learning process, but they forged ahead anyway, as David gently explained, "in the confidence of total ignorance." He summarized his very successful business philosophy like this: "Clarity of purpose and superiority of execution."

When Humana was criticized for "making profits off the sick" at a time when hospitals were mostly religious-based and non-profit, an irritated David Jones always had a ready answer: Humana offered better medical services at lower prices and paid taxes.

Along with the hospital growth, he and Wendell led the much-needed rebirth of downtown Louisville, including a new performing arts center, sprawling waterfront park, and classic Humana Building headquarters, a study in pink granite.

They supported public and private education at home and across the country. They created the world's first center for artificial hearts. Then David helped create and fund his final enduring legacy, the multi-purpose, 4,000-acre, environmentally secure Parklands of Floyds Fork at Louisville's eastern edge, whose existence David Jones proudly advertised almost daily with the logo on his shirts.

Yet standing in his old neighborhood in casual pants and shoes and said shirt, David Allen Jones is not given to talking about such successes. He never was.

He and Betty, who, between personal gifts and family and corporate foundations, have donated hundreds of millions of dollars to worthy causes—many of them educational—didn't want the Jones name attached to any of it.

That sincere modesty was part of their lives. Both kept their old friends and met them regularly for lunches, family travel, and book clubs. They stayed in, prayed in, and financially supported their Highland Presbyterian Church, living by the mantra: "You don't pray in public."

David drove slightly used cars to work, enjoyed eating at White Castle, and joked that he preferred his Timex watch over a Rolex because "it glowed in the dark." But not all his tastes were so humble. Later in his business life, he developed a strong taste for the most modern jet aircraft. But that, he said, was essential to building a big company with far-flung operations while still participating in his family's day-to-day life. And David fulfilled those goals at first with much more modest, propeller-driven aircraft taking off from a central Kentucky farm field.

I was a newspaper columnist and features writer for the *Louisville Times* and *Courier Journal* for thirty-three years, traveling thousands of miles across the state and southern Indiana, writing eight books and more than 4,000 columns and stories. Yet I had met Jones only twice.

The first time was the June 2, 1985, dedication of the Humana Building, the twenty-six-floor, pink-granite, pyramid style, Wendell-Cherry-led and Michael-Graves-designed building that dared to be so different in a world of aluminum box architecture.

I had written a column praising the building and its success in challenging the architects of future Louisville buildings to be bold. David was at the dedication, surrounded by sunlight, towering glass, and granite. He thanked me for that and other newspaper columns I did not know he had read. He shook hands—a memorable bone-crushing hold—and smiled that smile.

Years later, at our next meeting, he would ask me to write about the lives and family histories of the people who owned the almost eighty separate parcels of land purchased to create The Parklands of Floyds Fork.

Many of them would be deeply personal and unique Kentucky stories dating back to the late 1700s and land once owned by Squire Boone, Daniel Boone's brother.

My Parklands writing project lasted almost four years. After that book was published, those family stories—and photographs—would go to the Filson Historical Society to be kept forever. David Jones always wanted to preserve more than property.

We met often in his large, welcoming office to discuss those stories, the family histories that would someday become part of the Parklands book.

His office shelves were lined with dozens of photos of friends and family. He could sit back in his chair and talk for hours, careful and comfortable with his words but always willing to listen to mine. I always came away from our discussions feeling better than when I went in. He was leader enough to know that once he put his faith in you, there was no way you would want to disappoint him.

He asked me to help with this book while I was finishing writing those histories of the families along Floyds Fork. Our final agreement was more a handshake than any formal legal agreement.

Knowing his preference for short, incisive memos, I put together a short list of ideas for the book, some we had already discussed. They included writing of his business success, but only as told through family, friends, and co-workers. His book would include his business principles and life's observations. I suggested I would begin the writing process, but any final product would be all his.

I interviewed Betty Jones at their Poplar Hill family estate, with its 8,000 square-foot hillside home she and David had designed. It sat on forty-three acres east of downtown Louisville, a family escape with a tennis court, swimming pool, fountains, gardens, brick walkway, and iron fencing, all of it more welcoming than imposing.

Betty and I talked about their journey, her memory equal to her husband's, her quiet confidence and sense of family firmly in place. David had joked that with five children, the Poplar Hill house's many bedrooms and baths were a direct response to the limited number he grew up with.

During my many interviews with him, the bond between us grew into more than a mutual respect for our different abilities. We had lived shared lives in separate places. I grew up one of five kids in a small, rented, boxy house in a blue-collar neighborhood a block from the local stockyards. I shared our tiny bedroom with two younger brothers. They slept in a two-level bunk bed, while I—being six feet four inches—slept in a six-foot rollaway bed all through high school. We had our part-time jobs.

Our very caring Irish mother—the family storyteller, keeper of lore, and frequent dispenser of Band-Aids—had worked part-time as a waitress to pay the bills. Our father was an engineer, a thinker who loved beer and a good argument. But with only two years of college, he had limited opportunities at mediocre companies. At one point, he had worked part-time at a gas station to pay the bills.

As with the Jones family, book reading was a religion in our house. We made frequent trips to the library, many on foot. Education and family mattered. Four of us graduated from college. That was the family law. We didn't feel poor. We were just waiting for our chance.

David and Betty Jones would provide thousands of students with that same chance. David was always a forward-looking man, an endless optimist, a man who once said he could accomplish anything he set his mind to. There is ample evidence he succeeded.

My initial assignment on this book was to interview about twenty of David's old friends, co-workers, and family members, a number that grew to about forty. He insisted they had all contributed to his success, and this book had to be about them, too.

His list included family; grade school, high school, and college friends; neighbors, bankers, business associates, environmentalists; local, state, and national politicians; the educators he had helped; and the black activists and ministers he funded in continually trying to restore his old, ever-more-segregated and struggling neighborhood.

There were mentions of his kindness, his temper, his honesty, and his willingness to listen; that stubborn streak that appeared when he knew he was right; that readiness to just take over a meeting when necessary;

his competitive need to play knock-down, in-your-face YMCA basketball, handball, or racquetball and forget all that when the game was over.

No one interviewed said anything truly bad about him. One person who had worked with him on several transformational philanthropic projects went so far as to say, "I think he may be the most important Kentuckian ever." I would joke about those things and call him "Saint David"— a description he would take with a smile. Then he ordered me to "keep looking."

We continued to meet as the book moved forward, but he would also respond with personal notes. Over his life, he would send thousands of such personal, handwritten "Thank you" notes, most of them treasured by the recipients. I kept all mine in a separate folder.

We began serious work on his book in 2016. David remained very busy with civic duties, travel, private Main Street Realty ventures, and, in partnership with his son Dan, creating The Parklands of Floyds Fork, his ultimate legacy.

His wish continued to be to include as many people as possible, which required more interviews. Our meetings remained moments of living history, and as we got into 2019, a publishing date seemed close. Then he was diagnosed with multiple myeloma. His work on the book slowed, although he kept it at his bedside during treatment.

We would never meet again. Betty Jones, who also had health issues, died on August 16, 2019, at eighty-six. Dealing with her loss, and multiple myeloma, David Jones died just a month later, on September 18, 2019, at eighty-eight.

It took almost a year for the family to recover, to mourn as needed, and to begin again to fully honor David Jones, as we all wanted, by finishing this book.

This, then, is his story.

—BOB HILL, June 2023

Part I

THE EARLY YEARS

Previous page:
Yale, 1960, with Betty, Sue, and Dave.

Chapter One

GARLAND AVENUE

"Everybody in the neighborhood was in the same shape, so we didn't feel poor."

— DAVID JONES

I n the late 1930s, with the nation deep in the Depression, my mom, Elsie Thurman Jones, would load a wagon full of books and pull it from the family home at 1737 Garland Avenue to Louisville's Parkland Library, more than a mile away.

Our family's small, frame, camelback home had three rooms and a bath downstairs, and two small bedrooms upstairs, giving it a hump-like appearance. The house was part of a parade of small, frame, blue-collar homes in the middle of California, an area bounded by Broadway, Oak Street, Ninth, and Twenty-Sixth Streets in Louisville, Kentucky.

Settled by German immigrants around 1849—the time of the California Gold Rush—its original name was "Henderson Subdivision." It became "California" because, as the local jesters said, it was so far west of Louisville its settlers were people just hoping to head out to California someday to get rich.

Mom and my dad, Evan Logan Jones, would have six children. Dad was a gardener, steel worker, carpenter, and handyman who struggled to find work during the Depression.

To check out library books for herself and her family, Mom would pull her wagon along city sidewalks and across intersections for more than a mile to the solid-brick Carnegie-endowed library. The words "Free to All" were engraved above its arching windows. She would return a wagon full of books, then load up more.

At times in the late 1930s, Mom worked nights in a laundry. When she was free, her Saturday missions were to return books checked out the previous week and haul another batch home. Her book load grew over the years. Every time another child was born, she qualified for another library card—and more books for her growing family.

I would walk with her on many of those trips, helping her pull the wagon. Some days, my brother Logan, born in 1929 and two years older, would accompany Mom.

The daughter of an Irish immigrant, Mom was one of eight children: Seven finished college. Family and education were always the most important things in her life. Her children were never allowed to miss a day of school.

Never.

Always the educator and role model—she was brilliant and fearless—Mom would pick out some of the well-worn books for her children. The Depression-era library shelves were thinly stacked. As we grew older, the classics would become our favorites—*The Adventures of Tom Sawyer* and *The Adventures of Huckleberry Finn*. We would pick out other books, too, then pull them home in the wagon.

I liked biographies and adventure tales. I remember one book, *T-Model Tommy*, by Stephen W. Meader, a popular novel for children. *T-Model Tommy* was published in 1938, during the Depression. It told the tale of feisty, red-headed Tom Ballard, a recent high school graduate trying to find ways to get ahead and support his widowed mother.

By mowing lawns and working odd jobs, Tommy saved enough money to buy an ancient Model-T pickup truck. Keeping his truck running, he began hauling coal, blueberries, furniture, mushroom soil, gravel, and produce. Through hard work, resourcefulness, and horse-trading trucks along the way, he worked his way up to a Ford V8 and well beyond, eventually creating a trucking empire.

Tommy became a hands-on, risk-taking success. He was smart, resourceful, and as tough as he needed to be. His story was a sprawling tale that would include strikers, hijackers, highway patrols, gangsters, and a high-school football teammate who went off to Yale, then began competing for Tommy's girlfriend. Tommy had no fear of failure because he had started with nothing and thus had nothing to lose—a mantra I would come to live by.

I won't say that was a story that turned me into an entrepreneur, but it was the one that gave me the idea that you can start small and end up big.

Elsie Thurman Jones's love of education came from her mother, Jessie America O'Bryan Thurman. Jessie was born in America in 1885 or perhaps on the boat on the way over as her family emigrated from Ireland. Either way, the "America" in her name was a celebration of that journey and a sign of things to come.

Grandma Jessie became a schoolteacher in Bullitt County, south of Louisville, and married Clarence Younger Thurman, a supervisor at American Tobacco Company, the father of their eight children.

My mom was the second oldest, born in 1910 in Mount Washington, Kentucky. She attended Louisville Normal School, a two-year teachers' college, and married Evan Logan Jones during her second year. She was never allowed to teach in Louisville because married women were prohibited from teaching in its public schools prior to World War II.

Dad came from a long-settled and storied Kentucky family. Born in 1901 in Shelby County, he was distantly related to Alex McIntyre, who served with Kentucky frontiersman Simon Kenton, a friend of Daniel Boone, and Isaac Shelby, a soldier in the Revolutionary War and the War of 1812. Shelby was Kentucky's first governor.

Education was important in my dad's family, too. Two of his three brothers became lawyers and the third an engineer. My dad hadn't gone to college because he went into the Army right after high school, serving at the very end of World War I. His brother Charlie had been on a ship that was torpedoed on the way to the war, but was rescued. After the war, my father joined the Army National Guard, a role that became important in his future. He liked to read, earned a living with his hands, and strongly supported his family's education.

I never really got to know my dad's parents. My paternal grandmother died before I was born. My paternal grandfather lived with our family for a time but died when I was about four.

I attended kindergarten at the former Parkland Elementary School, a two- and three-story brick school with a peaked roof, turret, circular windows, and a white picket fence.

For first grade and half of second grade, I attended Brandeis Elementary School, a broad, distinctive structure at Twenty-Sixth and Kentucky Streets built in the Tudor Revival architectural style. It eventually landed on the National Register of Historic Places and became a fifty-unit apartment complex with a community learning center and garden.

I was always an excellent student, a leader, a good athlete whose competitive nature became evident at an early age in neighborhood games of football, basketball, baseball, and, when required, schoolyard fights.

The fights were fierce—knock somebody down, get on top, and keep flailing. But the fury rarely lasted. You would fight one day and forget it the next.

I remember Brandeis well because of my second-grade teacher, Miss Shauntz. I once did something to upset her, and she threw a hard rubber eraser at me. I had good reflexes, so I ducked, and it missed me and hit the girl behind me right in the eye, creating quite a stir. I remember that very well because I got blamed.

I also remember the most cataclysmic event in Louisville history— the 1937 flood, which drowned an already depressed city at a time when there was little state or federal help. Escape and recovery depended on the kindness of good neighbors, if not strangers.

Nineteen inches of rain fell on the city in January, with fifteen inches falling January 13–24. The waters crested at thirty feet above flood stage. Seventy percent of Louisville was buried—including the California neighborhood—with 175,000 residents, more than half the city's population, forced to flee. The river of ruin stretched from Pittsburgh to Cairo, Illinois, with one million homeless, 385 dead, $250 million in losses, and long years of recovery.

I was then five years old, living with my family in a small one-story house at 2234 Garland Avenue, now a vacant lot. My dad was working for General Box Company at Fourteenth and Maple Streets. The company sent a truck to evacuate us, and we stayed with another family. The Louisville newspapers were full of photos of desperate people sitting on rooftops or packed tightly into rescue rowboats.

When we returned to our house, I'd say the water had been within three or four feet of our ceiling. My dad, in the National Guard in those days, was on duty during the flood. We would see him every now and then in a rowboat down the street someplace.

In 1938, Dad lost his job at General Box. The family moved a few blocks to a more modest home at 1737 Garland Avenue. The rent at 2234 Garland had been $25 a month. It would be $15 a month for the new house. The home was owned by the Eckerle family, a close-knit, friendly bunch that owned a grocery store near Parkland Junior High School. Each month Logan or I would walk to the store carrying the $15 rent money and get a free piece of candy as a bonus.

There were now four siblings at home—Logan, Jr., born in 1929; me, born in 1931; Charles, born in 1934; and Lucy, born in 1938. Two more children would follow, Jean in 1941 and Clarence in 1944.

We four Jones boys slept in one room upstairs, the sisters in the other. Our parents would sleep downstairs in the middle room—a dining room by day.

Our family always entered the house through the side door. The front room—its door always locked—was kept tidy in case the minister showed up on a surprise visit. The kitchen and bathroom were in the back, with the small back porch overlooking Dad's garden.

We didn't have a refrigerator. Blocks of ice were delivered in horse-drawn wagons, along with bread from the Donaldson Bakery and milk from Von Allman's Dairy. The sights—if not smells—of the deliveries were as memorable as the "clip-clop clip-clop" of the sturdy horses.

We bought our groceries at Weller's, a nearby store that extended credit. You paid what you could afford at the time, the rest later. When the money got too tight and our electricity was cut off, another option was a store that sold kerosene at seven cents a gallon. At home, it would be poured—carefully—into a cooking stove and lanterns.

The neighborhood shopping area was at Eighteenth Street and Garland, with the nearby Dawn Bakery and Schreiber's pharmacy being the most practical and necessary stops. One Saturday morning a month, Mom, with one child in tow, would take a streetcar downtown to pay the water, gas, and electric bills. While there, she put one dollar a week in the family's Christmas savings account at the bank, which didn't draw any interest.

Mom would occasionally shop at the downtown department stores, Ben Snyder's or Bacon's, putting clothes on layaway. She'd always treat whoever was accompanying her to an ice cream sundae or a milkshake.

Occasionally, she treated us to a movie at one of the downtown theaters—Loews, the Strand, or the Kentucky. Closer to home were the Parkland Theatre and Oak Theatre, with all their cowboy movies and the Zorro serial. (The hero was always on the edge of some magnificent death but somehow reappeared hale and hearty the following week.)

On summer days, Dad occasionally offered his sons a rare treat: a trip to see the Louisville Colonels. They were the minor league professional baseball team that played at Parkway Field off Eastern Parkway, now part of the University of Louisville. Louisville's Pee Wee Reese played for the 1938 Colonels, and Babe Ruth occasionally appeared in exhibition games.

They had what they called the Knothole Gang, where we kids got in for practically nothing. The tickets probably cost a quarter, and I know we had to take three separate streetcars to get there.

My mind was always on athletics. The family yard was only twenty-five feet wide, much of it devoted to Dad's vegetable garden, so we played

18

games in other places. I would ride my bike down to Shawnee Park in the summer to play baseball in a league sponsored by Campbell-Summerhayes Lumber Company, a community-oriented retail and wholesale firm.

I played at nearby Victory Park, a busy neighborhood landmark and kid magnet two blocks long and one block deep. It had an ice cream shop on one corner. We kids would show up in the morning and stay all day, our parents never worrying about us. We all knew the neighborhood; each child had many watchful parents.

Softball games were a problem because someone was always hitting the ball into the streets, but few in the neighborhood owned a car anyway. I never saw a tennis racquet or a golf club in the neighborhood, but I would go on to play both sports. There was a beautiful golf course at Shawnee Park, but I never played there.

In the fall, we kids played tackle football with fierce adolescent intensity, no helmets or pads, and some inevitable flesh-and-bone damage. In such neighborhood turf wars, the players were selected in a time-honored pecking order of size, age, enthusiasm, and leadership. I soon moved near the top of the list.

Everybody knew everybody, so if you did something wrong, your mom heard about it before you got home. We never did anything terrible.

In one memorable incident, I was sent as a "Royal Ambassador" for two weeks to Camp Clear Creek, a fundamentalist Christian camp in eastern Kentucky. I was nine years old. Along the way, we were able to buy an ice cream cone that had three dips for a nickel. It was the highlight of the trip.

Not only did they have multiple church services, which wasn't bad, but they wanted me to rededicate my life. And I said, "I can't. I've never dedicated my life." I didn't know what they were talking about.

And they wouldn't let me go swimming until I rededicated my life. So for two weeks down there, I never got to go swimming.

Dad remained unemployed from 1938 through 1941. He was not alone.

There wasn't a man living on our block who had a steady job. The only automobile parked on Garland from Eighteenth to Twenty-Sixth Streets had "Morton Salt" written on the side—a salesman with a job owned it.

Almost every tavern in the area came with a bookie—someone who tended bar with a telephone and pencil handy, or who would come by every day knocking on doors to collect bets or make payoffs.

There was Henley's Saloon at Seventeenth and Garland, where out-of-work men hung out in mutual desperation and support. A pitcher of beer cost a dime, with a hard-boiled egg to come with it.

My mom didn't allow beer or anything alcoholic in the house, so my dad would go down to Henley's. When it was dinner time, I'd often run down there—or my brother would—and tell him it was time to come home. He didn't have enough money to do much drinking, but in the evenings in those days, you could send a seven-year-old boy down to get a pitcher of beer, and he could carry it home.

Everybody in the neighborhood was in the same shape, so we didn't feel poor. Our family dug in. Mom worked the night shift at Spalding Laundry on Twelfth Street. She walked a half-mile to work, crossing four train tracks on the way. The company would send her home by taxi at two, three, or four o'clock in the morning.

On some Saturdays, she walked downtown to work as a salesclerk at Kaufmann Strauss Department Store on Fourth Street, a Louisville institution from 1879 to 1969. Kaufmann Straus paid on commission, so in the Depression, sometimes Mom would work all Saturday and not sell anything. But she made a little bit of money. On her off days, she would walk the kids to the library.

Our family's politics were mixed. Mom was a staunch Democrat; Dad was a strong Republican. Both would get up very early to read the morning paper. Mom always made sure her children were up, fed breakfast, and off to school afterward.

Family income picked up in 1942 when Dad got a job across the Ohio River in Jeffersonville, Indiana, at Jeffboat, a company founded in 1834 as the Howard Ship Yards to build some of the great paddle wheel boats on the Ohio and Mississippi. Purchased by the US Navy in 1942, it produced 123 LSTs (Landing Ship, Tank) and twenty-three submarine chasers for World War II combat. The men who had to ride those LSTs to shore under heavy fire in the Pacific islands or the beaches of Normandy always thought LST meant "long slow trip."

Once at Jeffboat, Dad bought a 1930 Model A Ford and would pick up three other workers every day, taking them to work and back. Shipbuilding was tough, four-season outdoor work—welding, bolting, and hammering steel into place, with extra-long hours added for the war effort in rain, snow, or sunshine.

Then in his 40s, Dad was dealing with ear problems related to his job. He was not called to active duty but served as the neighborhood air raid warden. My dad was a very peaceful man. What is true of my family is we grew up without any resources but with a lot of love.

Mom was the disciplinarian, the parent who set the rules and the consequences. Along with family, she also did what she could to help the neighbors, including cooking meals for months for the family of a woman dying of cancer.

We lived directly across the street from the National Casket Company. An elderly lady lived in an apartment above it. On Mom's orders, Logan or I would carry coal up to her and fill the stove to keep her apartment warm every winter morning and afternoon, then take away the ashes.

Church was the social center of our lives. Every Sunday morning, Mom would lead her children on the walk to Calvary Baptist Church for the regular service and Sunday school. We would return on Sunday night for a service at the Baptist Young People's Union. Thomas Jefferson Barksdale was our preacher, and sometimes he'd get so excited that his false teeth would fall out!

The church also had prayer meetings on Wednesday nights. Just one of the kids was required to go, but Mom never missed.

Dad never attended church with his family. He would stay home and prepare a large Sunday dinner, much of it from his garden. He'd cook chuck roast or some other inexpensive cut of meat, add noodles and potatoes, and the result was a rare treat.

Like their politics, the family's religion had become mixed, adding an early ecumenical outlook to my life. When Grandmother Jessie America O'Bryan, an Irish Catholic, married Clarence Thurman, a Protestant, she was read out of the Catholic Church, but our family was happy with the Baptist side of life.

Church and Sunday dinners were a big deal, the regular bonding of the Jones family no matter what else was going on—a tradition that continues to this day. We had a strong religious upbringing. I don't know how well it took, but knowing right from wrong was crystal clear in my family and our neighborhood. My mom and dad tithed their meager resources throughout their lives. That was a given.

I learned from that. Later, when my income was high, Betty and I more than gave away our income every year. My experience has been the more you give away, the more you get.

✳

During World War II, my older brother, Logan, and I helped pick up the slack in the family's income. We would do odd jobs, mow the neighbors' grass with a push mower for thirty-five cents, and go door-to-door selling magazine subscriptions—a competitive neighborhood business in the best of times.

Logan was the leader in so many ways, the glue that held the family together, and so much of what I was able to accomplish later was literally following in his footsteps. We would go door to door, passing out handbills for Froelich Heating Company, a firm owned by Max Froelich, who had married our mother's sister Thelma. Our work ethic was established early. Froelich paid us only one dollar to deliver 1,000 handbills.

In those days, we didn't have a bank or checking account. If we had to make a telephone call, we'd walk to Grandma Thurman's house. Logan and I sold *Collier's* and *Look* magazines, and it was a hard sell. They cost about a dime, but nobody had any money.

We were allowed to keep any money we made, and I remember one time we finished up on the Loop on Bardstown Road, a long way from our house, and there was a Woolworth's store. We went in and bought Mom a set of mixing bowls. She was so surprised and happy.

Logan was always busy. He dropped out of school at sixteen and started working, so he didn't get a chance to play sports in high school, but as fast and strong as he was, he would have been terrific. After he dropped out, he bought a car. I think it was a 1938 Cadillac, a great big one that had a window that rolled up between the front and back seats.

Then he bought a 1947 Chevrolet, and when he went off to the Korean War, he left the car with me. I guess he'd saved all his Army money because he traded in that car when he returned and bought a new one, which was unique to our family. None of us had ever had a new car before.

Later, when I graduated from Yale, Logan had a little English car of some sort and brought my mom and two other family members up there in that little car, which was really, really nice. My memories of growing up and of Logan are all about how everybody helped each other, plus the fact I was always trying to keep up with him.

Our time together also gave Logan and me a firsthand look at Louisville neighborhoods, an education in itself. When we worked for Max Froelich passing out handbills, he would pick us up and drop us off in Germantown, in the Highlands, or someplace, giving us carfare home. Logan would go down one side of the street, and I would go down the other, and at the end of the day, instead of spending the carfare, we would walk back home. Those walks gave us a stark view of Louisville's strict racial segregation in the 1930s and '40s. Decades later, I would remember that in my commitment to my old neighborhood.

The lines were clear: from Fifteenth Street west, everybody was white. East of Fifteenth Street, the neighborhood was mostly black. Earlier in Louisville history, attempts were made to declare such segregation legal. The city fathers passed a law in 1914 forbidding black people from owning—or occupying—homes in a majority-white neighborhood. An NAACP challenge reached the US Supreme Court, which unanimously ruled the law unconstitutional in 1917.

All-black neighborhoods were the norm, even as the city's black population rose from about 47,000 in 1930 to 57,000 in 1950—about 15 percent of all Louisville residents. But the Depression raised the black unemployment rate from about 12 percent to 37 percent, with many African Americans living in the California neighborhood.

The neighborhood would be the scene of race riots following the 1968 assassination of Dr. Martin Luther King, Jr. Two people died, and 427 were arrested. Subsequent anti-school-busing demonstrations in 1975 added to the tension.

With white flight, the California neighborhood had become about 90 percent black by the 1990s—creating economic, social, and educational issues I would later respond to as a person who could make a difference.

※

Throughout the 1940s, Logan and I would walk three days a week from Garland Avenue to the YMCA at Third Street and Broadway in downtown Louisville for basketball, swimming, track, and gymnastics. The journey would take us through those black neighborhoods, where we never had a problem—and then over the fence at the L&N Railroad yards. We'd get chased by the railroad cops, but they couldn't catch us young kids.

I never heard a racial word in my life growing up. My mom and dad were accepting people and didn't seem bothered by their circumstances.

Logan and I would always find new ways to walk home from the Downtown YMCA. We would go by all the car dealerships, then along Broadway. The old train station near Ninth Street and Broadway was always busy as the war moved people in and out.

We didn't have two nickels to rub together. We'd walk by the Brown Hotel, put our faces up against the window, and look in at those elegant people eating there. I shot some pool at the neighborhood pool hall and had a friend who dealt the cards for the older generation in a back-room poker game.

There were neighborhood places to eat—Turner's Grill at Eighteenth and Kentucky Streets, where we teenaged boys would hang out, play pinochle, and tell stories, and the White Castle at Eighteenth Street and Broadway with its five-cent hamburgers—five for twenty cents when on sale. To tell you the truth, I don't even know if there was a real restaurant in our neighborhood. There were a lot of saloons and the hard-boiled eggs, but I don't think I ever ate in a restaurant until college.

As I grew older, our family often gathered at Grandma Jessie Thurman's house at 1365 Cypress Street—easy walking distance for kids with no other option. My granddad, Clarence, had managed to keep his job at American Tobacco during the Depression, providing some family security. Their two-story house, built in 1900, had a castle-like look made to create memories, with almost twenty windows that looked out in all directions and added to its charm.

All the Thurman children had interesting lives, many with a religious turn. Two boys became preachers; two of the daughters married preachers—one Baptist and one Methodist. The youngest brother, Clarence, graduated from high school in 1941, then flew B-17 bombers in World War II while still a teenager. He was shot down, spent fourteen and a half months in a German prison camp, then slowly recovered in hospitals and lived to age ninety-two.

The Thurman home was on a deep lot with two apple trees and a grape arbor—more fodder for my boyhood memories. In his 1940 campaign for his third term, President Roosevelt rode by in a train on tracks nearby, sitting in the back of the caboose, and I waved to him!

Grandma Jessie also raised chickens in the backyard. She would wring their necks, chop off their heads, and stick the carcasses in boiling water to remove the feathers. We'd help her pick off the feathers because we knew we were going to get some delicious fried chicken.

The family's frequent moves shuffled me from school to school. After

Brandeis, I continued my education through the sixth grade at California Elementary School, a three-story brick building with a silo-like structure that served as a fire escape. I was always among the first to finish my work and would be rewarded with a practice trip down the fire chute, a journey with a fun mission.

Every time it rained, the water would get inside the silo, and it would get rusty. So the teachers kept a potato sack handy, and I'd wear it while sliding down the chute to clear off the rust. We also had fire drills, where we'd all slide down. The boys would go first and then put their feet up against the wall to create a logjam, and the girls would start screaming.

I gravitated toward good teachers, and they adopted me. A favorite was my fourth and sixth-grade teacher, Mrs. Floor, a woman I remember as young, strong, slim, and pretty. She had a commanding presence—a trait I could appreciate and would try to emulate.

As I earned straight A's, always being first to get my work done, she gave me another timeless reward: a 1930s addition system called "ten by tens." Combined with "the rule of nines," it allowed me to execute complex computations quickly. I would use that skill for the rest of my life, performing math operations in my head. An excellent teacher can make a difference forever.

From 1943 to 1946, I attended Parkland Junior High School. My days all began the same. I would ride my Western Flyer bike over to Grandma Thurman's house, leave it in her yard, run in and give her a kiss, then walk the two blocks to school. After school, I would run errands for her, maybe to the local grocery store, and she would reward me with a slice of apple pie or a chicken drumstick.

I rarely got into trouble in school and was emerging as a leader, dealing with low-level turf wars and bullies. They were the result of students from five elementary schools—Parkland, Brandeis, Strother, McFerran, and California, the poorest—all feeding into Parkland.

The school fights, wild fist-swinging affairs with bare knuckles harking back to "Our Gang" movies, were inevitable. Always among the biggest of the students, I had an undefeated run at Parkland. I put down one challenger in a woodworking class on the first day of school. On the last day of school, I subdued another older kid, ending a long-simmering affair.

I played basketball at Parkland in a league with other junior high schools, returning to the gym at night to practice. I once scored thirty-three points in a game and was good enough to be quietly recruited to play at Manual High School.

I was also co-valedictorian of my class and delivered a graduation address. My one low grade in three years was a B plus in eighth-grade English, given to me by a substitute teacher who happened to be my aunt. I took this up with her, asking, "I earned an A. Why did you give me a B plus?" And she said, "I couldn't give an A to a relative."

Harold Gordon, a Parkland classmate, had his own school memories. He was the son of a Latvian immigrant, Irvin Gordon, whose father and siblings came to the United States in the early 1920s. Each of the seven sons started a neighborhood grocery store in a different section of the city, and each lived in an apartment above the store. That was the easiest way for a new immigrant to make a living and have a roof overhead with a steady source of food.

Chasing prosperity—and pushed out by the 1937 flood—Irvin Gordon moved his store four times, the last time not far from my parents' home. Gordon left his neighborhood mark in a special way: He was always willing to forgive the families that needed food and were unable to pay.

Harold Gordon recalled me as a kid the others looked up to—and the one who punched him in the mouth, knocking out a tooth. The punch came with provocation, and I threw it at Harold to impose discipline in a class that had been giving a teacher a hard time. The teacher, stressed with the class and anxious about her husband off at war, had put her head down on her desk and begun to cry. I was the peacemaker, but my mom had to come to school and straighten that out. But Harold and I remained friends all our lives.

I still recall other early friendships that were more in passing. Jimmy Mayes went on to be a Louisville police captain. Jimmy Flood, my co-valedictorian, became a salesman for a printing company. Alfred Plamp, nicknamed "Ears," was a friend from elementary school. Many years later, when Betty and I bought a house on Lowell Avenue and needed fireplace tongs, I heard Plamp sold them. Plamp and I hadn't seen each other in about fifteen years, but the old neighborhood bond held. When Betty went to buy the tongs, he remembered our friendship and wouldn't let her pay.

✳

On my final day of school at Parkland, only fourteen but soon to be fifteen, I talked my parents into letting me drive their Model A Ford to school. The one condition was that Logan had to ride with me. But I drove around the block, honking the horn.

Things were much the same when I drove myself to get my driver's license at sixteen. I took the family car to the testing station and easily passed the written test. When the examiner saw I had driven myself down for the driving test, he gave me a license without any behind-the-wheel bother.

During World War II, teenaged Logan and two of his friends bought a 1932 Nash. All the boys would tool around in it at night. The car's tires, worn thin in an era of strict rubber rationing, were rarely equal to the task.

We'd have a flat tire at least once a night. We carried a patching kit with us. We could break that tire down, get the inner tube out, fill it with air at a gas station, see where the leak was, put a hot patch on it, and off we'd go.

As World War II began to dominate everyone's life, the Jones family's connection to the military—which would also play a huge role in my life with three years of service in the US Navy—became more evident. Every neighbor had somebody off at war, and the country rationed food, gasoline, and car parts.

Mom loved Eleanor Roosevelt. She read her column in the newspaper, along with that of famed war correspondent Ernie Pyle, who wrote about the troops in combat—stories about the men and women from places like the California neighborhood. All the other war news, heavily censored, came from the radio or in newspapers being hawked on street corners.

＊

Despite Manual High School's interest in my athletic abilities, I chose to go to Male High because it was the school of my uncle Clarence Thurman, the bomber pilot shot down in World War II and then held in a German POW camp. It was almost as if I owed him something. Uncle Clarence was somebody I respected. I didn't even know Male was a college prep school.

Many of my old friends would go on to Manual, but the friendships I made at Male would also last a lifetime, as many became involved in my community work—a tradition among Male graduates.

My favorite teacher at Male was Harrell N. Teague, a Yale graduate who would astonish his English students by balancing on two legs of a chair while flipping their finished papers at them from across the room—papers on which each student had been ordered to write sentences using ten vocabulary words. On Fridays, we had to use all forty words in a theme.

Mr. Teague taught a lesson beyond the wonder of chair balancing. Throughout my personal and business life, I would come to appreciate—and demand—brief and concise writing, the right word in the right place at the right time.

At Male, I played basketball and football. It was challenging to play both because the last football game, the annual Male-Manual slugfest, wasn't played until Thanksgiving Day, cutting into basketball practice. In football, I was a linebacker, safety, and blocking back in single-wing formations. That was a style where they centered the ball to a tailback, with the blocking back leading the charge. It was in-your-face football.

My football career ended in my junior year when I was hit by a streetcar while riding my bike on Fourth Street. I was in the hospital for a few days, on crutches after that—and still bear the scars. But that accident led to my brief career as a Golden Gloves boxer.

Again, I was following my older brother, Logan, a Golden Gloves champion. We were trained by Joe Martin, who was a revered figure in Louisville boxing history: He later guided Cassius Clay to Olympic glory, setting the stage for Clay—better known as Muhammad Ali—to become the most recognizable person in the world.

Logan and I trained after school or after one of our many jobs. We worked out in the basement of the historic Columbia Gym, now part of the student center at Spalding University. We never lifted weights; our day jobs added the muscle. Our training was old school—running for miles and pelting punching bags. We would lie back on the floor as Martin and another coach, Stu Gibson, hurled medicine balls at our stomachs to tighten our abdominal muscles. Then came our turns to spar in the ring.

Logan fought at 135 pounds. My first bout was at 160 pounds, and then 175. Both weights were difficult to make, as my natural weight was 180 pounds. My only hope was to spend time in a sauna or steam room or do extra running. And you could even lose weight by spitting if you had to make your weight.

Outside of baseball, college and professional sports did not hold sway in Louisville in the post-World War II 1950s. The amateur and Golden Gloves fights were tough, old-school events, an extension of problem-solving that had begun with flying fists in the schoolyard after class. They drew crowds of over 1,600 into the snug Columbia Gym and even more on the road.

Martin, a former fighter himself, was a Louisville police officer, very sturdy, straightforward, and a strict disciplinarian. To him boxing was a craft, an art, not just hurling punches. I did well against many opponents because I could outbox them, out-think them, and dodge their heavy blows. The fights went three rounds, each lasting two minutes. The gloves of the day were much heavier than they are now, the punches more labored. The only time I ever got knocked down was sparring with my brother.

Louisville was heavily segregated in the early 1950s, but in that tightly defined little world inside the ring, race did not matter. What mattered were results. The teams Martin put together were white and black. Of my eleven fights, ten were against African Americans. They were good guys, nice guys. They tried to hit me as hard as they could, and I tried to hit them as hard as I could.

Logan and I occasionally worked out in what was then the "colored

YMCA" at 920 West Chestnut Street. Joe Martin took us to fights on the road in his car. We fought some in Louisville, but we traveled a lot. Joe would pile us four or five in his car, and we fought as far away as Toledo. Joe would buy our lunch or breakfast because none of us had any money.

Martin wrote a boxing column in the *Louisville Times* called "The Ring." He wrote of boxing matches and personal experiences, including one in which he was fleeced out of $50 by a disreputable promoter in Nashville.

The *Courier Journal* and the *Louisville Times* devoted heavy coverage to the fighters and the matches. The various weight classes defined the participants. Many of the mentioned fighters were teenagers—thirteen, fourteen, and fifteen—including "Sluggin' Harry" McKenna, of whom the *Times* wrote: "In his last half-dozen efforts, the 14-year-old McKenna, 133 pounds, kayoed five opponents."

Logan and I were featured in one *Courier Journal* photo, our faces locked in posed, concentrated mock anger. We leaned into each other—young, muscular, nose-to-nose, bare knuckle to bare knuckle. The story labeled us the "Fighting Jones Brothers."

In one scheduled event in Seymour, Indiana, we were matched against another set of brothers, Charles Booker, at 130 pounds, and Paul Booker, at 160 pounds, with the rematch set for Louisville. Logan won decisions in both matches, and I lost both decisions. My moment of boxing glory came later.

My best fight was up in Toledo. I was sitting next to the guy. I was eighteen, maybe nineteen, and he was about twenty-three, a muscular young guy. He was talking about the fights he had won, and I was a little nervous, so the first thing I did was hit him as hard as I could and knock him out. I think it was mainly from fear.

Logan was always the better fighter, the brother Joe Martin saw with the most potential in the Golden Gloves lightweight division. That dream ended in January 1951 when Logan received his induction notice for the Korean War. A *Louisville Times* photographer posed him standing at the mailbox of our Garland Avenue home, checking the mail for his notice just before his last fight. The headline on the accompanying story read:

Golden Gloves Aspirant Keeps Up
With His Training, All the Time
Wondering If Call to Army
Will Hold Off Until Tourney Time

It didn't. A full year of heavy combat in Korea awaited him. He returned to Louisville with a case of malaria and briefly attempted a comeback before he left the ring. Somewhat fittingly, and after all the family goodbyes, I had driven Logan in our well-used Ford to the induction center at the Federal Building at Sixth Street and Broadway. The date was February 1, 1951, the week "The Great Ice Storm of 1951" dropped temperatures well below zero and covered Louisville streets with snow, sleet, and ice.

The car got stuck in the deep snow at the Federal Building. I said goodbye to Logan and walked the mile back to our Garland Avenue home. The car was ticketed for illegal parking, but authorities tore up the ticket when they learned Logan was going into the service.

My fighting career was short-lived; I was too busy. I had maintained my straight-A average all through Male High school, played any sports I could, and worked nights at the Surety Gas Station at Seventh and Oak Streets.

Looking back on all that and what I had learned growing up and used later in life, Humana's success was neither luck nor a dynamite product like Apple's smartphone, Facebook, or Amazon. It was the long-term product of strategic thinking and excellent execution, a risk-taking culture in which leadership was trusted. It wasn't accidental; it came about because I could recognize when it was time to change and was willing to act.

I also would say that one of the most difficult challenges with such success is finding the best and most rewarding ways to give back. We supported many efforts, but education was the greatest need. Betty and I—and the family foundation we started—created and funded, among many endeavors, programs to prepare preschool and kindergarten children to read. We also thought it was important to create conditions that improved school success through effective teachers, principals, and governance and supported at-risk students as they entered college.

That need remained evident in a trip back to the old neighborhood. I revisited the narrow patch of grass on Garland Avenue where my family had lived until our home was buried beneath the Great Flood of 1937.

The house we moved to is also gone, now part of the Brown-Forman Corporation's parking lot, with the distillery's massive water tower, painted like a bottle of Old Forester, rising into the air on forty-foot metal legs. Across Garland Avenue, a row of old frame houses remains, faded and worn, their occupants another generation of blue-collar residents with children needing education and guidance.

The big sign at the edge of the California neighborhood says, "Established 1849—Reflect, Reform, Rebuild, Renew." That connection— the memory of my mother pulling books home in a wagon—has always remained. Mom sparked my lifelong interest in education, my knowing what it takes to succeed, and my need to reach back to where I came from and pull people along.

All Mom wanted was for me to go off to college. I always believed I would go to college—even while pumping gas at night. The success of my uncle Earl was always on my mind. My father's brother was a lawyer for General Box Company in Louisville until the firm was acquired by Continental Box Company, in Houston. Earl moved there and eventually became CEO.

But when I graduated from Male in 1949, my family had no money for college. Only about one in four of my classmates went on to higher education. College still seemed much more a dream than a possibility.

Chapter Two

LEAVING HOME

"The ever-curious Jim Thornton—about four years older than me—walked over to the Surety station to watch me at work. He waited around, bought a Coke, then finally introduced himself—two founders of eventual multi-billion-dollar companies in gas stations and insurance first meeting over a Coke in the early hours at an all-night gas station in downtown Louisville."

— DAVID JONES

D reams deferred were never part of my agenda. My goals after graduating from Male High School were clear: college, then law school.

The credentials and competitive mindset were there: excellent grades, athletic success, leadership skills combined with an opportunistic outlook, and a willingness to throw a solid punch when necessary. The family expectation was always there: Education mattered. My work ethic was never in doubt. Risk-taking came naturally. All that was missing was the tuition money. The jobs I had didn't pay enough.

My working life had begun with passing out handbills alongside my brother, cutting grass, pumping gas, and even putting together bedsprings one summer at Leggett & Platt bedspring company—a rare skill that came in handy when I scrambled to open my first nursing home years later. There would be many other such jobs along the way, work offering a mix of honest sweat and responsibility, helping me develop my business perspective, the best ways to deal with people—and incidentally—the intricacies of applying weather-stripping.

That last opportunity occurred in the summer of 1945 when, with World War II almost over, my father and uncle were laid off from Jeffboat. With metal once more available, my uncle restarted his company, weather-stripping schools and churches across southern Indiana and southern Illinois. At age fourteen, I joined them.

It was all done with brass and copper, and there was a huge demand because no metal had been available during wartime rationing. I learned to take those huge windows down, plane them, level them off, and replace the ropes. Later, I didn't tell many people about that, and I pretended to be kind of klutzy so I didn't have to do that kind of work again. But back then, I made $20 a week, which was a fortune in 1945.

There was a bonus to learning how to plane windows: It gave me the opportunity to spend more time with my father, including a train trip one Sunday from the town of Olney, Illinois, to the St. Louis Zoo. My dad could do almost anything with tools. I can't. I remember that trip so well because when you have so many siblings, you don't get much time alone with one parent.

Still searching for tuition money, I found a few jobs that didn't produce much income but did fully convince me of the need for higher education. One such job was in Louisville on the eleventh floor of the massive L&N Railroad building. The L&N was a legendary line chartered by the Commonwealth of Kentucky in 1850. It grew into a 6,000-mile behemoth covering thirteen states and hauled troops from both sides during the Civil War.

In the late 1940s, passengers on trips from, say, Louisville to New Orleans received double-wide tickets, each segment a different color. At the time of sale, the ticket agent tore the long strip into two pieces and dropped one half into a big box. The train conductors would then tear off one segment of the passenger's strip at each stop and drop it into a smaller box that was returned to the Louisville L&N office.

It became my job—along with a few dozen other very bored people seated in a large room—to match up the torn tickets with the original long strips, proving not much of anything. And to this day, even though I am a certified public accountant and have been involved in complex financial matters, I still cannot fathom why they did that. My best guess was it was just a maneuver to save jobs during the Depression.

In what I came to consider a stroke of good economic fortune, United Mine Workers president John L. Lewis led Kentucky coal miners on a strike in the summer of 1949, reducing coal production and train traffic and costing me that job. I've always loved John L. Lewis because I got laid off from the most boring job imaginable.

I found a second pre-college job with another behemoth, the R.J. Reynolds Tobacco Company. It was started in Winston-Salem, North Carolina, in 1874 by R.J. Reynolds, a tobacco farmer's son who eventually became the wealthiest man in that state. I played a small part in the company's growth—and the job contributed to my future golf game. I worked in a tobacco re-drying plant, and unless the markets were open, we really didn't have anything to do. The warehouse was so big we practiced hitting golf balls.

After about a month's training in Louisville, I was sent to Wilson, North Carolina, and later to Georgia to work on tobacco markets. My trip to Wilson was my first commercial airline flight, in a Piedmont DC-3. We took off from Louisville and landed in Lexington and London, Kentucky; Bristol, Tennessee; Roanoke, Virginia; then Raleigh, Elizabeth City, and Goldsboro, North Carolina. Eight hours and then I had to take a Greyhound bus to Wilson. It took the whole day, and it was fun. While there, I learned a lot about the tobacco business. I was offered a raise and promotion to stay, but I was more than ready to move on to college.

The opportunity came in the spring of 1950, courtesy of the Navy's ROTC Holloway Plan, which was created to add officers to a Navy depleted by World War II. Serendipity—a lifelong ally of mine—played a part. While seeking information on attending the University of Louisville, I saw a notice on the bulletin board at Gardiner Hall about the Holloway Plan, which offered a scholarship for successful test-takers.

It was a nervous time in post-war America. The Cold War was just beginning. In March 1946, Winston Churchill had given his ominous "Iron Curtain" speech at Westminster College in Fulton, Missouri, warning of the perils of the Soviet domination of Europe after the war.

The Korean War would begin on June 25, 1950. My brother Logan served as a combat infantryman for a year and never got to college. I took the Navy ROTC test at U of L with twenty to thirty other candidates. It was similar to the SAT but also had a spatial relationship section and was heavy on math. I did well and received the results in time to begin school in September.

About thirty NROTC freshmen enrolled in the College of Arts & Sciences at U of L, and a slightly higher number in the Speed Engineering School. Each student would take a naval science course each semester, serve on Navy cruises each summer, and spend three years in the Navy after graduation.

During my freshman year, all ROTC members were required to wear uniforms every day, and to participate in marching drills and training. The Korean War presented the possibility of being called into active service at any time. As the fighting drew to an end, in 1953, uniforms and drills were required only once a week.

The ROTC scholarship was a happy bargain for me, eagerly made and forever cherished. It would provide a lifetime of benefits, high among them seeing the world beyond Louisville and developing and maintaining life-long friendships for both Betty—who I met at U of L—and me.

My sense of military duty would be passed on to our children. One of our sons, Matt, a career Marine, would be wounded in Desert Storm in 1991 as part of serving his country for twenty-seven years. Another son, Dan, would serve in the Navy, and their brother David would serve in the US Department of State.

When I entered U of L in the fall of 1950, I still lived at home to save money. While a full-time student, I worked several part-time jobs, including stints at W. T. Grant's dime store on Saturdays and the US Post Office during the Christmas rush.

I continued to work nights at the same Surety gas station where I had worked during high school. I worked summer jobs alongside my father at Robert Lear & Son, a firm that did tuckpointing, a process that involves putting colored mortar between bricks to solidify a wall.

My job there was to drive a truck, carry bags of cement, and then deliver small amounts of cement to the bricklayers. It required me to join the hod carriers union, giving me a card and a distinction I would value all my life. The pay was $1.50 an hour, or about $60 a week—big money in the early 1950s. By comparison, my first full-time pay as a Navy ensign was $220.30 a month, plus allowances of $47.88 for food and $85.80 for housing because I was married.

But the University of Louisville came first. My freshman year, placement tests were an indicator of my academic abilities—and deficiencies. My scores were very high on the verbal and mathematical side but very low on fine arts.

I eventually majored in accounting and naval science. I also took general courses in physics and math, as well as Spanish, English, and history, with my writing skills a great help in those disciplines. I never got below an A in any course I really cared about. I also served as business manager of the *Louisville Cardinal*, the student newspaper.

I met a lot of good people at U of L. Many would become part of my future life, but my best friend was Carey Thompson. We were fraternity brothers at Lambda Chi Alpha, kindred spirits who had a lot of fun together with great plans for our futures, and then he died in 1962 at age thirty-two of leukemia.

His girlfriend, Carol Cochran, had been the Sweetheart of Lambda Chi. The two had married in 1953. They both loved to travel and, with little money, still managed to spend a marvelous summer in Europe on the cheap. Thompson joined the Army, then met up with Betty and me again at U of L while he was in law school. The four of us didn't have much money, so we hung out and played bridge. Later, we couples traveled to Florida and Virginia Beach, taking the kids, who grew up to become friends. We loved golfing together; Carol, a great athlete, often beat me.

Carey died just twenty-one days after being diagnosed with leukemia and just a month after their third child was born. It was an incredible blow for all of us. Carol was left a widow with three little kids. She lived only a few blocks from us and was one of Betty's best friends. Carol always said I felt obligated to help her because of my friendship with Carey, but she also helped us deal with his death. We stayed close. I helped her with the life insurance settlement, and we traveled together with our children, driving to Florida to enjoy swimming and playing on the beaches.

Four years after Carey died, Carol married Joe Ferguson. I helped them finance a small travel agency they built into the very successful Woodside Travel Company, which he sold just before 9/11. Joe paid me back with interest. He had no experience in this business but would joke about it as I had with the nursing home business: "Saying, 'I've done all this travel, so I have a travel business,' is like saying, 'I go to a lot of movies, so I'll be a great actor.' "

The Fergusons would later make a generous contribution to a favorite project of mine, The Parklands of Floyds Fork, the almost 4,000-acre park in eastern Louisville that would become my son Dan's work and legacy. We always stayed in touch with the Fergusons as best we could. Carey's death was never far from my mind as I thought about how lucky I was to be able to move forward.

As a student at the University of Louisville, my shortcomings in the fine arts took a great leap forward in a Shakespeare course taught by Dr. William Ekstrom, who also twice served as interim president of the university. The school library is named in his honor.

He was the first outstanding liberal arts professor that I remember. He was a very trusted and loved man with high expectations. Dr. Ekstrom awakened my interest in great writing and literature. What I liked most about Shakespeare were the vocabulary and the plots. I mean he pretty much wrote the English language.

In my sophomore year at U of L, I met Betty Ashbury, then a freshman. Our relationship would grow into a perfect partnership and marriage of love, loyalty, and commitment. I would describe her as not just my wife but my "pal"—a bonding affection over and above what would become sixty-five years of marriage.

We had good role models. Betty's parents, Prosser Lee Ashbury and Lillias Estelle Hutchins, began dating as teenagers at Woodrow Wilson High School in Portsmouth, Virginia. After high school, Lillias attended Westhampton College—now part of the University of Richmond. She graduated in 1922 as class valedictorian and Phi Beta Kappa while studying Greek and French and majoring in Latin. She taught for two years at what was then Averett College in Danville, Virginia, and then at her high school alma mater, Woodrow Wilson.

Prosser, son of a Portsmouth shipbuilder, came to Louisville to attend the Louisville College of Pharmacy. In 1947 it merged with the University of Kentucky and then moved to Lexington. He graduated in 1923 and took a job in Louisville with the Taylor Drug Company. Through all that time and distance, Lillias and Prosser kept their relationship alive with summer visits and letters. They married in the Fourth Street Baptist Church in Portsmouth in October 1925. She was twenty-four, and he was twenty-five.

The newlyweds took a steamer to New York City for a honeymoon, then a train to Louisville, where Prosser worked in several drug stores. He bought a pharmacy at the corner of Jackson and Market Streets in the 1940s. In 1948, he and business partner Abe Berman opened the Ashbury-Berman Drug Store at Breckenridge Lane and Shelbyville Road in the east Louisville suburb of St. Matthews. All the local customers came to know Prosser as "Doc."

It was genuine affection, well-earned. Prosser was very much part of the era of neighborhood drug stores, with pharmacists working seventy to eighty hours a week, late into the night if the occasion demanded, getting out of bed to deliver medicine to needy patients. For a time, while I was in college, I would help make deliveries.

Betty was one of the three Ashbury children, all college graduates. When we met, the family rented at 2319 Sycamore Avenue in Crescent Hill, an old-fashioned, middle-class, two-story home in a neighborhood lined with many such houses, most with broad, white-columned front porches. The Ashbury family grew up as faithful members of the Crescent Hill Baptist Church.

Married women had not been allowed to teach in Louisville public schools before the war, but with a dire shortage of teachers both during and after the war, Lillias Ashbury began teaching part-time. She taught math, English, and Latin at the Masonic Home orphanage, which then had classes K–12. When Eastern High School opened, it offered four years of Latin, which she taught, along with algebra, until she retired.

"And she was so happy with it," Betty would say of her mother's dedication to education. "She loved it."

Betty attended Clark Elementary School—now condominiums—on South Galt Street. She went on to Barret Junior High School, just down the street, and then the old Atherton High School on Morton Avenue. She was in the last all-girls class in the school.

After graduating from Atherton in 1950, Betty considered going to Westhampton—her mother's alma mater. She also looked at William & Mary but decided on the University of Louisville, primarily because several of her close friends were going there.

The university, chartered in 1798, was the first city-owned public university in the United States. It remained a public municipal university until 1970, when it joined the state system. It was commuter-friendly, a "streetcar college" with enrollments of about 6,000 to 8,000 students in the early 1950s. Many were on the GI bill or recipients of Navy ROTC scholarships. Its four small dormitories on the tight-knit campus were named for the first four graduates killed in World War II.

One of Betty's high school friends who went on to U of L was Ann Cobb. Ann and her husband, Stew, have been good friends and travel companions with us for more than sixty years, as well as active supporters of the University of Louisville.

We first met at the University of Louisville, with Betty and Ann in the Sigma Kappa sorority and Stew and I in the Lambda Chi Alpha fraternity. Ann and Stew had a great sense of humor that we all tested the year our fraternity built a parade float featuring a mild version of the old 1950s advertising campaign of a lady dreaming of doing something in a Maidenform bra. I thought we would get thrown off campus, but people loved it. We always had a lot of fun with them, sometimes mixed with business. When our first nursing home opened, we took them to see it, and they patiently waited as I used my calculator to close the books for the week in about eight minutes.

My good friend Stew would also complain when I called on him over the years to fix a mechanical problem, assuming I could do it myself if need be. He was probably right.

Betty was a terrific student who often said she didn't want to teach. She watched her mother work the six hours a day teaching and then prepare the next day's session every night in addition to managing the house and three children. Betty, of course, later got into teaching at Jefferson Community College and the University of Louisville, where she was happy, respected, and admired.

Earning straight A's at U of L, Betty took courses in home economics, human anatomy and physiology, psychology, general chemistry, and organic chemistry. She graduated with a Bachelor of Arts degree in 1956. She continued her formal education many years later, completing a Master of Arts degree in French language and literature in summer classes in Vermont.

While still a college student, Betty worked part-time in the daycare center at the old Neighborhood House on First Street, and with Les Shively in the U of L alumni office, for fifty cents an hour. She also worked at the

Byck's store in St. Matthews on Saturdays and during Christmas.

She worked in the jewelry, scarves, and handbags department, where they gave a nice discount for purchases. Byck's had a certain quota you had to sell, but she was pretty good at it because she'd worked in her dad's drug store during high school. She and her sister would help him at the soda fountain.

Both Betty and I had dated other students at U of L in our freshmen and sophomore years, with Betty dating one of my best friends, Tom Bowling. We couples began to double date. Then, in the spring of 1952, I asked Betty out. She later explained she only said yes because I was a very handsome fellow and very persistent.

With my brother—and sparring partner—Logan in the service, I dropped my Golden Gloves fighting. At U of L, I played all intramural sports, including basketball and flag football. A young quarterback named Johnny Unitas refereed some of the games.

I also played regular lunchtime bridge games in the Student Union Building with fellow students John Alvey, Duke Heleringer, and Jim Patterson. Alvey became a CPA and went to work with a big department store company in New York. Heleringer became very much involved in the family's furniture business. Their lives would mirror my belief that you can find business success in Louisville as well as anywhere else.

Patterson grew up around Seventh and Hill Streets in Louisville and was the family's only high school graduate. He would always joke with me about his neighborhood being tougher than mine. He played baseball at U of L, sold insurance, became an Air Force ROTC member, then served in the Air Force during the Korean War.

Back home, he bought and remodeled an old restaurant, which he opened as Jerry's. Within eight years, he opened two more Jerry's, which led to his creating the Long John Silver's franchise. He became a Wendy's franchisee when it had forty-seven restaurants. Then he moved

43

on to Rally's hamburgers, Chi-Chi's Mexican restaurants, telephone and software businesses, and real estate ventures.

Patterson would later help found the School Choice Scholarship program in Louisville to help more than a thousand low-income students with private school tuition, and the U of L College of Business Emergency Loan Fund. Thanks to Jim, the University of Louisville's very successful baseball team now plays in Jim Patterson Stadium.

I joined the fraternity's choir at U of L but lip-synced the whole time. I couldn't carry a tune in a bucket. One fraternity brother was Bill Juckett, who also grew up in the 1930s in the Parkland area of Louisville and then lived on a small Indiana farm for a few years. He paid his way through U of L working in a Kroger store but would go on to become senior vice president of marketing for the multi-billion-dollar Brown-Forman Corporation, chairman of the Louisville Olmsted Parks Conservancy, and an early proponent of what would become The Parklands of Floyds Fork.

Juckett remembers the day I walked into the fraternity house during rush week. "David had gotten in a year before I did," he says. "He came through the front door, and he looked like he was chiseled out of a piece of granite. He had on one of those athletic jackets that has a cloth body and leather sleeves, and it had a patch up on the shoulder that said 'Golden Gloves.' And when you shook hands with him, you knew why he was in the Golden Gloves.

"What I always said about that meeting, and my initial experience with him, you sort of knew here was somebody who seemed to be made of pretty solid stuff."

Juckett also remembers me as confident, modest and polite, always thinking ahead and encouraging others to do the same. And I was respected in the fraternity, he says, for my judgment, fairness, and competitive spirit on the fraternity football team.

"He protected the quarterback and did a damned good job of it," Juckett explains. "It was pretty competitive stuff. David could knock people on their ass. . . . And he was an outstanding student. The only person I know who got better grades than David was Betty."

*

Betty would be named U of L's Outstanding Freshman Co-ed. At that time, men could live in fraternity houses, but the sororities had no on-campus residences. Both Betty and I lived at home all through college.

During my sophomore year, my family moved from Garland Avenue to 319 South Bayly Avenue in Crescent Hill. It was a classic two-story house with a broad front porch in a long row of Middle-America architecture. It cost $10,000, with an uncle and aunt helping with the down payment, and Logan and I helping with the monthly payments.

I always had some sort of car to get to school or to meet Betty, another reason to work so many part-time jobs. My first was a 1937 Ford, from which I worked my way up to a spacious 1948 Packard, the one I owned at college graduation. It looked nice, was a comfortable ride, and burned an estimated quart of oil every twenty-five miles.

Betty and I went to movies, fraternity parties, and dances, and to what was then KT's Restaurant on Lexington Road, where Wednesday night was date night with music from the jukebox. Another stop was Louisville's legendary Air Devil's Inn on Taylorsville Road, once a hangout for pilots training at nearby Bowman Field during World War II. The inn had opened in 1929 and offered a beer garden, a jukebox, and a chain of overhead lights. Betty remembered going to Bowman Field as a kid and watching the planes come in on Sunday afternoons.

She was less than enthusiastic about my old Packard. She hated it, remembering the times I lent it to her if she was late to class or had to get downtown, and it broke down every time. She was very frustrated with that, saying, "I would much rather take the bus."

Our relationship survived. We soon began to go "steady," and when I could finally afford one, I presented Betty with my fraternity pin the Christmas of her junior year. Marriage seemed inevitable.

Meanwhile, I continued with all my part-time jobs, including pumping gas at night. I also checked the oil and water and air in the tires, and wiped the windshield and rear window, always.

That night work at the Surety gas station led me to meet Jim Thornton, who would become another successful Louisville and southern Indiana entrepreneur. He and his family would build a chain of almost 200 retail service stations across the Midwest and Florida, with more than $2.3 billion in annual sales.

Our first meeting was beyond mere serendipity. It was more an unlikely plot to a movie filmed in early morning at a gritty, four-pump gas station from which a stocky kid emerged to do the pumping.

I was a college freshman, working from 10 p.m. to 6 a.m. for the small chain of six Surety gas stations. My role was to rotate from station to station, giving the regular night person the night off—and me the opportunity to do my homework in the quiet, early hours.

Thornton was a high school graduate who began working at his stepfather's small gas station in New Albany, Indiana. Having never attended college, he became a partner in Dixie Dance gas stations at age twenty-four and grew that experience into a chain of convenience store stations. Before it was sold in 2019, Thorntons ranked 194th on Forbes magazine's list of privately owned American companies.

The meeting took place as I was working at the Surety station at Tenth and Jefferson Streets near downtown Louisville. Thornton was working nights at a Transit station on the opposite corner.

Thornton recalls that his station was not very busy, but looking across the street, it seemed the Surety was very busy. He saw me over there boosting sales by selling Valve Ease—cans of gasoline additive that supposedly kept the engine running more smoothly. Not only that, but Valve Ease was also selling for thirty cents a can, with Surety making about fifteen cents on each can.

The ever-curious Jim Thornton—about four years older than me—walked over to the Surety station to watch me at work. He waited around, bought a Coke, then finally introduced himself—two founders of eventual multi-billion-dollar companies in gas stations and insurance first meeting over a Coke in the early hours at an all-night gas station in downtown Louisville. Thornton, the ambitious high school graduate, asked me—

soon to be a college graduate—if I wanted to partner up in the gas station business.

"David," he said, "I'm going to do a lot in this business, and I need somebody to join me who would like to share in it. And watching you operate, you fit everything that I know to ask. So give it some thought."

I did think about it. About two weeks later, I called back and said: "Mr. Thornton, I've given a lot of thought to your offer, but when I graduate, I'm going into the Navy. And when I finish service, I don't know what follows. I've got some things in mind, but I don't know whether or not any of it will take place. But we'll get together when I get out of the service, and we'll go from there."

And the two of us did get together to help community efforts, with our future meetings every bit as timely and interesting.

Navy ROTC trainees were required to take a summer cruise each year, a learning experience that I greeted with curiosity, enthusiasm, and great expectations. The first summer, Tom Bowling—Betty's old suitor, who would remain a close friend—and I were driven to Norfolk by Bowling's parents. After a few days at nearby Virginia Beach, we boarded the battleship *USS Wisconsin*, which had served in the Pacific Ocean in World War II and later shelled North Korean targets in that war.

We spent the first two days loading potatoes and supplies onto the ship for the 800 midshipmen who were on there in addition to the regular crew. We had about 3,300 sailors in total.

That summer's cruise would offer first-time sights and experiences a long way from Garland Avenue in west Louisville. I became enthralled by the sea, the big blue sky during the day, and the twinkling festival of stars at night. The ship's skipper was probably thirty-eight, and the rest of the crew ages seventeen to thirty-five—all young and healthy. Nobody ever got sick. You get seasick, but you don't get colds or other illnesses. There are no germs in that air.

Our first stops were Halifax, Nova Scotia, and then Manhattan, where we anchored in the Hudson River opposite Seventy-Ninth Street until the battleship pulled its buoy out of the river bottom. The captain summoned tugboats to pull the ship to safety before it went aground. The *Wisconsin* was moved to the aptly named Gravesend Bay, off Brooklyn, which was a two-mile walk to the Coney Island subway once the sailors were ashore.

We couldn't have cared less. We had liberty every day, and New York was a magical city in the summer of 1951. I had a wonderful time there attending plays. Our pay was $50 a month, but you could get a nice steak dinner for two dollars.

The *Wisconsin* headed south to Guantanamo Bay, Cuba, an island whose history includes being named by Christopher Columbus, a role in the Spanish-American War, the iron rule of Communist leader Fidel Castro, and the CIA's secret detention camp dating to 2002.

My first stay there would include the final match of my boxing career. It began after about 140 Marines and midshipmen had gone onshore in an LCI, or Landing Craft, Infantry. It was August. Accommodations were tight; all the sailors had to stand for a thirty-five-minute trip—each way.

Beer had been the refreshment of choice onshore, and a fight broke out as the LCI returned to the *Wisconsin*. The fight lasted most of thirty-five minutes.

One of the participants, a Marine sergeant, never did calm down, so when he got back to the ship, he was subdued with a two-inch fire hose, placed in a straitjacket, and allowed to sleep it off. Later, the Marine still wanted to fight, and I agreed to my last bout as shipmates watched, with a full-sized ring set up on deck.

The Marine was tough as nails, but he didn't know how to box. I thought I won. He may have thought he won. I don't know. It was just kind of fun. There was no discipline meted out. They just helped him calm down.

Another Guantanamo story—and I would make four trips there—involved the commodore of our six-destroyer escort fleet, whom the other officers found a little stuffy. Some of the young officers went out, caught an enormous fish, let it sit for a couple of days, put it in a gift-wrapped box, and sent the smelly gift to the commodore. He tried every way he could to figure out who did it, but there were six ships, and nobody was talking.

On a trip to Key West, a gunnery officer and friend, Dale Critz, whose family owned a big fishing boat, took me out to catch sailfish. I hooked a big one, watched it jump high out of the water and get away—but the memory lasted another sixty years.

My second summer cruise covered planning, serious training, some risk-taking, and problem-solving, with an early entrepreneurial spirit that would characterize my life. Later, I wrote a log of the journey that began in Louisville and ended in Corpus Christi, Texas.

In 1952, five of us received six cents per mile for the 1,000-mile trip, or five times $60 made $300. We bought a pre-war Buick for $200 and had enough cash left for food and the 25-cents-a-gallon gas. We planned to sell the car in Corpus Christi for whatever we could get and split the cash five ways.

Fate intervened. In Lake Charles, Louisiana, the transmission fell out. We sold the car for $75 and a meal each. After a fuss over whether a second glass of milk was included for one of our number, we made a plan:

Three would hitch-hike to Corpus Christi, while the short straw winner and I would catch a bus to Corpus Christi with all the sea bags, and with a night in Houston for all of us.

The reason was my Uncle Allen managed a hotel in Houston. He gave us rooms, fed us, and seemed happy to see us.

The Navy training in Corpus Christi was an adventure of a different sort:

We flew in trainers, with the pilots doing loops, etc., trying to make us sick. If you upchucked, you had to clean the plane. We also flew in large seaplanes and shot 20 mm cannons at targets on the water. Fun.

But one other lesson in military discipline awaited me:

> One morning at 5 a.m. reveille, our CO [commanding officer] asked the assembled group if we had anything to report. Not realizing our Marine CO was near in the semi-dark, I reported that colleague Matt Fagan had been carried off by the gigantic ants that resented our living in their quarters.
>
> That resulted in my being confined to quarters (after the day's work) until I wrote a report on how to thwart the ants. That caused me to miss a phone call that I had promised Betty. There being no reference book on gigantic ants available, I provided a fictional account which was accepted, and Betty forgave me since duty had required my sacrifice.

I didn't drink, but My ROTC buddies did. We all spent two days and one night on a miserable beer-laden train trip to Little Creek, Virginia, to spend three weeks training with the Marine Corps.

That typically brutal, in-your-face boot-camp Marine training came with the option of choosing the Marine Corps or Navy for your three years of active duty. My buddy Tom Bowling chose the Marines. I stuck with the Navy, which came with a third summer cruise in 1953, on the *USS Worcester* to Bergen, Norway; Copenhagen, Denmark; and again to Guantanamo.

The *Worcester* ran into a heavy storm in the North Atlantic, with waves towering above the bridge. The crew could track the *Worcester*'s roll with a device called an inclinometer. It indicated the ship was tipping sixty-two degrees. A destroyer in our group lost a man overboard; there was no way to recover him in the surging storm. We didn't know what might have happened had the *Worcester* tilted more than sixty-two degrees. Nobody would tell.

Europe was still recovering from World War II as I toured Copenhagen, Denmark's capital. It was a good-sized city but with very few automobiles on the streets. Denmark being a very flat country, we rode our bikes the twenty-five miles from Copenhagen to the royal castle of Helsingør, popularly known as Hamlet's Castle at Elsinore.

It was a wonderful experience. I loved the Navy and the constant training. They take boys like me, who have never been any place, and give them lots of training and discipline, and before you know it, they work as a team.

Among the hundreds of ROTC recruits on this cruise—including many Ivy Leaguers—I was one of three chosen for advanced leadership positions. I spent two weeks each as midshipmen executive officer, the top job; as head of damage control; and as head navigator. Navigator was a job I'd come to enjoy—I turned out to be very good at celestial navigation.

Back home at U of L after the cruises, I had about 150 credit hours— thirty more than I needed for a degree. I had a particular interest in accounting classes taught by Bill Thompson and economics courses taught by Dr. Carl Abner, whom I regarded as a brilliant, iconoclastic teacher and a wonderful disciplinarian. They made me eager to get up and go to class in the morning.

My accounting skills also enabled me to get a part-time summer job with a Louisville accountant, Irving L. Wasserman. "We did mostly what we called 'shoebox' accounts," Wasserman recalled. "That's where people brought up all their stuff in a shoebox at the end of the year, and you would have to sort it all out."

In his memoir, *Seventy-Five—and Still Alive*, Wasserman described my solution to a client's very messy problem:

> I had a client who sold and erected prefab houses and who was in dire straits. He had built some fifty houses or more and had kept poor or nonexistent records. I assigned Dave to this account to prepare a record of the client's transactions, and Dave and I went to see the client's attorney.
>
> She was an energetic lady who shared an office with her

mother, also an attorney. . . . We came into her office and explained our mission. After she checked with the client, she said, "Here are all my files. Scattered through them are your client's closings, and you are welcome to look through them as long as you want. . . . By the way," she added, "I was looking through them the other day and I found a $100 bill. You are welcome to keep anything you find in them."

I left Dave to the assignment . . . and he spent a month on that job. When he was finished, he had a complete record in detail of every transaction, which satisfied both the client and the IRS. The revenue agents were charging our man with a large sum in taxes, but they backed off when they saw Dave's amazing record.

Chapter Three

MATRIMONY AND MARITIME

"Only later did I appreciate just how important my Navy experience would be in the corporate world. Those of us who had been privileged to serve our nation received a big head start in learning how to lead. In my case, I led a group of forty men as a Navy ensign by age twenty-three. That sort of youthful leadership opportunity is very rare outside the military, and it's truly precious. Once you've been a leader, you're generally ready for more and don't fear responsibility."

— DAVID JONES

As I neared graduation from U of L in the spring of 1954, marriage was on my mind—and Betty's. After my junior year, I bought Betty an engagement ring, but the Navy would not allow us to get married until I was commissioned into service.

There was also the matter of Betty being about a semester behind me in school and her mother's concern that if she married before she completed her degree, she might not finish at all.

I applied for the Navy's supply corps school and was accepted. That meant I would be in training as an ensign in Athens, Georgia, for six months, but with long trips aboard ship and away from home after that.

Betty discussed the situation with her mother. She promised she would get her degree. The University of Louisville normally would not offer a degree unless the final thirty hours were completed at the school, but she got a waiver.

All her family loved me, but her mother knew many women without an education and the difficult time they had if they were left alone with children. Yet it was not in her mother's nature to interfere with our marriage. I was twenty-two, and Betty was twenty-one. She accepted our decision and gave us her blessing.

I got my Bachelor of Arts degree with a double major in accounting and naval science and was named outstanding senior in my class. Betty and I were married soon after, on July 24, at Crescent Hill Baptist Church amidst a big celebration of family and friends. Already stationed in Georgia, I had driven home on a forty-eight-hour pass. I wore my white military uniform for the ceremony. The groomsmen and bridesmaids were lifelong friends and siblings.

The men were Lee Ashbury, Bill Dohrman, Howard Dohrman, Charles Jones, Logan Jones, and Ray Schnurr. The women were Barbara Ashbury, Jane Ann Dudgeon, Ann Ford, Lucy Jones, Helen Mohlenkamp, and Pat Tucker.

The day after our wedding, we drove to Athens where, the next day, Betty enrolled at the University of Georgia, taking courses in bacteriology, education, and psychology. I continued in the Navy supply corps school.

In Athens, I had already met a nice man named Shelby Clark, a Naval Academy graduate who invited me to dinner with him and his wife, Jeanne. The Clarks were also newlyweds. We instantly bonded in our young married lives over all things large and small.

We remained close friends. We have often visited the Clarks in the "gently shabby" neighborhood of Pawleys Island in South Carolina. They have come to Louisville for the Derby, among other things.

Family is the most important thing, but friends are important, too. Getting together on a busy schedule took organization. I give Betty a lot of credit for this because our friends have been longtime friends. Almost everything we do in Louisville we do with people we have known for a long time. We knew most of them before we were successful. And you can't put on airs with people who knew you back when.

In Athens, we lived for five months in a two-room apartment. The bathroom was down the hall, and we shared it with some nurses living in the building, a situation we later jokingly gave as the reason each bedroom has its own bathroom in our Louisville home. Our Athens apartment, which we would drive by years later on a fond-memory tour, rented for $49.50 a month.

※

While living in that two-room apartment, I made a carefully studied decision that would have a lasting effect on the rest of our lives. It would allow us to begin a family while helping pay the mortgage on my parents' home and eventually led me to my business success.

I had earned my degree in accounting in June 1954 and had been working in Louisville for Wasserman before our marriage. I wanted to take the CPA exam, but Kentucky required two years of accounting experience before a candidate could take it. Only two states exempted candidates from that requirement: Tennessee and Rhode Island.

Looking at a map of my future—literally—I learned that the Soldiers & Sailors Relief Act allows someone about to be inducted into the military to choose a home of record. I chose Tennessee. To make that work—and having been assigned to Athens as my first posting—I stopped off in Chattanooga on the way to Georgia and listed my official home of record as the Lambda Chi Alpha fraternity house at the University of Tennessee-Chattanooga. My fraternity brothers gave me a "pigeonhole" for my mail, which gave me a Tennessee address—and a home of record for the CPA exam.

In November 1954, Betty and I left Athens at one minute past midnight, with a Navy pass giving me three days to complete my CPA mission. I drove to Nashville and dropped Betty off at a Greyhound bus station at 6 a.m. so she could take the bus to Louisville. I then took the CPA exam in Tennessee over the next two and a half days.

Afterward, I rushed nearly 200 miles to Louisville, picked up Betty, and we both got back to Athens in time for her Monday classes at the university and my Navy duty. I passed all four parts of the CPA exam and, in January

1955, was given CPA license number 1212 by the State of Tennessee. That CPA license would allow me to earn much higher wages in off-duty civilian jobs during my Navy career and, in another twist of fate, would lead me to law school at Yale.

The following January, I was assigned to the *USS Greenwich Bay* in Norfolk, Virginia. A seaplane tender launched at the end of World War II, it would serve as flagship for the commander of the US Middle East Forces, eventually deploying through the Mediterranean Sea to the Suez Canal, Persian Gulf, and Indian Ocean. The *Greenwich Bay* carried about fourteen officers and 250 crew. I became coach and captain of its basketball team, which played against teams of several nations.

Meanwhile, Betty and I moved into a small second-floor apartment in nearby Craddock, Virginia, as the *Greenwich Bay* underwent shipyard engine repairs from January through March.

With my nights and Saturdays free—and having taken my CPA exam in Tennessee—I found part-time work at a Norfolk CPA firm, doing about the same type of tax returns I had done in Louisville. My non-CPA starting pay was one dollar an hour. A week later, I received word I had passed the CPA exam, and my pay was raised to $2.50 an hour, a big addition to my Navy salary. That was a lot of money in 1955.

I also tried to leverage that degree on a trip to Washington when I spoke to an officer who assigned men to their ships. I mentioned that the Navy was paying civilian CPAs about $7,500 a year, and I was doing the same thing for $222.30 a month.

"How about me having one of those shore-based jobs?" I asked the officer.

"Jones," the officer responded, "you're going back to sea."

The CPA experience was a great help when I launched my business career. It also offered me a lasting life lesson as I read a large sign outside a Norfolk real estate company I was auditing. It showed a Rip Van Winkle figure of a man with a beard that reached all the way to the sidewalk. The sign's wording told of a young man who had waited for the price of real estate to come down. I've never forgotten it.

In March, its engines repaired, the *USS Greenwich Bay* sailed down to Guantanamo Bay for a shakedown and training cruise and a test of its weapons. It returned in May and then left for a seven-month deployment to the Middle East. I was the assistant supply officer on board, helping to buy supplies, balance the books, and change money in foreign ports—easy work for a CPA.

Betty returned to Louisville during my deployment to the Middle East. She took several courses at the University of Kentucky, wrote a senior thesis for U of L, and graduated just a few months late.

The Korean War ended in 1953; I never saw a shot fired in anger in my Navy career. But with the commander of the US Middle East Forces on board, I saw a lot of the Middle Eastern world—Alexandria, Egypt; Port Sudan, Sudan; Asmara in Eritrea. We visited Djibouti, French Somalia, and Yemen, and sailed down the west coast of the Indian peninsula to Karachi, Pakistan and then Bombay and Cochin, India. We stopped at Sri Lanka, visiting its cities of Colombo and Trincomalee, then sailed south and enjoyed the traditional celebration that came with crossing the equator.

That ceremony traditionally includes the transformation of slimy "pollywogs" (seamen who have never crossed the equator) putting on a talent show with skits and songs before King Neptune, receiving a "subpoena" from Davy Jones, and being mocked and harassed by the Shellbacks, the veteran sailors.

Along with accounting, my duties included celestial navigation, using a sextant for sun and star sightings to determine the ship's location. The ship was also equipped with radar-based navigation, but Navy tradition required us to use the sextant at dawn, noon, and twilight. It was a challenge but great fun.

With an admiral on board, British and French diplomats often joined us for feasts hosted by the Arab leaders. They would serve whole sheep on an enormous bed of rice, providing a unique gastronomical experience.

We were surrounded by guards with huge swords, often with a falcon on their arms. We never met in a permanent building; the feasts were always in large, beautifully decorated tents.

We all sat on the floor, left hand behind us, and slowly ate the delicious meal with our right hand (observing the tradition that the left hand was for the toilet, not the table).

The admiral's number one aide, a lieutenant commander, once said to me, "Jones, the sheep's eyeball is a delicacy, and when they hand it to the admiral, if he doesn't eat it, you have to eat it."

Well, the admiral ate it, and I've never known whether that was really a delicacy, or they were having fun with us.

The admiral and the ship's captain loved to play tennis, with the ship's chaplain and me joining them. We would play matches at 6 a.m. to beat the heat on Bahrain Island in the Persian Gulf at a British naval station, where the Scottish bagpiper played "Taps" at sundown.

I got back to Norfolk—and Betty—just before Christmas in 1955. Two weeks later, I left on the *USS Darby*. That World War II destroyer escort had served in the South Pacific when the United States took back the Solomon Islands, Guadalcanal, and Eniwetok from the Japanese.

The *Darby*'s mission was to seek out Russian submarines in the Caribbean Sea. The ship became caught in hurricane winds with forty-to-sixty-foot waves that surged above the bridge deck, itself thirty-four feet above the water.

In those situations, you fill the fuel tanks with seawater to lower the center of gravity; if you head into the wind, you are normally safe. You button up the ship—all the hatches are closed so it resembles a bottle with a cork in it. When you see those waves coming up over the bridge, it's frightening, but we had a skilled skipper who led us through safely.

At yet another stop in Guantanamo, I spent a day on a submarine, where I experienced instant claustrophobia, with no wish to do it again. In 1957, as I neared the end of my three-year service, the *Darby* was sent to New London, Connecticut, where it performed maneuvers with the *USS Nautilus*, the world's first nuclear submarine. Its skipper would surface right in the middle of our ships and then dive, and we could never catch him. Its speed was classified. Our old Navy ships had no chance against that kind of submarine.

Back home, Betty taught seventh and eighth grades in Norfolk, sang in the choir at a Baptist church, and found companionship with other Navy wives and with extended family in Portsmouth, a closeness that mattered.

Religion would always be a strong and bonding force in our lives, although it took some searching to find a church compatible with our beliefs. The religious environment in 1950s Georgia was then very much Old South. Our first Sunday in Athens, we attended a Baptist church, but were turned off by the preacher's rant against the Supreme Court's *Brown v. Board of Education* ruling, which outlawed "separate but equal" public education, a doctrine that had allowed segregated public schools. We attended a Methodist church the following Sunday, where another minister delivered the familiar anti-integration rant.

Beginning that December, when I was assigned to the *USS Greenwich Bay* from Norfolk and then the *USS Darby* out of Norfolk and Key West, we attended a progressive Baptist church when I was in port. We both enjoyed that experience, but future changes in churches awaited.

As my tenure in the Navy ended, I was determined to fulfill my dream of law school. Only later did I appreciate just how important my Navy experience would be in the corporate world.

Those of us who had been privileged to serve our nation received a big head start in learning how to lead. In my case, I led a group of forty men as a Navy ensign by age twenty-three. That sort of youthful leadership opportunity is very rare outside the military, and it's truly precious. Once you've been a leader, you're generally ready for more and don't fear responsibility so long as you receive the required authority.

My law school role model remained my Uncle Earl, who, as an attorney, had kept his job all during the Depression. I applied and was accepted at Harvard, the University of Chicago, and the University of Michigan, with Harvard always my first choice. Then serendipity—and my CPA degree— again came into play. While my ship was stationed at New London, a fellow officer who had applied to Yale Law School invited me to ride down to New Haven with him.

While my friend was being interviewed, I spotted an opening on the law school bulletin board. It was for an accounting teaching position at Quinnipiac College in nearby Hamden. I quickly applied for the job and got it. I then applied to the Yale School of Law and was accepted.

Harvard still beckoned, but Yale could provide a nearby job to help support us. It also offered affordable veterans' housing and a partial academic scholarship. All that, and my $110 a month GI Bill income, would help with school and could get us home for Christmas. Yale Law School tuition was $1,350 a year, an amount almost equal to my GI Bill stipend.

Yale it was. I turned twenty-six just before starting law school in 1957. There were about 175 students in my class, approximately one-fourth the size of that year's Harvard class. About half of them were veterans.

As I entered Yale, the most useful purchase Betty and I made was a large, reconditioned typewriter we bought at Sears, Roebuck for $25. I had learned to type at Male High School—another skill filed away for future use. I had already typed papers for Betty while dating her in college and would use the bulky model as I took my law school exams. I would write out my points and then type them up. You can type a whole lot faster than you can write.

One vital benefit of Yale was its guaranteed financial support. Our respected contact became Associate Dean Jack Tate, the man we saw when we needed money. Later in our lives, Betty and I established a Yale fellowship in Tate's name to help students with similar financial needs.

Tate Fellows tend to be like we were—students who come to Yale and have young families. They have some life experiences. I have wonderful memories of that. We always get a nice letter from each of them at the end of the year. We had lived that need.

We had returned home to live with Betty's parents the summer before I went to law school. We were then expecting our first child, David, Jr., with a second, our daughter Sue, to follow, both born while we lived in New Haven.

Betty explained our reasons for starting a family: "We thought we were just so old, and whatever we were going to do, we didn't want to put the babies off."

To earn money that summer in Louisville, I worked at Irv Wasserman's CPA firm during the day and taught accounting classes at U of L at night. Our strong relationship with the university would later lead to my becoming a donor and playing a role in school issues.

Each of these summer jobs had rewards. Every job that I had, I learned more and more. I met interesting people. I think that's why I'm a good fund-raiser today. I like people, I like to hear their stories, and I don't mind sharing a relevant part of my story with them.

Meanwhile, Betty again worked at the U of L alumni office and audited a few humanities courses, which were free because I was teaching at the school.

Chapter Four

HALLS OF IVY, HUTS OF METAL

"He walked fast, stopped, and chatted with whoever was up and about at that early morning time. He inquired about our future plans and discussed our military service. He encouraged engagement—political and societal—and was just extremely nice."

— DAVID JONES remembering a walk at
Yale with former president Harry Truman

Betty and I went to New Haven in the fall of 1957 and moved into Yale's affordable housing—exactly half of a metal Quonset hut. Our quarters were twenty feet wide and twenty-two feet long—440 square feet of living space. The structure had a curved metal roof with no insulation, two ten-by-ten-foot bedrooms, and a bath.

Our front room had a kitchen on one side and a living room on the other. It was heated by a Franklin stove. The main rule was never let the fire go out because the water pipes would freeze and burst. The rent was $43 a month with all utilities—such as they were—paid.

Betty would remember those quarters were "cozy and warm"—provided you kept enough nuggets of coal in the stove—with the coal being stored in a box by the clothesline. There were 132 units in this married student housing. Most of our neighbors were other veterans who shared life stories and financial status that created lifelong bonds and relationships.

Among those friends were Allen and Lucy Duffy. Allen later practiced law in New Haven but died in 1986 of myelogenous leukemia when he was only fifty-six, a death I would think about all my life.

Our entire family has stayed in touch with the Duffys. Lucy, the daughter of a minister, had attended Brandeis University, where she met Allen, whose father was a caretaker on the huge DuPont estate on Maryland's Eastern Shore. They met their junior year, got married in August 1954—the same summer as our marriage—and finished college living on the campus as proctors. Allen played soccer at Brandeis and became student body president.

Lucy's parents had met in France during World War I. He was an American medic who wanted to learn French, and Lucy's mother, then sixteen, obliged. Their classes lasted only six weeks. After he returned to the States, the two sent hundreds of love letters back and forth, finally marrying in 1921.

After Brandeis, Lucy was accepted at Yale for graduate school, but family life intervened. With a military draft in 1955, Allen enlisted in the Marine Corps and served two years. They had their first child in 1956. After his service, Allen started law school at Yale. Lucy had taken summer courses to become a teacher and support the family.

"We arrived in New Haven in 1957," she said, "with a thirteen-month-old child and poor as church mice. I taught, my husband took care of the baby part-time, and we sent him to daycare part-time. We lived in the basement of a big old house that was converted into apartments. And best I can remember, it was terrible, but we were young and optimistic."

In their second year at Yale, the Duffys were able to move into half a Quonset hut of their own, and the friendship bloomed. We would attend a lot of off-Broadway shows together, always getting the cheapest tickets. Allen and I began playing golf together, then squash. We were so evenly matched that after three years, we ended up tied in games won.

I remember one last squash game where best friends and best rivals collided: We played five games in a set. We were in the fifth game, just about dead even, and Allen swung really hard at the ball. The racquet slipped out of his hand and crashed against the wall.

What did I do? I took the point.

Betty and I hosted parties in our Quonset hut. Betty and Lucy became active in the Yale Law Wives, a group of spouses who met regularly in the evening for a stimulating lecture by a Yale law professor or visiting professor. At exam time, the spouses would serve coffee and doughnuts to the men. Allen, who loved American traditional music, was a mix of intelligent, Yale-educated lawyer and country boy. He kept bees, pruned apple trees, and loved Leadbelly, Big Bill Broonzy, and the blues. After Allen died, I helped raise $1.5 million to endow a professorship in his name at Yale Law School.

"I think back about our years at Yale. It was a difficult time," says Lucy of our deep friendship, "but I don't think we thought it was difficult. I think, 'My God, how did we do that?' But it was a marvelous education. We were very close to Dave and Betty."

When Allen died, I sent a plane to carry close friends and family to the funeral in Harwich, Massachusetts. Our plane would later pick up Lucy for trips back to Louisville and other places. She would bake cookies for the pilots.

Lucy grew very close to the four Jones children who went to Yale, especially Dave, who would call her when Yale had a food workers' strike and ask to come to dinner. Betty and I, in turn, invited the Duffys to the Kentucky Derby several times, hanging out in the infield just for fun. Lucy, Betty, and I flew to Berlin just as the Wall came down, chipping off a piece. Then Lucy and Betty went to Paris, rented a car, and went to Lucy's mother's hometown in France.

Allen was a runner, and Lucy began running in her mid-forties. She completed her first marathon at age forty-eight and went on to run a total of fourteen, after which she took up triathlons. When Allen got sick in 1985, she ran the New York City Marathon in a hand-printed "Lucy Against Leukemia" shirt to raise money for leukemia research. Allen, in remission, was with her in New York but died a month or so later. Lucy continued to support leukemia research through her runs, eventually raising hundreds of thousands of dollars and being credited as one of the founders of the Leukemia Society's "Team in Training" fundraiser.

The Quonset hut that Betty and I lived in was right across from the iconic Yale Bowl, the first bowl-shaped football stadium in the country. Built in 1913–14, it was the nation's largest—with 70,896 seats—at a time when the Ivy League was the football power. It became a gathering place for older students and we could walk across the street and go to games.

Our intramural games were played on fields right below where we lived. They were used as parking lots on football weekends. That's the first time I ever saw tailgating. People would come with their Rolls-Royce and butler.

In New Haven, I went to work for Irv Lasky, an accountant who became a good friend as well as an employer. Irv suggested we open a McDonald's together in Louisville in that company's early franchise years. It didn't happen. Somebody beat us to it.

Along with working at a CPA office in the morning doing taxes and teaching at Quinnipiac at night, I taught an economics class for two years at Yale, Analysis of Financial Statements. My office was in Yale's seven-story Sheffield-Sterling-Strathcona Hall, a quiet place where I would do all my homework.

The class added another layer to my knowledge and plans for the future. It was a required course for industrial engineering majors, taught by a team of four professors and instructors. All four of us would meet on Fridays to discuss new textbooks and create exam questions. I still remember how proud I was the first time one of my questions was accepted.

My teaching led Ralph Jones, the department head, to recommend me to the Travelers Insurance Company in Hartford for a summer job analyzing the effects of price-level changes and inflation, the subject of a book he had written. Twice after I graduated, Ralph asked me to come back to Yale to teach.

My office was on the top floor of the twenty-three-story Travelers

Tower, then New England's tallest building. My companion up there in those bare-bone days of insurance analysis was a weatherman keeping an eye out for damaging storms.

It was a pretty conservative place. They paid me a handsome sum. I wrote a report I was very proud of, and I learned a lot about insurance, how claims came in, and how long it took to process and pay them. It stayed back there in my memory bank and came in handy as Humana moved into health insurance.

My final report, which detailed the fact the company was doing a lot of dumb—but easily correctable—things, received high praise from my boss, who told me, "If I show it to anybody higher up, I'll lose my job."

The other half of that summer, I found a job with an Indianapolis law firm, Ross, McCord, Ice & Miller. I gained great experience with talented colleagues, had lots of fun, and was offered a position upon graduation, but I chose to return home to Louisville.

In New Haven, Betty worked for a time for a man named Richard Lee, who was running for mayor. She had wanted to teach school in New Haven, but being pregnant with our first child prevented that. Our first two children, David, Jr., born in January 1958, and Susan, born in April 1959, arrived while we lived in the Quonset hut.

Betty had been taking new mother classes at the Yale School of Nursing, where a nurse taught the values of natural childbirth—the less anesthetic, the better. When Dave was born, Betty, almost twenty-five, shared a hospital room that had six beds. It cost $25. The attending physician reminded her not to pay the $50 anesthetic fee because she didn't use it—a savings we needed.

"I've always joked that David was the cheapest of our babies," she would say.

I have my own memories of that birth. The night that Dave arrived, I drove Betty over to the hospital. My first law school exam was the next morning, so I'm sitting there timing her contractions and reading *Prosser on Torts.*

Dave was born. I went down to get in the car to go take my exam. The car had been towed away because we had come in the middle of the night, and parking, as always around hospitals, was tight. It was only about a mile or so to the law school, so I hustled over there, took the exam, and then my friend Jim Johnstone drove me to the impoundment lot and loaned me $10 to retrieve my car.

Sue was also born in New Haven. Our other three children, Dan, Matt, and Carol, were born in Louisville, with Betty taking only a muscle relaxant because she wanted to witness their births.

In New Haven, the young families living in the Quonset huts had developed a non-cash babysitting barter system. We took turns helping each other.

Betty recalled, "It was a babysitting pool, and one of the moms was the rotating bookkeeper. You had a roster of people, and you would be credited when you babysat for somebody. We would call somebody to come sit if we wanted to go out. And then we would owe three hours. We were able to go to a play or movie every now and then or play bridge."

We played a lot of bridge. Betty was a natural, and I had honed my skills in the Navy. We shared dinners with friends, but the menu didn't change much. We made a lot of good meals with hamburger. I think Betty has about fifty ways to fix hamburger.

We survived—even thrived—in our new environment. I was more than ready for scholarly pursuits after a few years away on Navy duty. As always, school—even law school at Yale—came easily for me. I enjoyed my classes in contracts, civil procedure, and constitutional law. Looking ahead, I was one of the few in my class who took a lot of classes in business. I was still teaching at Quinnipiac and Yale.

After Dave was born, Betty ran a nursery school for the children of Yale graduate students. With no Southern Baptist churches available in New Haven, we began attending a Congregational Church. We loved it, partly because Sunday School for the children was at the same time as the sermon. And it only required an hour of attendance compared to the three hours it often took at the Baptist churches.

When former president Harry Truman came to Yale in 1958 to deliver one of its historic Chubb Lectures, I got a 4 a.m. call from a friend, Burt Griffin, who was an editor of the *Yale Law Journal*, asking if I would like to join him and Truman for a walk.

"Yes, sir," I said.

Students always wore a coat and tie to classes back then. Betty got up, quickly ironed the collar and cuff and the front of my shirt, and sent me off to meet the president.

Every morning about six o'clock, Truman took a long walk. He was still fairly young and vigorous. He had only one or two Secret Service guys. Burt Griffin and I were the two students who went walking with him. A brisk walk in the morning with a former president of the United States is something that sticks in the memory. I would write about it later:

> He walked fast, stopped and chatted with whoever was up and about at that early morning time. He inquired about our future plans and discussed our military service. He encouraged engagement—political and societal—and was just extremely nice.

The walk with Truman was a wonderful experience that would help me think about my own politics. I was a young socialist at that time, politically, not formally but in my views and beliefs, having grown up in what today would be called poverty, although we didn't know it at the time since everyone in the neighborhood was just as poor.

Burt Griffin, my walking partner, would later serve on the Warren Commission, which investigated the Kennedy assassination, and helped write its report. Later he was the first director of the national Legal Aid program. He then practiced law for a while in Cleveland before becoming a judge.

Along with a law degree, I picked up other skills in New Haven that would become a part of my Louisville business life. A friend taught me to play golf at the Yale course, where students could play for a dollar. I played squash almost every day, golf when I could, touch football in the fall, and basketball in the winter. Given a chance, Betty said, my first career choice would have been to become a professional football player. I maintained a B-plus grade average, which was pretty good, while working and teaching between my classes and in the evenings. I didn't have any real problems with Yale. I loved it! We always found ways to balance our personal and professional lives. The advice I have given people about marriage is try not to go to sleep at night with any unresolved grievances.

But in the spring of 1960, we were ready to come home to family and friends in Louisville. Both sets of parents were there, and I was eager for new opportunities. Our New Haven connections always stuck, too. We attended class reunions every five years, and four of our five children went to Yale.

I had several job possibilities. During Christmas in my third year of law school, I had been offered a job with the Wyatt, Grafton & Sloss law firm in Louisville—at $425 a month, or $5,100 a year. I had been offered other jobs in New York and Washington law firms for about $7,200 a year, but the Louisville lure was too strong.

I had already taken a bar review course in New Haven and would pass the Kentucky bar exam later that summer in Frankfort. While there, I shared a $10-a-night hotel room with another law candidate—and eventual congressman—Ron Mazzoli.

Wyatt, Grafton & Sloss advanced me $300 to help with the move home—the money to be paid back at $25 a month the first year. We packed all our possessions into an old two-wheel trailer we had purchased in 1957 for $15 and had often lent to other Yale students. We said our goodbyes and took off for Louisville, 800 miles away, in an orange 1952 Dodge station wagon. It was a modest replacement for our somewhat newer Chevy, which had been smashed by a driver running a stop sign.

Our fan belt broke on the Pennsylvania Turnpike, so we stopped by the side of the road and waited for somebody to radio for assistance. There were no cell phones then. An authorized repairman eventually arrived, put on a new fan belt, and charged $20. That depleted our cash, so we were unable to spend the four dollars for a motel room. We drove all night as the children slept, and Betty dozed off. When we got to Cincinnati, we didn't have enough money to buy gas to finish the trip to Louisville.

I had three options: pawn my watch, call brother Logan and ask him to meet us in Carrollton, Kentucky, or go ask the AAA auto club manager to cash a postdated five-dollar check. The nice AAA manager cashed the check. Upon arrival in Louisville, I borrowed five dollars from Betty's dad and deposited it so the check would clear.

We were practically broke—but we were home.

Part II

GETTING DOWN TO BUSINESS

Previous page:
Behind David, from left: William T. Young, William Ballard, Jr., Carl Pollard, Joseph Greene, H. Linden McLellan, Wendell Cherry.

Chapter Five

Meeting Wendell Cherry

"When I graduated from law school, I was probably close to being a young socialist. I'd learned a lot about regulation and how wonderful it was. Then I saw it in action, and probably within two weeks of starting to practice law I realized I'd been taught a lot of stuff that really wasn't accurate. People are people, and human nature doesn't change."

— DAVID JONES

Upon returning home to Louisville, Betty and I moved in with her parents for a few months, then bought a two-story red-brick home at 2239 Lowell Avenue, just off Bardstown Road in Strathmoor Village, a solid middle-class area lined with similar red-brick homes. The house cost $15,000—$500 down and mortgage payments of $85 a month—payments just in balance with the family income.

I augmented that income by teaching two courses three times a year at the University of Louisville, mostly in its MBA program. I enjoyed teaching, plus it was night work, earning me another $2,400 annually. I taught almost anything they had to offer, so I was kind of a utility infielder. I taught math and income tax. I taught algebra. I taught statistics. The only course I ever turned down was child psychology. I taught five or six years because we needed the money. It put a big burden on Betty. She was always there taking care of the kids and me.

My teaching did allow Betty to audit U of L courses for free or take them for credit at half-price, and she attended a wide variety of classes. Another bonus: U of L basketball tickets in the early 1960s were only one dollar for faculty.

I was the ninth lawyer hired into the firm of Wyatt, Grafton & Sloss, small by today's standards but at the time the largest law firm in Louisville. My mentor was Bob Sloss, a leading lawyer in real estate, an area that very much interested me. With his long list of connections, Sloss was the firm's "rainmaker," the man who attracted the money.

He came by that naturally. He graduated from the University of Michigan at age twenty, where he had been editor-in-chief of the student newspaper. He was a good writer, detail-oriented, with an upbeat personality, a demanding attitude, and strong work ethic. He would toss me things and expect me to do them. It was a leadership technique that I would use to great effect throughout my life. I think the confidence I showed in people created the sense they didn't ever want to disappoint me.

Sloss was also a great mediator. He could bring angry people together in the same room to talk and reach a settlement without lawsuits. I developed the same skills: negotiations done in private and out of the media spotlight until we reached a settlement. I would also come to understand the power of a press conference: inviting the public for a look at some issue but always giving credit to others. Praise in public, criticize in private was another enduring lesson learned.

My law colleagues also had interesting backgrounds, with deep and lasting connections in Louisville and Kentucky. Brothers Arthur and Chip Grafton were the sons of a missionary to China. Chip was the father of the late Sue Grafton, a prolific and popular mystery author.

Wilson Wyatt was a very prominent Kentuckian with a national reputation. A 1927 graduate of the University of Louisville School of Law, he served as Louisville mayor from 1941 through 1945. After World War II, President Truman appointed him to a cabinet-level position as United States housing expediter to help find and build homes for millions of returning GIs.

Truman sent Wyatt a letter noting that:

> Veterans and former war workers have come back to their
> hometowns and have found no place to live. . . . It is urgent that
> every available temporary living quarter be used in overcrowded
> communities [and] that the production of homes be hurried.
>
> I am asking you . . . to make the machinery of housing
> production run as smoothly and speedily as possible.

Very active in Democratic politics, Wyatt became campaign manager
for Adlai Stevenson's presidential campaigns in 1952 and 1956, both
ending in losses to Dwight Eisenhower. Wyatt later served as lieutenant
governor of Kentucky from 1959 through 1963 and headed the Kentucky
Economic Development Commission. He ran for the US Senate in 1962
and lost to incumbent Thruston B. Morton by 45,000 votes.

I primarily worked in real estate, with some work in tax and general
business. I was also a volunteer for the American Civil Liberties Union. In
my five and a half years with the firm, I handled only two criminal court
cases, each providing an education of a sort.

My first ever trip to court—the "Great Bowling Ball Case"—involved a
friend of Bob Sloss who owned Parkmoor Bowling Lanes on Third Street.
His friend's wife had been bowling there, and somebody stole her bowling
ball. She was fairly certain she knew who had taken it, and Sloss assigned
me to go to small claims court to get it sorted out.

Mission accomplished.

The guy had to give her thirty bucks for the bowling ball.

My other case—in federal court—gave me some early practice in the
art of the legal bluff. It involved the husband of a maid who worked for a
friend of Wilson Wyatt. The husband was a retired conductor for the L&N
Railroad, an African-American man with a law degree who, in those days,
could find steady work only as a railroad conductor. He had also worked
part-time as a waiter at Kapfhammer's Party House, a catering company
in Louisville, and had been charged with hiding that income so his railroad

retirement income would not be reduced.

Before trial, I asked my client if he had ever been in trouble before: "Oh, no, Mr. Jones, everything is fine."

I had already negotiated with the prosecutor, who had ample proof of my client's transgressions. But because of the client's prior clean record, the deal they offered was to plead him "nolo contendere"—legalese for "you could probably convict me if we went to trial, but let's avoid all that and I'll take probation."

So we get over there and tell that to the judge in federal court. It's kind of an awe-inspiring thing. I'd never been before a federal judge. The judge was okay with the deal until a probation officer testified that my defendant had three prior felony convictions. I was caught totally off guard. Things were looking grim until the prosecutor said he couldn't go to trial on the case; he wasn't ready.

I responded: "The judge set the trial date, and I'm prepared. Come on, let's go at it."

The prosecutor—wanting to move on—agreed to the probation deal.

I wasn't prepared either. It was a total bluff.

My writing skills proved useful in appellate briefs, almost all of them successful. My method was to find the previous research of a lawyer who knew more about a very narrow bit of that particular law than anyone else in the world and use that information. It was all about due diligence.

Other than malpractice, reimbursement, and acquisition cases, we never sued anybody in my forty-four years at Humana. We did sue the government time after time and won most of our cases against them because they would try to cheat us on reimbursement, and I didn't put up with that. But as far as getting sued or suing anybody, I just didn't do that.

I got my finest legal advice from law school friend Allen Duffy, a litigator who had to calm me down after I got upset about a case I considered pursuing in court. He told me that before I did anything, I had to remember that judges are wrong about half the time. You can win a lot of cases that you shouldn't win, and you can lose a lot of cases that you shouldn't lose. But I enjoyed law. I think I would have been a good lawyer.

In terms of religious advice, Betty and I were helped by a young law firm partner, Gordon Davidson. Upon returning to Louisville, we were turned off by the anti-Catholic rhetoric in the Kennedy-Nixon presidential race in 1960, with some Baptist churches posting signs that said, "Attend the church of your choice while you still have a choice." Those signs reflected the widespread concern, especially in the South, that Kennedy, a Catholic, would be a more faithful servant to Pope John XXIII than to the American people.

Davidson suggested Betty and I attend Highland Presbyterian Church on Cherokee Road. It not only fit our beliefs, but it was also a one-hour church, with the children in Sunday school and parents in the worship service at the same time. We became dedicated, generous members for almost sixty years. For nearly half of those years, we were held spellbound by Henry Mobley, Jr., the church's beloved, caring, funny, golf-playing minister whom I once described as "smart, kind, progressive, and a bit tough, or perhaps curmudgeonly."

Mobley was a regular on a longtime TV and radio program named *The Moral Side of the News,* along with Rabbi Herbert Waller of Temple Adath Israel and the Rev. John Rowan Claypool of Crescent Hill Baptist Church. Their weekly discussion was popular and effective in lowering the anti-whatever rhetoric. We need something like that program today.

It was at Wyatt, Grafton & Sloss that I first met Wendell Cherry, a man who would become my partner in the creation of Humana and my dearest friend. We had very different personalities, enabling us to mix vision, passion, and prudence to build a great company.

I was the visionary, willing and able to deal with people and inspire them to take chances but not get too tightly wound up about it. I tend to see the humor in things. At the end of the day, I've always been able to deal with whatever comes up. In terms of the big picture, if you're a baseball pitcher and you think you're going to strike somebody out, and he hits a home run instead, it's not the end of the world. It might be the end of your contract, but business is like that.

Wendell was a brilliant man who always brought an honest, intense, focused reality into the picture. He was prone to saying exactly what was on his mind to whomever he thought should hear it—four-letter language included.

I'd been hired at the Wyatt firm in December 1959 while on Christmas vacation from law school. I had been taken to the then very private Pendennis Club by a partner in the firm, who offered me a job. After that meeting—and having been introduced to all the other lawyers in the firm—I went back to talk to Wendell, one of the firm's few young lawyers.

We closed the door, and I said, "Wendell, you've been here six months. Tell me about this place."

"It's terrible," Wendell responded. "They work you like a dog, and they don't pay you very much."

The mutual bond that led us to found Humana two years later was pretty much established in that moment: I, a man who would eventually back many civic endeavors; Wendell, whose legendary art collecting, imagination, and architectural skills became part of Louisville's marble-and-mortar community fabric. We were well-matched. We wanted success, but we also liked to see other people succeed.

Wendell's life mirrored mine in its Horatio Alger storyline. He was born in 1935 in Depression-era Riverside, Kentucky, in Hart County, and grew up in nearby Horse Cave, in the cave-rich area called Caverna. He was the son of grocery wholesaler Layman S. Cherry and his wife, Geneva.

Wendell's interest in art took root when the Caverna community gave members of the state semifinalist basketball team, their parents, and chaperones a trip to Washington, DC, in a yellow school bus. They visited the National Gallery of Art. Wendell saw a John Singer Sargent painting and said it changed his life. The rest of the crowd went off to the Smithsonian and the monuments. Wendell spent the whole two days in the National Gallery.

He received a business degree from the University of Kentucky in 1957 and his law degree in 1959. As with me, when he began at Wyatt, Grafton & Sloss, he taught night classes at the University of Louisville to augment a slim income.

Friends and family described Wendell as alternately shy, talkative, charming, laser-intense, very decisive, generous, caring, short-tempered, quick to laugh, as profane as he had to be, self-effacing, and not particularly interested in law or how much money he made. Occasionally, he was a man who just wanted to be by himself.

He reached out and touched people in his own way. He took the longtime family housekeeper, Rose Fugit, to the Metropolitan Museum of Art in New York, where he spent an hour with her talking about paintings and other art. When he was dealing with cancer later in life, Fugit took him for his weekly cancer treatments.

She wrote of that experience:

> He always sang, "Swing low, sweet chariot, coming for to carry me home," on the way there and then again on the way home.
>
> Mr. Cherry loved peaches, and he would always have me slice them up for him. About a month after he died, there was an aroma of peaches in the house. I always think of him when I see peaches.

Wendell would become very deeply involved in the Louisville arts community. He helped create, fund, and oversee the construction of the Kentucky Center for the Performing Arts, was instrumental in designing and constructing the Humana Building, and became one of the nation's leading art collectors. He was a lawyer for the group sponsoring world heavyweight champion Muhammad Ali. He was part owner of the Kentucky Colonels basketball team with me and was once president of the American Basketball Association.

His friends nicknamed him "Horse Cave Harry," but his sophisticated ascent into the art world defied the label. At a Manhattan auction in 1981, Wendell outbid other collectors for the self-portrait *Yo, Picasso*, paying what was then the highest price ever for one of Picasso's works.

The night before the purchase, Horse Cave Harry had called his banker, Bert Klein, and asked if his credit was still good for $5 or $6 million dollars.

"Sure," Klein said.

The next night, Klein was watching a national newscast where it was announced an "unknown" collector had purchased *Yo, Picasso* for $5.83 million. The next morning, Wendell called Klein and told him where to wire the money. Eight years later, Cherry sold the Picasso for $47.9 million.

"Good old Wendell," said London art dealer Desmond Leon Corcoran. "He always lands on his feet."

In many Wendell Cherry stories, the name Horse Cave Harry was a perfect fit. One story is told by David Grissom, a lawyer I hired for the firm. It involves the time Wendell, still struggling financially, purchased a used Studebaker Lark from Louis J. Herrmann at Summers Herrmann Ford. The car had constant problems, including a balky ignition system.

One Monday morning, Wendell drove the car into the dealership's service area, where he met Herrmann, a believer in personal customer service. Wendell leaned out the window and asked Herrmann, "Louie, do you stand behind your cars?"

"I certainly do," said Herrmann.

"Good," said Wendell. "Get back behind this car 'cause I'm going to run over your ass."

Wendell stepped out of the car, laughing, handed Herrmann the keys, and left.

Grissom became a partner, business success, and friend who also fit the blue-collar mold. One of four children, he moved to Louisville when he was a child. His mother was a homemaker. His father, a manufacturer's representative for DuBois Chemicals, was the first in his family to earn a college degree. A great athlete at Atherton High School, Grissom attended Centre College in Danville, Kentucky, where he would later serve as chairman of the board for more than twenty years.

Grissom married his childhood sweetheart, Mary Ellen Wilhoite, just before his junior year at Centre. He was nineteen, and she was eighteen.

They lived over a furniture store in Danville, sharing the single bath with three other apartment dwellers. While playing football and competing on the track team—in seven events—he worked in the school cafeteria, graded papers, and drove the campus school bus, picking up students at the Kentucky College for Women on the other side of town and taking them to classes at Centre.

Grissom left Centre after his junior year to attend the University of Louisville Law School in a program where Centre would give him his Centre degree upon finishing at U of L. To earn money while in law school, he worked construction jobs at the new Ohio River locks and dam and in the Kentucky highway department's legal section. He was twenty-four when he got his degree.

Mary Ellen Grissom would tragically die in an automobile accident at age thirty, leaving David with three children ages ten, eight, and eight months, as both of their families rallied to help.

He and his present wife, Marlene, would later establish the Grissom Scholars Program, a four-year, all-expenses-paid scholarship to Centre for "exceptionally talented, high-need, first-generation" college students.

Grissom, Wendell, and I instantly bonded at the law office. We were three of its youngest, most dynamic members. In Humana's early years, Grissom played a key role with Wendell and me.

Wendell and I were like brothers, our occasional, if not inevitable, disagreements only drawing us closer. One day Wendell and I met with three older and allegedly wiser gentlemen, one, the president of a small college; the second, the chief executive of a large bank; the third, a very successful politician.

After some obligatory small talk, it became evident to Wendell that what the three men really wanted was a $1 million donation from Humana, in return for which the college president offered to name its business school the "Humana School of Business."

The words were barely out of his mouth when Wendell looked him in the eye in that steely way of his and said, "If you gave us a million dollars, I wouldn't let you name your school Humana."

On another occasion, Wendell and I were having discussions with another college president who had a faculty member who—in our view—was impeding progress on an important matter. When we suggested the president use his authority to remove that roadblock, the president responded that the faculty member was "indispensable" and could not be removed.

"I drive by Cave Hill Cemetery every morning," Wendell said, "and it's filled asshole-to-elbow with indispensable men."

A corporate partner once analyzed the Cherry-Jones partnership: "The way they work is this: Wendell says, 'Go f—— yourself,' and Dave says, 'Come on, let's sit down and talk about this.' "

Wendell and I did talk. About everything. Almost every day we would find time to sit down together, shut the door, and discuss what was going on. Not just about the company but events around the world that could impact our business.

Thinking is incredibly important. I'm action-oriented, and it's action that changes the world, but I'm also a thinker. I think about what I am doing. If there are problems, you solve them. You get to the point.

Wendell and I always had a lot of fun together, beginning with our early days at the law firm. We worked five-and-a-half-day weeks in the law office and would alternately work one hour apiece on Saturday mornings handling the law firm's switchboard. You could listen in on everybody's calls.

In our early years with the firm—we had small children then—we gave each other rides to work to save money. We also took early stabs at outside money-making ventures. I always had an interest in real estate. While I was in college, my brother Logan and I rebuilt homes, borrowing money from local banks. Wendell and another friend, Stuart Jay, opened The Scene, a coffee house at First and Barbee Streets on what's now the U of L campus. The venture lasted about a year.

The first Jones-and-Cherry deal involved a possible Holiday Inn franchise. I had represented, through Bob Sloss, a group of men who had built four very successful Holiday Inns in Louisville in the early 1960s.

Wendell and I optioned a piece of property from a small grocery store at the Glendale exit off Interstate 65, about forty-five minutes south of Louisville. Wendell's father had been aware of the property and helped set up the deal. We hoped the proposed new Western Kentucky Parkway would come through the land, but it was routed north to Elizabethtown.

We were paying about $50 a month for six months on the Glendale land option. We could barely afford the $50. We each had three children, and we were very, very busy. Our more successful business—using expertise gained from Bob Sloss—was developing a subdivision on Blue Lick Road. The land was very wet—literally dubbed "crawfish land"—and a septic system would not work there.

With the help of Ken McGee, a student of mine in an MBA course at U of L, I formed a sewer district and sold sewer bonds. We hired someone to install sewers and created a subdivision. The lots sold for $4,000 and $5,000, about a year's salary each. We made a fair amount of money on it, and we improved the value of that land by bringing sewers to it.

Our friendship also led Wendell and me to a place we never thought we would be: politics. In 1961 I became a speechwriter for Democratic mayoral candidate W. S. Milburn, my principal at Male High School. He was chairman of the Louisville board of aldermen and a heavy favorite for mayor.

Wendell wrote speeches for county judge-executive candidate Thomas L. Ray, a Democratic leader in the Kentucky House of Representatives. He was also a local favorite for an elective office that had been controlled by Democrats for the past twenty-eight years. Milburn lost in a landslide to Republican William O. Cowger, and Ray lost to Republican Marlow Cook by 20,000 votes, giving Republicans the clean sweep after almost three decades of Democratic control.

Another lesson learned. That was the end of my political career, and I think Wendell's, too.

My politics moderated after I joined the law firm. I had grown up with a mother who was a staunch Democrat, and a father who was staunchly Republican. We children would tease our parents, saying they should just stay home on election day because they only canceled each other's votes.

When I graduated from law school, I was probably close to being a young socialist. I'd learned a lot about regulation and how wonderful it was. Then I saw it in action, and probably within a few weeks of starting to practice law, I realized I'd been taught a lot of stuff that really wasn't accurate. People are people, and human nature doesn't change.

✳

The story of our creation of Humana starts with a favorite phrase: "the confidence of total ignorance."

It began in 1961, shortly after I returned to Louisville. The city's housing market was dealing with a surplus of executive homes due to the departure of Reynolds Metal Company. The firm, founded in Louisville in 1919 as US Foil Company and eventually the third-largest aluminum company in the world, left Louisville in 1958 in bitter circumstances.

Reynolds had developed plans for a research park near suburban Anchorage that would employ about 2,000 people, many of them executives. Famed architect Eero Saarinen, designer of the St. Louis Gateway Arch and the main terminal at Dulles International Airport, was hired to design the park as more of a university campus off Westport Road, near Central State Hospital, a mental institution.

Reynolds was then the largest company in Kentucky, with more growth promised. Upscale Anchorage area residents fought the plan. Good idea, they said, but not in my backyard, and the proposal was twice defeated in angrily contested zoning hearings.

Reynolds also had tentative plans to create a renewal project along the city's decaying rust-belt riverfront, using urban renewal funding. Louisville Mayor Andrew Broaddus tried to persuade the company to build a new headquarters along the waterfront, but that plan was also denied. Reynolds Metal was run out of town by the same kind of people who later wouldn't let a proposed East End bridge get built—delaying the project for decades. In a way, the short-sighted stupidity of Louisville's leaders in losing Reynolds stunted the city's growth for many years, but it also led to the creation of Humana.

At that time, I was helping Bob Sloss prepare the possible closing of a home owned by Billy Reynolds, the company CEO. The prospective purchaser was Brian McCoy, a lawyer who had been two years ahead of me at Male High School. I remembered McCoy. He had grown up in Louisville's blue-collar South End, with limited family income. Now he was looking to buy the home of the CEO of Reynolds Metal, a home priced at about $85,000 in 1961, perhaps worth several million dollars now.

Curious, I asked McCoy how he could afford the house.

"Dave," answered McCoy, "I built a nursing home last year."

I immediately gave that some thought. I was still earning low wages, and our third child, Dan, had just been born. After our talk, I went to Wendell's office with an idea: "Let's build a nursing home," was the essence of my suggestion.

"Why not?" was essentially his answer.

And Humana was born, though the name itself was years away. Our decision came five years before the passage of Medicare and Medicaid, which now fund much of nursing-home costs. There were very few dedicated, regulated nursing homes in the country then, especially for the elderly who needed long-term care. Many still lived with their children or in older houses that had been converted into nursing homes, with minimal care regulation and a shortage of qualified medical staff.

A national government survey in the 1950s showed the country had 9,000 nursing homes with about 250,000 beds. A federal Government Accounting Office estimate showed a shortage of between 250,000 and 500,000 beds, with little funding available for them unless the new facilities were associated with hospitals.

I had a personal experience with such makeshift nursing homes, and it would strongly affect my approach to the business and patient care as Wendell and I moved forward. My beloved grandmother Jessie America O'Bryan Thurman—the woman I kissed every day after parking my bike in her yard on my way to Parkland Junior High School—eventually reached the point where she could not be cared for at home.

In 1956, the final year of her life, she was moved to a three-story house on South Third Street, built at the turn of the century. Many of the residents had been tied into their chairs, presumably for their own safety. There was little physical therapy or any other services so common today. If a fire broke out, there's no way in the world the staff could have gotten the residents out. There were no elevators, and I didn't like it.

I saw a similar situation with Betty's grandmother as we visited her in a nursing home in Portsmouth, Virginia. Old house, well-intentioned, kindly people, but, again, it was distressing to see in person. In both those cases, women who had been so brilliant and vital and wonderful were in a place of total dependency and not much else. But at the end of life, if there's nobody home to take care of them, they have to be placed where they can receive care. So that was on my mind.

Sensing an opportunity, Wendell and I discussed the nursing home business, with Brian McCoy's nursing home next to the Jewish Community Center as a basic model. We had no idea where it would lead us, but I was certain it would be much better than the conditions I had seen with my family. Wendell had had the same experience with a grandmother. After seeing those situations, we vowed that anything we built wouldn't be like that. The Golden Rule would be in place. And we built a really beautiful nursing home where nobody was ever tied in a chair.

Our start to what would become a company with $64.89 billion in 2019 sales was like something out of an American Dream book—maybe *T-Model Tommy*, the inspirational stories I had read as a boy. I borrowed $1,000 from Household Finance. Wendell borrowed $1,000 from his father-in-law. I wrote a business plan, which would later be encased in Lucite by a mutual friend, Carl Pollard, and kept on a shelf in my office.

I put all my sales skills to work. There would be four other partners in the venture—Louisville businessmen and realtors Sonny Bass and Charlie Weisberg, and Bill Rommel and Jim McFerran, of Rommel–McFerran general contractors. All had met through Wyatt, Grafton & Sloss. Bass,

Weisberg, Rommel, and McFerran also put up $1,000 each.

The company was incorporated on August 18, 1961, with the name Wendav. The land for the first nursing home was at 2000 Liverpool Lane, at Bardstown Road. The property was on Louisville's 1960s urban-suburban edge, directly across from what would become Bashford Manor Mall. (The shopping complex was built on a fifty-eight-acre parcel that was once the site of a Thoroughbred horse farm that produced three Kentucky Derby winners, Azra, Manuel, and Sir Huon. It has since gone out of business.)

Bass and Weisberg knew the Liverpool Lane landowner, Caesar Bertoli, a large, engaging man who owned a Louisville tile company—a man prone to suddenly breaking out in arias made famous by Enrico Caruso. I persuaded Bertoli—and his attorney, Bill Mulloy—to lease us the land on a long-term basis and then allow us to place a first mortgage on it. That meant Bertoli would lose the land if we and our partners didn't pay the mortgage. Our group paid a higher rent to account for that possibility. Having Bass, Weisberg, Rommel, and McFerran sign the lease created the financial credibility we needed.

I delivered our business plan to Charlie Will, the CEO of Portland Federal Savings. He believed in our vision, eventually becoming a vital lending partner in the company's future growth. With all six partners signing the note and the initial land lease, Portland Federal and Will lent us 80 percent of the appraised value of the land and proposed building, which was $256,000.

Still needing more money, I then persuaded Jack Zehnder, owner of Zehnder Mechanical Contractors, to accept a five-year note for $100,000 at 9 percent interest, high for those days. Zehnder would provide all the plumbing, heating, air conditioning, and ventilation for the home.

Zehnder and I were also a natural fit. He was a 1934 Male High School graduate and a 1939 graduate of Jefferson School of Law. He was also a licensed master plumber and a former B-25 bomber navigator in World War II. Later in life, he raised Thoroughbred horses and gave generously to many local organizations and charities.

Zehnder's help completed the deal. With willing partners, a helpful banker, and a guy who sang Caruso songs, Wendell and I had $356,000 to build our first nursing home: $320,000 for construction plus $36,000 to pay for furniture and equipment. So that's how the company began. Betty used to worry about all the loans I signed, and I've always told her, "You shouldn't worry. The bank should worry."

Bass and Weisberg introduced architect Kenny Mock, who designed the building—the first of several he would design as the chain expanded. There was one little bump along the way. Wendell and I decided to name our first nursing home "Hermitage House" after President Andrew Jackson's home in Nashville. We hired a young artist, Keith Spears, for $35 to create a Hermitage House logo. Somehow it came out "Heritage House."

We couldn't afford to have it done over, so we said, "Heritage House sounds fine."

Construction on the home began in December 1961, with contractors Rommel and McFerran, who had been brought in as partners, agreeing to build at cost. The home opened on August 10, 1962, with seventy-eight beds. It was later expanded to 120. We purchased furniture from the American Hospital Supply Corporation, whose salesman had promised good service. The furniture delivery was late. The night before the opening, many of us were frantically putting together furniture, hauling in bed springs, and preparing the rooms. The next day, ten pre-registered guests were checked in, each solicited by ads in the *Courier Journal*.

Bernie Rosenthal, the head of advertising and in charge of copy and layout at the *Courier Journal*, helped us write the first ad. Rosenthal remembers Wendell and me walking into the advertising department wanting to place that ad—two young men with a plan and no real idea where it would take them.

"We just spoke in general terms," Rosenthal recalls. "They said they wanted to open up a nursing home, they had an address and a phone number, and that was about it."

The first ad wasn't large. Rosenthal found illustrations of a very attractive couple to promote the home. The copy above the couple read:

A wonderful new concept in

NURSING AND
CONVALESCENT CARE

The copy below read:

Heritage House

"Their home away from home"

"I may have done it while they were right there," Rosenthal says.

The "well-managed" part of the first nursing home took a little more time. Wendell and I had hired a nurse to manage the operation. She put together a staff but had no experience running a nursing home. Who did? The night before the home opened, in the middle of all the bed-assembling work, the nurse stressed out and ended up in a bed herself—Heritage House's first patient.

So we opened the nursing home and just about went crazy. For a couple of months, it was chaos. I had a little leadership experience in the Navy, but I'd never run a nursing home or any kind of business. Wendell and I had different personalities. I would hire the nurses and the employees in the morning, and Wendell would fire them in the evening. I was pretty good at hiring, and he was pretty good at firing.

The solution—another lesson forever remembered—came in the form of Elmer Shaffner, a man I had met while working at Wasserman & Associates CPA office. Shaffner had later gone into hospital administration. I called and offered him the opportunity to manage our "beautiful nursing home." Fortunately for our partners and me, Shaffner agreed. Overnight, the chaos turned to calm. The lesson we learned was if you don't know how to do something, hire someone who does. That lesson paid off well for Wendell and me over the years. There's not enough good I can say about Elmer because, all of a sudden, we could go back to doing all those other

91

things, our nursing home was in great shape, and it gave us the basis for expanding to the next one. A lot of credit also goes to Betty, my always partner. She was in on some of the early planning and wrote most of the checks for the first few years of our business.

It was still a tough early climb. Seeking a $12,000 line of credit to keep the business flowing, we were turned down by Liberty National Bank officers, who advised us to "get our ducks in a row." Ed Waits, a vice president of Citizens Fidelity Bank, helped us borrow the money, and the company meandered forward.

Tommy Borders of Tommy Borders Restaurant Services was our meat supplier. Borders was a good friend of Bass and Weisberg. A US Army veteran of five major battles in the South Pacific, he was very patient with the nursing home payments, as were other vendors, who were usually paid on time.

The semi-private rooms at Heritage House cost $11 a day, the private rooms cost $20. Most nursing home costs are fixed, with payroll being the chief variable. Knowing the income from the rooms, I asked Shaffner to call me every Monday morning to report on occupancy and hours worked by the nurses. With this close approximation of earnings, I prepared a weekly estimated income statement, showing it to both Charlie Will at Portland Federal and Ed Waits at Citizens Fidelity—but there were still a lot of empty rooms at Heritage House.

Some weeks were good, and some were bad, but I earned a reputation for candor and honesty. It paid off because Mr. Will ultimately financed six nursing homes for us. And within a year, Heritage House was making a small profit.

Chapter Six

REACHING FOR THE SKY

"When I began working at Wyatt, Grafton & Sloss, my finances were so tight I would borrow $20 from my assistant, Wanda Ryan, so I could go out to lunch for a week while she ate peanut butter sandwiches."

— DAVID JONES

"He always paid me back on payday . . . but he didn't have any money at all. He more than made it up to me later on."

— WANDA RYAN

Our second nursing home, in Lexington, Kentucky, in 1963, came a little more easily, but with the inevitable complications that early success can bring.

Wendell and I were not necessarily thinking of expansion, but we were always tuned in and very opportunistic. Our own money remained very limited. This enterprise had begun just two years earlier when we each borrowed $1,000 to invest, but we could not pass up a chance to grow the company through a traditional business formula: Use other people's money. Our subsequent growth and success would involve many people, most of them a long way from Wall Street, with farm, coal-country, and blue-collar Kentucky backgrounds.

The long and the short of it is: Hunger is a great motivator. If you don't have anything, your choice is to earn it or steal it. And stealing will often put you in jail.

Wendell and I relied on the business mantra that would sustain us, although it was increasingly less true: the confidence of total ignorance. Each of the endeavors that we undertook—nursing homes, hospitals, insurance, and moving into the digital age—was something we knew absolutely nothing about.

We had no developed long-range goals in mind in 1963 when Gladys Bass, the wife of Sonny Bass, introduced us to her cousin Maury Kaufmann, a Lexington allergist who wanted a first-class nursing home there. Kaufmann had led a group of Lexington doctors on a tour of Heritage House in Louisville, and they were impressed by the building, the staff, and the financial possibilities.

The Lexington group—seven or eight doctors and a few of their friends—had a good sense of the need for a nursing home in Lexington. They helped find a suitable piece of land for the home and made a $100,000 subordinated loan, a loan that ranks after other debts if a company goes bankrupt or insolvent. Charlie Will at Portland Federal again stepped in to make the first mortgage loan.

The driving force behind the second nursing home was Hilary J. Boone Jr., whose life and work history paralleled my own. A native of Springfield, Kentucky, he paid his way through the University of Kentucky, delivering newspapers and working as a hotel night clerk while also serving as captain of the tennis team.

He was a bombardier in the Army Air Forces in World War II and afterward created a successful career in the Massachusetts Mutual Life Insurance Company. He eventually did very well with Humana stock and developed Wimbledon Farm, where Kentucky Derby winner Spectacular Bid and English Derby winner Golden Fleece were foaled and raised. He then gave back generously to the University of Kentucky and other organizations.

Wendell and I had learned from our Louisville nursing home experience. The Lexington home started with a good manager. Its staff was ordered to treat patients as if they were their own parents or another loved one. They were supportive, and Lexington really took off.

Boone then stepped in and said he and his colleagues—many of them Massachusetts Mutual general agents—could help build two more nursing homes in Connecticut. Boone helped form the local investment group, which invested $5,000 for 50 percent of the common stock and provided $100,000 in subordinated debt. Heritage House (the Jones-Cherry group) paid $5,000 for the other 50 percent of common stock.

Meanwhile, Bass, Weisberg, Wendell, and I had agreed to buy a home in Virginia Beach, Virginia—a transaction that brought me back to my Louisville roots. The connection would be Sam Klein and his brother Izzy, who owned used-car lots at Broadway and Eighth Streets in downtown Louisville—National Auto Sales on one side of the street and King Auto Sales on the other. If you got mad at one of the car lots, you went across the street and bought from the other. Nobody knew they were owned by the same people.

In the early 1940s, my brother Logan and I often stopped by the lots as we walked home from the Downtown YMCA. Having never had a car in our family until 1942, when Dad bought a Model A Ford, we were perhaps a bit inspired. We would admire the polished sheen of the cars, the opportunities they represented, and daydream of owning one.

To finance their car lots, the Klein brothers had to create a reserve fund at the Royal Bank & Trust Company. As a result, they became the bank's largest creditors. When the bank owner went to jail for income tax evasion, the brothers purchased the bank, which became the Bank of Louisville-Royal Bank and Trust Company.

Fast forward to 1963, when our group had contracted with George Holmes in Virginia Beach to buy his nursing home. Holmes orally agreed to carry a second mortgage of $35,000 to make the deal work, but the day before the scheduled purchase—and after the banks had closed—Holmes called me to say our deal was off. He had a better offer, which he would accept unless the Louisville partners came up with $35,000 by nine o'clock the following morning.

Charlie Weisberg immediately called Sam Klein—then well out of the used-car business—about our problem. Klein, who had never seen the

Virginia Beach nursing home, told Weisberg that I should prepare a note, and he would meet me at his bank at Fourth and Market Streets at six o'clock that night.

Sam was there at 6 p.m. He didn't know how to operate the cashier's check machine, but he brought along his nephew, Bert Klein, who did know how to use it.

Meeting the 9 a.m. deadline meant I would have to drive all night, much of it over mountain roads. Armed with a thermos of black coffee and No-Doz, I stepped into my white Ford station wagon and set out on the fourteen-hour journey. I listened to music on the radio—country and gospel—to stay awake. While stopping for gas, I refilled my thermos. The trip from Louisville to the Virginia coast—almost 700 miles—was familiar. I had made it many times during my Navy days in Norfolk.

I was accustomed to long night watches in the Navy and was young, so the trip was manageable. I arrived an hour early. George Holmes, the owner, was astonished to see me. Holmes got his money on time, and the Louisville partnership had its fourth nursing home. After the transaction, I slept several hours in the nursing home I had just bought, then drove home. George couldn't believe that we were able to close, but we did, and he ran that nursing home successfully for us for many years.

Not long afterward, in April 1964, Sam Klein and his wife, Hattie, invited Betty and me to their home on Village Drive—a street off Bardstown Road in a leafy area of Louisville's Highlands. The Kleins showed us through the house and offered us tea. As we sat and talked, the Kleins made a totally unexpected offer: They wanted us to buy their house.

It was an absolutely gorgeous place. It was 1964. I'm still at the law firm, and my company's still small potatoes. I told Sam, "We're living in a $15,000 house on which we paid $500 down. Our payments are $85 a month, and we can barely make that. There's no way in the world that we can buy this house."

Klein was not deterred. He told me they had bought the home for $35,000 in 1948, sixteen years before, and would sell it for the same price.

"This is a lucky house," said Klein. "I want you to have it."

Betty, who was always part of the nursing home and family discussions, was even more adamant: "No, we can't do it."

Klein wouldn't accept "no." He had come to believe in my character, honesty, business skills, and work ethic. He said I could borrow 80 percent from Charlie Will at Portland Federal Savings and Loan for the house— which we ended up doing—and he, Klein, would accept a note for the rest. The new house payments would be $200 a month, well above the $85 we had been paying. I wasn't yet making any money from the nursing homes, for which I was CEO and keeping the books at home at night. And we had three small children. But the future looked good.

Both Betty and I had grown up in Depression-era families in which debt was not an option; their incomes were too low to attract creditors. But I was willing to take that chance. In the low-inflation economy of that time, we would end up selling our $15,000 home for $14,500, and we acted as the real estate agents. But Klein, who would later step in again to help me save my struggling company, insisted I would be able to pay the more expensive house mortgage. He was right, and I was confident about our future. I can't tell you where that confidence came from, but I've always had it. I'm always optimistic. I don't think I'm overconfident, but I tend to see what can be done.

The Village Drive house did turn out to be lucky. The business and family prospered during our seven years there, with the children playing in Cherokee Park, which spread out near our home. We lived in that four-bedroom house until our fifth child, Carol, was born in 1971. Six weeks later, we moved to our present home off Blankenbaker Lane.

I thrived on being busy. I continued to teach two night classes at the University of Louisville, kept the nursing home books at home in a little room beside our kitchen, and followed my philosophy of clear communication to keep our lenders and equity partners informed. Confidence in Wendell and me grew, which was vital because other people's money was the key to our growth. All while practicing law full-time.

The night classes I was teaching at U of L earned me $2,400 a year and added to my extensive background in accounting and analysis of financial statements. Our mortgage was manageable, and our credit was good. A pattern was established. Confidence in the nursing home business, combined with the frugality practiced by my family, enabled me to borrow against my nursing home stock to buy out early partners Bill Rommel and Jim McFerran. Wendell did the same, and Rommel and McFerran each received $64,000 for their $1,000 investment.

But by 1964, the growing nursing home business had become cumbersome, unwieldy, and difficult to manage. It had morphed into four separate private nursing home companies in three states, with forty individual owners. And it wasn't the operations that were complex—it was the ownership.

This was driving me crazy, because, as a young lawyer, I had to bill somebody for every working minute of my time. If Wendell or I was spending the law firm's time on our nursing homes, we had to pay for it, and as we grew, it was becoming difficult to know who to bill among our four different ownership entities. So I started working on putting us all together in one company.

This was the toughest and most important negotiation in the history of the company that became Humana. I had to get all forty investors to agree on the value of their personal shares so they would swap them for shares in a single new company. The work required to simplify our business was difficult, time-consuming, and seemingly endless; Wendell and I traveled to Lexington frequently.

If numbers are a language, I'm fluent—a skill that helped throughout my forty-four years with Humana. Still, the package we were putting together was complex. Wendell and I owned two-thirds of the Louisville and Virginia nursing homes and two-thirds of one-half of each of the other two nursing homes. Sonny Bass and Charlie Weisberg's shares involved similarly complicated mathematics. I was convinced I could make the company grow if it had a simple, common ownership.

I think there were twelve people in the Lexington group and ten to twelve people in each of the other groups. I told them if we could put it all together, we had a chance to really grow. We knew what we were doing by then, although the company was only three years old, and instead of most of us owning one-tenth of one-half of a nursing home, we could make a successful company.

After all these far-flung group negotiations, there was one holdout, a Lexington lawyer who argued against such mutual ownership. At a company meeting, he angrily charged that I would soon be earning $150,000 a year, Wendell $100,000, and Boone $50,000—and the other shareholders would not make nearly as much.

Hilary Boone then stood up and told the lawyer, "If you don't want in, I'll buy you out."

The lawyer agreed. The ownership problem was solved. The four nursing homes were soon one company—still named Heritage House. I was CEO.

I later ran the numbers and estimated that if the Lexington lawyer had agreed to the original deal and stayed through all the subsequent company dealings and stock divisions, his original $10,000 investment would have been worth about $140 million in 2017.

Returning alone from Lexington late one night, I fell asleep and went off the road. No harm done, but Betty then insisted I stop the crazy driving trips, which led us to charter pilot John Landrum and his single-engine V-tail Beechcraft Bonanza. I learned a lot flying with John to Connecticut and elsewhere for these negotiations. Those early trips together showed me the benefit of a company plane.

I enjoyed flying and would study the various models as new planes became available. To monitor our far-flung ventures, Wendell and I purchased our first company plane in 1968, a second-hand, four-year-old Beechcraft King Air twin-turboprop, serial number 15. Our pilot was Landrum, who would fly for the company for forty years; his co-pilot was Gene Van Meter. The plane could cruise to 25,000 feet, above much weather, yet Landrum still needed an air traffic controller on the ground to alert him to coming storms. He was ready to fly it alone, but Wendell and I insisted on a co-pilot. Landrum would always argue that "all a co-pilot does is add weight to the airplane."

Landrum and the other Humana pilots who flew with me for many years became devoted friends of mine and one another. Landrum grew up amid the coal dust of Harlan County. He began flying at age sixteen, attended Centre College, and enlisted in the Army Air Forces when he saw World War II was coming. He served as an aviation instructor throughout the war, after which he vowed never to fly again. He thought he'd used up all his luck teaching would-be pilots dangerous maneuvers and was living on borrowed time.

But he kept flying into a life worthy of a book in itself. After the war—with the family's coal business failing—he started an insurance agency and a charter flying service in Harrodsburg, Kentucky. He kept his plane at a nearby 3,000-foot farm-field runway used mostly by crop dusters. From there, he began flying Wendell and me on our business trips as we developed our nursing home business. It was another scene from an up-from-nothing movie. Landrum was soon leaving the farm field for the twenty-minute flight to Louisville three and four days a week—a pilot in farm clothes—sometimes scrambling to the landing strip on thirty minutes' notice.

We started flying with him after driving proved impractical and dangerous, but we had some issues flying, too. We took off once from Bowman Field in the Bonanza, got about thirty feet up, and lost power. We landed on the plane's belly, skittered to a stop, jumped out, and chartered another plane to get to our meeting.

Landrum's ready and able partner was his wife, Vivian, who had grown up in Pineville, Kentucky, the youngest of twelve children. They married in 1948. She was a feisty, competitive five-foot-two-inch woman and top tennis player, often playing mixed doubles with her six-foot-four-inch husband, the second-best player in the pair. Vivian was a Tulane University graduate who earned her pilot's license and, later in life, flew all over the world with John, from South America to Iceland to Europe.

Landrum led my companies from a single-engine plane to a twin-engine propeller, a turboprop, and then jets. He also put together a strong team of company pilots. His early relationship with the company turned out to be very profitable.

"I was cheaper," Landrum explained of his charter pilot relationship with Wendell and me, "and I was willing to wait for them to pay me because they didn't have any money. I never worried. It was just a matter of sometimes waiting a month or two before you got paid."

Happily for him, some of those late payments came in company stock. He also received stock options over the years as he joined Wendell and me in our explorations, adding his own business savvy. At my request, Landrum joined the company board, eventually serving for thirty-seven years and becoming the company's chief pilot—and a large shareholder. A flying career that began with a teenager wearing goggles and flying a Piper Cub ended with his piloting the Humana company jet on business trips for hospital purchases in Switzerland and London. The occasionally dusty rural pilot came to own 2,000 acres of valuable farmland as well.

"David Jones had an energy level that just kept going," Landrum remembered at age ninety-six. "I was used to people who were going to form a committee before doing something. If David and Wendell decided to do something, they would just do it."

"Just doing it" eventually meant reaching for the sky. To Humana, a private plane wasn't a luxury but a necessity. Airline service in Louisville was often lacking. The company's nursing homes and hospitals were spread out, many in smaller towns with no commercial air service, so private planes were the best option. They made it possible for me to do a whole lot of things.

And I don't remember ever being tired in my life. I mean occasionally,

101

if I'm in a ball game, or I'm running a long way, I might get a little bit tired. But as far as working, I try to finish my work every day. And when I go home at night, I'm there for the family.

Another Humana pilot—and mechanic—Ken Machtolff, recalled that I knew about as much about the aircraft as they did. Machtolff, who flew co-pilot with Landrum, was another blue-collar fit. His father was a World War I artilleryman who fought in the battle of the Argonne Forest and came to work at Seagram's Distillery. His mother took care of the family. They lived in a small house in the Louisville suburb of Shively.

Machtolff attended Parkland Junior High School, as did I, and graduated from Valley High School in 1949. He joined the Air Force, then served in a reserve unit during the Korean War.

He used the GI Bill to earn his pilot's license in 1958. He became a civilian mechanic for the Kentucky Air National Guard and then director of maintenance at Humana, where he oversaw the company's purchase of a Hawker-Beechcraft 125-700 twin-engine jet. He always reported directly to me.

"David knew what he was talking about," Machtolff always said. "He knows his airplanes."

Humana bought the first of the Challenger 600 business jets. When the plane was first flown to Louisville, Landrum had the Humana company logo taped on the bulkhead with double-faced tape. I ordered it taken off. I didn't want any Humana advertising on the plane.

Sometimes the company scouting forays were a little more undercover. When Wendell and I would fly somewhere—in a plane not bearing the company name—to inspect a hospital, I would often dress in a pair of jeans and wander around the building, quietly checking it out.

Other private trips to help others were made without fanfare. I authorized the company plane to fly a badly burned child to a hospital in Boston after his parents were killed in a fiery wreck on I-71. Machtolff and family members were on a bicycle trip in Iowa when they learned of the death of a relative. I sent a company plane to fly them home. When a family tragedy involving Machtolff's daughter resulted in large legal bills, I paid them.

"Those things happened lots of times with various people," Machtolff said of those incidents. "We never told anybody. It was not advertised."

✳

By the end of 1964, with all participants on the same page, Heritage House began negotiating with First National Bank in Louisville for a $500,000 loan to accelerate growth. Bank president Henry Offutt lined up a loan through Marine Midland, a big New York bank that offered a partnership with the Small Business Administration. The bank would put up 25 percent, the SBA the rest. The loan would have required Wendell and me to grant significant equity to the banks.

Hilary Boone had a better idea. He went to W. T. "Bill" Young, a Lexington friend and business colleague who had been invited into the original Lexington group but said he didn't want to own 10 percent of half of a nursing home.

Young's story was also a perfect fit for the ever-evolving company. He was born in Lexington and attended the University of Kentucky, graduating with a Bachelor of Science degree in mechanical engineering in 1939. After serving as a major in the US Army from 1941 to 1945, he married his college sweetheart, Lucy Maddox, an artist whose father was president of a small bank and owner of a peanut-processing business in South Georgia.

His sage business advice to his new son-in-law—somewhat akin to the memorable word "plastics" in the movie *The Graduate*—was a little longer: "You should make peanut butter."

Young had saved some money, and, with a loan from his father-in-law, started Big Top Peanut Butter Company. Their approach was to market peanut butter in jars that could also serve as drinking glasses. His wife created sets of those glasses, one design for each state. Young piled them into the back of his car and drove around the country, selling peanut butter in glasses. His very successful company was sold in 1955 to Procter & Gamble, which renamed the peanut butter brand Jif and promoted it with "Jifaroo," a blue kangaroo. It has been the largest-selling peanut butter in the United States since the 1980s.

In later years, Young became executive chairman of Royal Crown Cola; I served on its board. In 1972, he established Overbrook Farm, near Lexington, where he bred 1996 Kentucky Derby winner Grindstone, as well as Storm Cat, one of the world's highest-priced sires.

In 1964, Boone's Massachusetts Mutual Insurance office was right across the hall from Young's office in a building Young owned. Boone asked Young to consider a major investment in the company. Young saw the future. After a few months of negotiations that carried over into 1965, he agreed to invest $500,000 in subordinated debentures. He received warrants to acquire common stock that gave him less equity interest than the banks, Marine Midland and First National, would have acquired.

Young's one insistence was that I had to leave the Louisville law firm and spend more time with Heritage House. Young would invest only if I paid full-time attention to where his money was going. The deal allowed the nursing home company—by then with the grander name Heritage House of America—to acquire nursing homes in Columbus, Indiana, and Owensboro and Paducah, Kentucky, and build another one in Waterbury, Connecticut.

Young and I became close friends. I admired his unflappable nature and his ability to stay calm in good times or bad. He probably knew me and my capabilities as well as anybody because, unlike a lot of people, he had real skin in the game. The best directors are always those who own stock in the company because then it's their company, their business. And it turned out to be a great investment for him.

"He is the creative genius, the dynamic soul of Humana," Young would later say of me in a *Louisville Magazine* profile.

I left Wyatt, Grafton & Sloss on December 31, 1965, intending to spend full time on Heritage House business. But many of my clients asked to continue with me. So I hired a young lawyer I admired, Jack Hardwick, to help.

In February 1967, Wendell joined me, forming a new firm called Jones & Cherry. David Grissom came on board in 1969, creating the law firm Jones, Cherry & Grissom. It ultimately became Jones, Cherry, Grissom & Boone and quickly grew to twelve attorneys and lots of business, including many unsolicited clients who had stayed with me.

Among them was John Y. Brown, who had just acquired Kentucky Fried Chicken. He would bring me onto the KFC board, which included "Colonel" Harland Sanders, whose work ethic and attention to detail I would always admire. He was an old curmudgeon who was as real as real can be. I liked him. When he went into one of his stores and found anything wrong, he'd let you know about it. He knew that business just as I knew our business.

I opened my first law office on the seventh floor of a downtown building at 310 West Liberty Street, bringing along Wanda Mudd, my secretary from Wyatt, Grafton & Sloss, who had grown up on a dairy farm near Springfield, Kentucky. She would become the fourth employee of that budding corporate giant Humana. In time, her husband, Mike Ryan, a Marine Corps veteran, would also play a role in the young company.

Wanda Mudd Ryan would stay with me for over forty-six years. She was one of seven children who grew up working the 170-acre family farm, with its dairy cattle and tobacco fields. The children were all automatically involved in the process, earning their spending money—maybe $200 to $300 a year—in endless farm chores. Her parents were very religious Catholics. Wanda graduated from what was then St. Catharine High

School near Springfield, where she developed the skills most often taught to women in the early 1960s: typing, accounting, and shorthand.

She spent one year at St. Catharine College in Springfield, where she was an excellent student, with a business degree in mind. But she was nineteen, money was limited, and in 1963 she and a few friends moved to Louisville to find work. They lived in a Catholic-owned boarding house on Fourth Street called The Visitation Home, where many other young women from the Springfield area lived.

Wanda had never been out of Kentucky except to cross the bridge over to Indiana. She planned to work in Louisville for a summer and earn enough money to go back to college. She found a secretarial job with Vulcan Hart Corporation, which manufactured commercial stoves at Eighteenth Street and Northwestern Parkway.

Her plans changed in May 1964. On a blind date, she met Mike Ryan, a farm kid from Lebanon, Kentucky, newly discharged after four years in the US Marines. They would date for three years before getting married. Wanda's new plan was to work at Vulcan Hart for a short time, then find a better job. On August 17, 1964, I interviewed her for a legal secretarial position at Wyatt, Grafton & Sloss. She was quickly hired—going two-for-two in her lifetime career employment quests.

"I was a good student," she would explain. "I caught on quickly. And Mr. Jones wanted someone he could train."

Over the years, as Wanda moved with Wendell and me into our new firm, she would do more of my personal accounting and tax work. She became part of the family, babysitting our three children, and taking them to visit her family farm near Springfield as Betty and I took our first trip to Europe.

When I began working at Wyatt, Grafton & Sloss, my finances were so tight I would borrow $20 from Wanda—her lunch money—so I could go out to lunch for a week while she ate peanut butter and jelly sandwiches.

"He always paid me back on payday," she said, "but he didn't have any money at all. But he more than made it up to me later on."

As her family grew to three children, her workload was reduced to a few days a week to accommodate her duties as a mother. She later came back to work full-time. For all of her years with me—nearly half a century—she always called me "Mr. Jones."

When discharged from the Marines, Mike Ryan bought a bright red four-speed 400-horsepower Oldsmobile. He had a job at the L&N railroad. He would pick up Wanda after work and give me a ride home in the back seat. When Ryan was considering leaving the L&N and using the GI Bill to go to college, I offered him a job during a ride home—assistant administrator at our first nursing home. He could then attend night classes at the University of Louisville to earn a degree.

Decades later, when asked why I entrusted so young a man with so much responsibility, I replied: "He'd been a Marine!"

Ryan justified my faith many times over. He took the job, saw it expand into a career, and eventually owned some homes himself. He never did finish college—the constant travel of his new job ended any possibility of night school—but at one point, he was managing forty-five nursing homes.

Most of the nursing home acquisitions happened due to the company's sound business plans, but some were a matter of almost accidental timing. Mike Ryan recalled that he was sitting in his office one day when three doctors walked in and said they wanted to sell their nursing home in Owensboro. Ryan called Wendell and me, and we quickly negotiated a deal using stock. Those Owensboro guys became mega-millionaires.

One of the young company's best deals was buying a struggling eighty-four-bed nursing home in Columbus, Indiana. A group of doctors with no experience in the field was running it. They had been managing the facility as if it were for acute care, which resulted in overstaffing and unnecessary medical procedures. Wendell and I instituted the proper management, staff, and rates, and the facility quickly became very profitable.

In 1966, after sweeping new Medicare legislation defined a nursing home as an extended-care facility, we changed the nursing home company's name from Heritage House of America to Extendicare.

Neither Wendell nor I had foreseen the advent of Medicare or Medicaid when we started the business. It wasn't that beneficial to our bottom line, but its arrival added greater possibilities to our business.

By then, we were dealing with eight homes; we had doubled the size of the company and were looking for other opportunities. The biggest came when Pye Conway, a broker with Stein Brothers & Boyce in Louisville, and a Yale and Harvard Business School graduate, approached me in 1967 with the idea of taking the company public.

I was already anticipating where to take the company in the far future—perhaps into hospitals. I was thinking seriously about that in 1966 when doctors in New Haven began sending patients to our nursing home during a flu epidemic. We were getting about $14 a day, and I discovered hospitals were getting about $100 a day. We didn't do surgery at the nursing home, but we did rehab. We had physical therapy; we had occupational therapy. We had nurses who could administer medicines to patients. So we did a lot of what goes on in hospitals, which made me think, I'm in the wrong business.

Meanwhile, Conway proposed to take our nursing homes public, and I had a more immediate thought: "This is crazy. What's he been smoking?"

The early numbers for the nursing homes were good. Total revenue from the eight homes in 1967 was a little over $2 million, with about a 10 percent pre-tax profit. They were doing well only six years after their start, but I was very skeptical the numbers could be big enough to attract strong interest in public stock.

At that time, even the idea of public companies was rare in Louisville, with many of the bigger companies family-owned or keeping a low profile about being public. Conway argued that with the advent of Medicare and Medicaid, several other nursing home companies had already gone public. With nothing to lose, Conway set up a meeting in New York with Tubby Burnham of Burnham & Company.

Burnham also had strong Kentucky ties. His grandfather was I. W. Bernheim, who had founded the I.W. Harper Distilling Company in Paducah and donated the land that became Bernheim Arboretum and Research Forest, south of Louisville.

Also instrumental in the deal was Steve Mann, a high-powered New York lawyer and good friend who had been the top student in my law school class; he would represent the company in its public offering. His office was in the Seagram Building at 375 Park Avenue in Midtown. The 38-story, $100 million tower, designed by Ludwig Mies van der Rohe, was the world's most expensive skyscraper when constructed in 1958. We would occasionally eat at the iconic Four Seasons Restaurant in the building.

Steve and I had played basketball together on the married men's basketball team in law school. He was very aggressive and feisty. He was a substitute, I was captain of the team, and he thought I didn't play him as much as I should. Mann and other law school buddies often came to visit our family for the Kentucky Derby. One year, we played a game of H-O-R-S-E for money in our backyard on Village Drive, where I usually shot baskets with my kids. Mann kept losing—and kept doubling up on his bet—until it reached $400,000.

"My ball and my court," I said, explaining my success.

Mann wrote me a $400,000 check, which somehow failed to pass bank muster. I had the check encased in clear plastic; it sat on a shelf in my Louisville office.

The meeting in New York to take Extendicare public included Mike Gellert, a Burnham & Company partner who would join Wendell and me in other ventures. Also along was Carl Pollard, a CPA and partner with Yeager, Ford & Warren, a large Louisville CPA firm founded in 1933 that had been doing all of Extendicare's accounting.

Pollard was yet another perfect fit for Kentucky boys on a roll. He was born on a farm near Lancaster, where his parents had been living with his grandfather, a tenant farmer. His father moved to Lancaster in the early 1940s, taking a job as bookkeeper and then a manager for a company that built tobacco warehouses and owned farms. His mother stayed home to raise their five children.

Like me, Pollard had a knack for math, bookkeeping, and accounting. After graduating from Lancaster High School in 1956, and with limited funds, he would regularly hitchhike the thirty-five miles to Lexington to attend the University of Kentucky. Pollard worked nights at Kroger stocking shelves, kept books at a used-car lot, and worked one summer in a North Carolina tobacco warehouse. He earned a degree in accounting, and had a job offer from Ernst & Ernst Accounting in Chicago and with Yeager, Ford & Warren in Louisville. He chose Louisville.

His long-range goal at the time: "I was thinking how I was going to pay the rent."

He began working at Yeager, Ford & Warren on June 13, 1960, the same day I went to work for Wyatt, Grafton & Sloss. We met over a very complicated tax case involving Sam Nally, who owned several construction companies, quarries, and a lot of heavy equipment. He was seeking some tax relief at a time when the highest marginal tax rate was 90 percent. Pollard and I worked on the case for many months using fourteen-column worksheets because there were no computers. Making matters more complicated, the information had to be passed through about twenty-five Nally company partners. So, when Wendell and I opened our first nursing home in 1962, we hired Pollard to audit its records. When the first home was being built, Pollard's job included auditing the contract work to ensure contractors were not padding the cost.

As a newly minted partner of Yeager, Ford & Warren, Pollard was a member of the Louisville group that met with Tubby Burnham in New York. Each of the nursing home companies that had already gone public had used one of the "Big Eight" accounting firms—the giants in the accounting world until merger and scandal cut it down to the "Big Four." At our first meeting, the Louisville men and the Burnham leaders wore mostly sedate Wall Street attire. Pollard showed up in his red and purple sports coat the rest of the Kentucky contingent had accused him of buying in Lancaster.

Tubby Burnham was a character. He kind of took to us and liked that we were from Louisville. But he said if you go public you have to ditch that local firm, Yeager, Ford & Warren, and use a Big Eight accounting firm.

Pollard didn't say a word, but I did. I fired back that Yeager, Ford & Warren had been our accountants from the beginning. They were first-rate, and I was not going to dump them.

"If you don't want to take us public, that's fine," I told Burnham.

Burnham agreed to that—but only on the condition that Pollard buy a gray suit.

So, with hometown loyalty winning the day, Louisville's Yeager, Ford & Warren stayed in the game. George Fritz was the Yeager, Ford & Warren partner who handled the initial public offering (IPO). He later became a senior partner with PricewaterhouseCoopers in New York.

Fritz nicknamed me "Speeding Bullet" for my ability to get things done. We would stay in contact for the next fifty years, occasionally reminding each other of the miserly pay, long hours, and little respect we received at our firms when first hired.

"What wonderful memories," I would write in an email to Fritz. "At Wyatt, Grafton & Sloss, we'd be called in at 3:30 p.m. on Christmas Eve, given a truly miserly bonus, reminded how green and useless we were, and sent on our way, too late to buy presents for our kids and not enough money anyway."

But during the IPO process, Fritz went to work on the complicated public sale, along with an Arthur Young & Company accountant flown into Louisville on Burnham's recommendation. To make an initial public offering, you must have a brokerage firm with super bright, or so they believe, investment bankers and lots of expertise and lawyers. But the long and the short of it is that lawyers love to talk. They get paid by the hour, so they talk and talk and talk.

The process was complex, requiring specialized legal and accounting assistance. A totally honest and transparent offering circular had to be created, giving the other brokers and possible buyers a sense of the company's history—and its future. Securities and Exchange Commission (SEC) guidelines added complications to the process.

Adding our input, Pollard and I met with the experts one night until 4 a.m. With our hotel almost thirty blocks away, we hailed a cab and were treated to a lightning-fast ride down New York City streets. We hopped in, took off, and the guy flew down whatever street we were on. He said the lights were all coordinated, so we either had to do twenty-two miles an hour or forty-four or sixty-six to catch all the lights.

Burnham & Company became the lead underwriter for the sale, which would take almost four months to complete, with several other firms added to the group to find enough buyers. It was here that Mike Gellert of Burnham & Company took the lead in facilitating the move. That leadership made such an impression on Wendell and me that Gellert would become a member of Humana's board for thirty-seven years. He also became good friends with Betty and me.

Gellert's history was another interesting fit in the rise of Humana. He was born in 1931, one of five children in a well-to-do family in Prague, Czechoslovakia. In 1938, just as the German army marched in from Vienna, much of his extended family of twenty escaped by train through Italy and France before making their way to England. In 1940, they took a boat to Havana, where they obtained a visa to the United States. Gellert eventually attended Harvard, where he joined the Army Reserves to help with finances. He studied business at the University of Pennsylvania's Wharton School, then served two years in the Army before joining Burnham & Company in 1958.

Gellert described his first meeting with Wendell and me as "love at first sight." It was obvious the two of us complemented each other. "They just had a lot going for them," Gellert said.

On January 31, 1968—less than six years after our first Louisville nursing home opened on August 10, 1962—250,000 shares of Extendicare were sold to the public. The initial $8 public offering—worth $2 million— opened at $16. With the mania for nursing homes, it ended the day at $20.

By December 1968, it reached $84 per share.

Most of the original Extendicare stock buyers would be retail customers. After the initial public offering, there were a million shares outstanding. The public owned 25 percent of the company; the many other partners and warrant holders owned about 45 percent. I owned a little over 17 percent, and Wendell about 13 percent. We didn't know whether to be upset with Burnham & Company for underpricing us or ecstatic because we collectively owned the other 75 percent of the stock.

We celebrated the 1968 deal at the Waldorf Astoria in New York, with Wendell, Charlie Weisberg, Bill Young, Hilary Boone, Mike Gellert, and me in attendance—a happy moment with so much more good and bad yet to come, celebrated in a photo on a shelf in my office.

After Wendell, Pollard, and I picked up the $2 million check, we came home to Louisville on an early-morning American Airlines flight. The plane was almost empty, but Wendell and I insisted Pollard sit between us. Our message was clear: Pollard would leave Yeager, Warren & Ford and work for us.

"Okay," said Pollard, who became a close friend.

He went on to become president and chief operating officer of Humana, CEO and chairman of Galen Health Care, and chairman of Churchill Downs, Inc. He later purchased the famed Hermitage Horse Farm, about sixty miles north of where he grew up in Lancaster. Pollard would also establish a $10 million scholarship fund for first-generation students—primarily the children of full-time workers on horse farms—enabling them to attend the University of Kentucky, and a similar $2.5 million fund for the University of Louisville.

He, too, remembered where he came from.

Chapter Seven

ZIGGY AND THE COLONELS

"The Colonels were ahead by one point with thirty seconds left, and the clock was suddenly turned off—giving the home team more time to score. I rushed down to the scorer's table and raised hell, and a great big beefy cop got me in a bear hug. The next year we had an official on the clock. We got homered. We lost that game by one point."

— DAVID JONES on part ownership of
the ABA's Kentucky Colonels

I t wasn't all nursing homes and hospitals for Wendell and me in the late 1960s. We were ever on the lookout for a new venture. Our often-serendipitous intersection with other business enterprises was never far away—and the sound of a bouncing basketball accompanied the next one.

Stuart Jay, a friend of ours, would explain that his five-year co-ownership of the Kentucky Colonels ABA basketball team with Wendell, David Grissom, John Y. Brown, and me started with his courtside conversation with a woman seated next to her dog. The woman was Mamie Spears Reynolds Gregory, an heiress with a reputed $50 million fortune and a long line of family connections.

She was the granddaughter of Evalyn Walsh McLean, the last personal owner of the Hope Diamond. Her father was US Senator Robert Reynolds, a controversial man who blamed the British for the Japanese attack on Pearl Harbor. She was the goddaughter of FBI legend J. Edgar Hoover and a world-traveling, successful member of the American Kennel Club. She also raised miniature horses and pygmy goats.

According to a book on the Kentucky Colonels by Gary P. West and Lloyd "Pink" Gardner, the team trainer, her Kentucky Colonels connection began when, at age twenty-two, she married a Cloverport, Kentucky, dog handler named Joe Gregory. His love of basketball, she explained, prompted her to buy him a franchise in the American Basketball Association (ABA) in March 1967.

The ABA was an upstart challenger to the National Basketball Association (NBA). It tried to attract fans using goofy, well-worn team promotions such as bikini-clad ball girls, wrestling bears, and half-time basketball games featuring local celebrities and personalities—including, just one time, myself. The initial Louisville franchise was awarded to ABA co-founder Don Regan for $30,000. The Gregorys and a minority owner then paid $65,000 for the franchise in a sport that, by 2019, was paying individual NBA stars more than $40 million a year.

The ABA brought to basketball-mad Kentucky the red-white-and-blue basketball, the three-point shot, and the Gregorys' prize champion dog, Ziggy, who attended all the games, team business meetings, public gatherings, and ticket promotions. Indeed, Ziggy—a Brussels Griffon whose full name was Gaystock LeMonsignor—had more words written about him in the original promotional material than the Colonels' star and the eventual all-time ABA scoring leader, University of Kentucky legend Louie Dampier.

Dave Kindred, the *Courier Journal* sports columnist, wrote a book, *Basketball, the Dream Game in Kentucky,* that captured the special nonsense that came with the ABA and the Kentucky Colonels, a team that played its first season wearing chartreuse-green uniforms.

One of the league coaches was fired when he won a fistfight with his team's owner at an All-Star game in Louisville. Another coach said the league's red-white-and-blue basketball belonged on a seal's nose.

Kindred wrote that Ziggy had twenty-nine different uniforms to alternate for home games and would share ice cream cones with Mamie, each taking a lick. Season ticket holders had the luxury of taking half-time breaks in the "Ziggy Room."

"Joe taught me everything I know about basketball, which isn't much," Mamie told Kindred. "I played a bit in grade school and always hated it. I couldn't see the point in just throwing a ball so it would fall through the hoop."

In its first year, Colonels management picked players partly because of what they read in basketball magazines. Dampier was signed for a $3,000 bonus and a $12,000 salary. Another signee, Orb Bowling of Sandy Hook, Kentucky—who had played college ball at Tennessee—signed a no-cut contract with the Colonels. He turned out to be so bad he didn't go on road trips and sat on the bench in street clothes at home games.

The team played a few games at Freedom Hall, but most were held in the old Louisville Gardens, a dim, sixty-two-year-old former National Guard armory with 6,000 seats and not much parking. The team reportedly lost about $100,000 in 1966–67 and averaged only 3,225 fans a game, many on one dollar discount tickets. Some nights, Ziggy was the star attraction.

Stuart Jay was a Colonels fan with a broad background in law and education. He had joined the Wyatt, Grafton & Sloss firm in 1958, a year ahead of Wendell and two years before me. Jay was a successful Louisville businessman and entrepreneur with several electronics and correspondence schools, including General Educational Services. He was also Wendell's next-door neighbor and good friend. Jay's seat at the Colonels games in the early years was close to those of Mamie Gregory—and Ziggy.

"Over time I knew her," said Jay, "and I got to talking to her. One day, just out of the blue, I asked her, 'Would you like to sell this team?' And she said, 'Yes.'"

Jay then came to see Wendell and me about the deal. We were intrigued, especially Wendell, who took the lead. We also brought in David Grissom. The fifth partner was John Y. Brown of Kentucky Fried Chicken fame.

The West-Gardner book labeled us owners the "Fab Five." We were all young men in our thirties. Wendell, Grissom, and I were at Extendicare,

116

which was growing rapidly in size and profits. Jay was doing very well with his electronics schools. Brown had purchased Kentucky Fried Chicken from Colonel Harland Sanders for $2 million in 1964 and would see it boom to 3,500 fast-food restaurants by 1971, including 863 added in 1968 alone.

The Colonels were not all about money, which turned out to be a good thing. Civic pride was involved. We new owners were sports fans and Louisville boosters. We already had a lot of personal business in town and wanted to see the team thrive as a business—perhaps someday leading Louisville into the NBA.

The five of us bought the team on October 30, 1969, for $500,000. Years later, I would offer a more realistic appraisal of our few years of basketball ownership. We had gotten involved with the team primarily because Wendell was so interested—and knowing that he would do the same for us if we needed a partner in an investment. We were young guys who had made a lot of money—and we didn't know what we were doing.

I put together a lettered-stock business deal in which, by SEC requirements, the stock is not intended for resale. Jay noted that the team and its finances did improve some in our four years of ownership, but profits, and a possible NBA franchise for Louisville, remained dim-to-distant. He said:

> We thought we could turn it around. It wasn't losing that much money. When we bought the team, they started to progress, to get better athletes, and we started paying bigger salaries.
>
> At one point, somebody from North Carolina wanted to buy the team. I think his offer was $3 million. I'll never forget it. We met at the hotel by the airport, and I fell in love with John Brown because I wanted to sell, and he wanted to sell.
>
> And Jones, Cherry, and Grissom said it's going to be worth a lot more than that. We're going to the NBA someday. So we voted, and as I remember, the vote was three to two not to sell.

Ever the competitor, I helped put together an Extendicare company basketball team that played a team from St. Joseph Infirmary at halftime of a Colonels game in 1970. I made two baskets and a free throw in a five-minute period, but we got waxed by the St. Joseph team. They had several kids who could handle the ball a whole lot better than we could.

My competitive instincts boiled up when the ever-improving Colonels were playing the Utah Stars in an early 1970s playoff game in Salt Lake City. The Colonels were ahead by one point with thirty seconds left, and the clock was suddenly turned off—giving the home team more time to score. I rushed down to the scorer's table and raised hell, and a great big beefy cop got me in a bear hug. The next year we had an official on the clock. We got homered. We lost that game by one point.

Our ownership group found better management—including hiring Mike Storen from the Indiana Pacers as president and general manager. He signed or re-signed future Hall of Famers Louie Dampier, Artis Gilmore, and Dan Issel. Attendance at Freedom Hall climbed to 8,811 a game, with a league record sixty-eight wins and sixteen losses in 1971–72. Only six teams in the older, established NBA had a larger average attendance.

I took Betty, her mother, and our children to the Colonels games and U of L games to see interesting, exciting basketball. But the Colonels lost in the first round of the playoffs to New York, four games to two. In 1972–73 the team went 56–28, averaged 7,113 fans per game, and lost to the Indiana Pacers in the ABA championship series, four games to three.

About that time, a reporter asked Wendell how many fans it would take at the 19,000-seat Freedom Hall for the team to at least break even.

"Thirty thousand," Wendell answered.

Wendell's interest in the team and his focus on the league's shortcomings eventually led him to become the ABA president. He helped develop the anti-trust lawsuit against the NBA that eventually led to an ABA-NBA merger, and, somewhat ironically, the end of the Colonels—the team he wanted to get into the NBA.

Steadily losing money, the "Fab Five" sold the Colonels to a group from Cincinnati after the 1972–73 season for $2.5 million, about five times what we had paid for it. I can't tell you how much money we lost with the

118

franchise. Nobody made any money. The only way you make money in sports ownership is to find a greater fool to sell to.

On July 31, 1973, after John Y. Brown learned that the Cincinnati group might move the Colonels to Cincinnati, he and his wife, Ellie, bought a majority interest in the team to keep it in Louisville. In the 1974–75 season, the Colonels, loaded with talent such as Issel, Gilmore, Dampier, Jim McDaniels, and Darel Carrier—and with Hubie Brown, now an NBA commentator, as coach—finally won an ABA championship.

In 1976, in a settlement reached with the NBA following Wendell's antitrust suit, the NBA allowed ABA teams into its league—after they each paid a $9 million franchise fee. But the NBA accepted only four ABA teams: Denver, San Antonio, New York, and Indiana. Brown, not wanting to pay the $9 million anyway, began selling his best and favorite players, Issel, Gilmore, and Dampier, to other teams. He then folded the Colonels franchise to the eternal dismay of its fans.

Brown then got heavily into franchise-flipping. Using the money from selling players, he bought the Buffalo NBA franchise. He then traded that team for a half-interest in the San Diego team. He and his San Diego partner then traded that team to Irv Levin, the owner of the Boston Celtics, who lived in San Diego. Brown and his partner ended up owning the Celtics. He got the NBA's most storied franchise without having to spend a penny of the $9 million entry fee. But the team struggled, and Brown began making deals without consulting legendary coach Red Auerbach, whom he fired. He was pilloried in Celtic-crazed Boston and sold the team in 1979.

Because the NBA had TV revenue-sharing, Louisville might have had a chance to support an NBA franchise, but it would have taken somebody with a lot of money to sustain it, and I would not recommend it now. We were in it in the Model-T age, but it was fun, and I think it was a good thing for Louisville.

Chapter Eight

MAKING MISTAKES AND MOVING ON

"One of our attempts to diversify led to a disastrous venture into mobile home parks. We learned a lot from that. The most important lesson is that just because you're good at one thing doesn't mean you're going to be good at something else.

"We also learned that it is a bad strategy to try to do two disparate activities at the same time. You spend all your time on the losing proposition, trying to make it work, when you should be spending your time on the successful proposition, where you could get a lot further ahead."

— DAVID JONES

By the late 1960s, the business ambition was there, the path was open, and Wendell and I were picking our way through a new step every day. But moving our new nursing home company forward wasn't easy. Competition was fierce. Speculation was worse. Many people had plunged in with no real interest in, or understanding of, the business; they just hoped to cash in on the craze.

Extendicare was the third of eighty-three nursing home companies with initial public offerings between 1967 and 1969, mostly because everyone seemed to believe that Medicare and Medicaid would provide quick financial bonanzas. For Wendell and me, at least, that did not turn out to be true.

But the belief did fuel rapid growth in our nursing home business. Extendicare owned eight nursing homes at its January 31, 1968 IPO. By the end of 1969, it owned thirty-five nursing homes with 4,078 beds and almost 10,000 employees, making it the nation's largest nursing home company.

In 1969 we hired Jim Beckham to be vice president of finance and treasurer of Extendicare. He had a first-hand look at that rapid expansion with Wendell and me. Beckham was one of eleven children who had lived in an apartment converted from a two-story World War II barracks at Bowman Field. His father, Howard, owned a service station near the Air Devil's Inn, across the road.

Jim had been working for Carl Pollard's former CPA firm, Yeager, Ford & Warren, while attending what was then all-male Bellarmine College. We first met when he began working on annual audits for Extendicare.

At times Beckham felt overwhelmed by the frantic pace of growth, with trips to Memphis, New York, and St. Louis, and then preparation for the company to offer some public securities.

"They don't train you in college, at age twenty-five, to be treasurer and vice president of a company on the New York Stock Exchange," he said. "There's no course for the pressure. There wasn't a mold or a pattern to follow. I later told David we were growing faster than money or manpower could keep up with."

Beckham left the company in 1974 after five years to start a CPA firm with other accountants and then founded a successful business on his own. Before he left, he would join me in noon basketball games at the old YMCA at Third Street and Broadway, across from our Portland Federal Building office. He remembers I could handle the ball and was a good shooter, but what distinguished my game was aggressive play. In our most memorable encounter, I knocked him to the floor, breaking one of his fingers.

"None of us were that good," Beckham said of the basketball games. "When David came in for a rebound, he would just come plowing right over you. That's the way he thought the game should be played. Of course, you could play that way, too. There were no hard feelings. That was sports.

When the game was over, the game was over."

Off the court, in our business, Beckham described me as mostly polite, mild-mannered, leading in a way that always made others feel responsible. But he noted that sometimes I could get upset, taking over when the moment required, always with a clear idea of what to do, although some change of direction might be required later.

"Gentlemen," Beckham remembered me saying, "I may not always be right, but I'm always the boss."

✳

We had grown faster than the other eighty-two nursing home companies because, first, we had enough cash for our base business, and second, our stock went from $8 to $84 a share, and we used that as currency to buy other nursing homes. So we were really on a roll. The 1969 profits of $1,113,384 were six times the 1967 profits of $173,936, with ten new nursing homes being built in Canada.

But with eighty-three nursing home companies crowding the market, the looming problem was one of supply and demand. So I thought, what are we going to do now?

The rapid growth of our company did allow me to merge our law firm—Jones, Cherry, Grissom & Boone—with Greenebaum Doll, giving me more time with Extendicare.

The $84-a-share stock was exhilarating, although, unknown to us, a steep drop lurked ahead, with the real possibility of bankruptcy. But in that booming period, Wendell and I were in the mood only to keep growing the company. Our rampant enthusiasm had even led us to choose "XTC" as Extendicare's stock symbol on the American Stock Exchange—which, when spoken fast, sounds like "ecstasy."

That's how unsophisticated we were.

For all that, the need to move our company into other areas of business was continually evident, but finding the path took a little more time. It seemed like every place in the country that needed a new nursing home had one. So we were doing well and had capital, but no place to deploy it. The nation's need for modern, skilled nursing homes was quickly being filled, and the only way to build our initial business was to buy other people's nursing homes.

One attempt to diversify led to a disastrous venture into mobile home parks. By then our company included me, Wendell, Carl Pollard, and David Grissom, who in 1973 would take an offer to become president of Citizens Fidelity Bank, the largest in Kentucky, eventually becoming its chairman and CEO.

In the late 1960s, Grissom took the lead in Extendicare's development of the mobile home parks—something we again knew absolutely nothing about. Our rationale was that mobile home parks seemed to fit our successful nursing home business model. That included finding well-located property in areas where people generally didn't want such an enterprise, then finding a way to get the required zoning. Because that land could be expensive, it could also require having to sell stock or borrow money, a skill at which our company had also become adept.

With the neighborhood resistance, getting proper zoning was tough, and financing the real estate side of it wasn't easy, either, but we pushed on. Wendell and I would visit as many of the parks as we could before any purchase or development. Grissom helped with the overall planning and financing. He did a really good job at what we asked him to do.

I wish he hadn't done such a good job.

In a year's time, we built a dozen mobile home parks. We discovered, though, that the next thing you have to do is sell the mobile homes to fill the parks. It turns out that people rarely move trailers from one place to another. You have to set up a sales lot. You sell the trailers, and you fill the park. Suddenly we're in a used car-like business about which we know nothing.

Also bad, the banks then required the seller of a trailer to co-sign the buyer's loan. They charged $14\frac{1}{2}$ percent interest. We were paying only 6 percent on our company borrowing. We should have loaned the money at $14\frac{1}{2}$ percent ourselves.

We lost $5 million in 1970 in the mobile home park business, at a time when the company was very small and could hardly afford it. We learned a lot from that. The most important lesson is that just because you're good at one thing doesn't mean you're going to be good at something else.

We also learned that it is a bad strategy to try to do two disparate activities at the same time. You spend all your time on the losing proposition, trying to make it work, when you should be spending your time on the successful proposition, where you could get a lot further ahead.

Having made the really bad decision to go into the business and having grown fast and executed poorly, we made a better decision: cut our losses and get out of it.

But that was easier said than done.

We first had to deal with a case of fraud within our operations. Back then, the mobile home manufacturers paid rebates for homes that were sold, but one Extendicare manager in North Carolina was stealing the rebates. He was also writing bad checks while losing $600,000, speculating in the stock market. His game was to buy a lot of stock, sell it before paying for it, and take the money to pay his bank loan—and money owed Extendicare—leaving his Merrill Lynch broker with the huge loss.

In the midst of this scheme, an Extendicare internal auditor arrived in North Carolina on a routine visit. The manager panicked, wrongly believing that the auditor was aware of his rebate-stealing, and repaid Extendicare and covered the bank checks. This move caused the entire loss to fall on Merrill Lynch, where the manager's broker had incautiously allowed him to purchase $600,000 worth of stock, then sell it and collect proceeds before paying for it.

So the North Carolina banker and I went to New York to meet with Merrill Lynch. I offered to split the loss three ways, but the Merrill Lynch executive refused, saying his company was the full victim.

I offered to "flip a coin, double or nothing" on the loss. The executive said that wasn't possible. I replied I was my company's CEO, and, yes, it was possible; I had the authority. The executive excused himself, then went out to talk with Donald Regan, Merrill Lynch's executive vice president and later US Treasury secretary and White House chief of staff under President Ronald Reagan. Regan agreed with me: The best answer was to split the loss three ways.

The losses in the mobile home parks were painful but hardly lethal.

We earned more than that in our health care business that year, but that was the first year in the company's history that we didn't have an increase in earnings. We actually had a decrease, so the stock took a hit. But we made one of the great decisions in the company's history: to shut down the trailer parks. It was a bad business for us. We took our losses, learned a lesson, and moved on.

Our nursing home profits grew steadily throughout the 1960s, and I enjoyed building that business. Occasionally, as the company built new nursing homes, some personal footwork was required to meet and greet the new neighbors. Before constructing a nursing home in Northfield, then one of Louisville's more elegant areas, Wendell and I met, listened to, and reassured the neighbors. The nursing home parallels the Watterson Expressway, so it actually shields the neighborhood from expressway noise. The first street of the neighborhood was built just east of nursing home property, so it was a good arrangement. There's a beautiful nursing home out there, but I can't imagine a neighborhood like that allowing a nursing home today.

But nursing home margins were small and threatened by the sector's rapid growth, which led me to think continually about moving the company into hospitals. I knew nursing homes were a real need in a new age when children might be living far away. Even if they did live close, parents did not always want to move in with their children, and the children might not want that arrangement either.

But I kept thinking about hospitals. I usually made a decision only after giving the matter a lot of thought and talking it over with Betty and Wendell. An eternal optimist, I could usually see the big picture, excepting the venture into mobile home parks.

If I were to describe myself—and I know I'm as likely to be self-delusional as anyone—I'd say I am an action-oriented thinker. Betty says I can be impulsive, but I never act without thinking. That's part of who I am. I'm not always correct, but I don't just go off and do something. Almost every night, whatever is going on at that particular time, I'll think about it. It doesn't keep me from going to sleep, but if I get an important thought, I'll jot it down on a notepad that I keep beside my bed.

Another part of my thought process dates back to my part-time job while I was a student at the University of Louisville in the early 1950s, working part-time at First National Bank. This was long before computers, when we did all accounting with pencil and paper. I would start at 4:30 p.m., after the bank had closed, joining a team of workers who would hand-record every loan, and every payment, made that day.

They had thousands of them. So we started with a number, added that to new loans, and subtracted from that all payments. We got to go home only when everything was in balance. So I learned about doing today's work today. And I implemented that system at Humana from the very first day. I've taught my kids to do the same because it's a very orderly way to do business.

So I thought hard about hospitals and then acted. By the late 1960s, Wendell, Extendicare, and I were already purchasing and building hospitals before we had decided to get out of the nursing home business. We concluded that the only way to learn the hospital business was to get into it. The changeover to hospitals started in 1968 when Extendicare, using its stock, bought a 300-bed hospital under construction in Huntsville, Alabama. The hospital, which didn't open until 1970, had been poorly financed, and the doctor-investors were a little nervous about the project.

We committed to going into the hospital business having more confidence than experience. It had worked for us in nursing homes, so why not hospitals? Again, using mainly stock as capital—with some cash obtained on a second stock sale—we acquired four small hospitals in 1969 and sixteen more in 1970. Most had been financed and built by doctors, but the doctors didn't like to run them, preferring to practice medicine. The doctors also made healthy profits on the sales.

✳

For Extendicare, 1970 would be a transitional year. Up to that point, Extendicare was considered kind of a "darling of Wall Street," a title that quickly vanished for investors with the sudden fall of Four Seasons Nursing Homes, the only nursing home company that was more highly valued than Extendicare.

It was a story of two continents. I did not immediately know about that fall when it happened. Seeking more money for hospitals, Carl Pollard and I had flown to Europe on a Saturday night for a first meeting with bankers on Monday morning. Along the way, we missed the headlines in *The Wall Street Journal* and *Financial Times* revealing that Four Seasons had serious financial problems and might declare bankruptcy. It soon did, in 1970.

The news rattled any likely Extendicare investors. Pollard and I were in Europe for eight days, visiting two or three banks a day, and not one would lend us money. All we heard was, "If the best company in the business turned out to be a fraud, why should we invest with you?" Carl said his ears got sore from hearing me tell the same story all those times, and we didn't raise a cent.

Having failed in Europe, I did find some financing from a New York bank to build Suburban Hospital in Louisville in a very expensive deal. But I hired Paul Gross, an experienced hospital executive, to manage the new hospital. He was successful and later became president of our Hospital Division and a corporate executive vice president. Gross knew what he was doing; he hired a good staff, and the hospital just took off.

Wendell and I continued to build new hospitals as our knowledge and training skills grew. The business practices we developed during the nursing home days continued to benefit the company. And what I learned from the mobile home debacle and about how I think and make decisions helped with another important decision: to abandon yesterday's success to focus on tomorrow's.

Extendicare sold all sixty of its nursing homes in 1972, receiving about $25 million—money that would be used to push further into the hospital business. The ten Canadian nursing homes were sold to the Canadian managers with a small down payment and a promissory note. The other fifty were sold to a nursing home company in Wisconsin, which ultimately led to several mergers. Eventually, Vencor bought those homes and returned their ownership and business to Louisville.

Looking ahead, that kind of thinking would later lead Humana out of hospitals—where its business practices revolutionized the industry—and into the insurance business, where new thinking and procedures would again lead to revolutionary success. But that came only after a nine-year period when the insurance and hospital businesses existed together in an uneasy balance that ended with the spin-off of the hospitals in 1993.

The '70s would be a good decade for the company, though 1970 proved to be a very difficult year for me personally. I had arranged for my parents to attend the famous Passion Play, held every ten years in Oberammergau, Germany. Afterward, they visited London, where my sixty-year-old mother, Elsie—who had diabetes— slipped on wet cobblestones at the Tower of London, falling hard and breaking her left leg.

Taken to Westminster Hospital, she had complications that required her leg to be amputated. She also suffered a stroke and remained in the hospital for two and a half months (at no cost, thanks to the British National Health Service). My dad stayed in London in an apartment nearby, where he was joined by my sister Jean. Because my mother did not like hospital food, Dad became a fixture in the small London grocery stores nearby, and he and Jean cooked for Mom.

As was often the case in my family's history of chance meetings, the medical emergency led to new relationships. My mother was first treated in the hospital emergency room by Dr. Malcolm Glasgow, with

128

the amputation performed by Dr. Paul Aichroth. I came to know both men well as I visited my mother often in London. As she recovered, we made plans to fly her to Baltimore, accompanied by Dr. Glasgow. Once in Baltimore, they were all met by Humana pilots John Landrum and Gene Van Meter in the company's Beechcraft King Air.

Many friends and family members greeted the plane when it landed at Bowman Field. Mom was then taken to St. Joseph's Infirmary, where she spent several more months and experienced an almost complete recovery from her stroke, having learned to speak, read, and write again.

But the story didn't stop there. In September 1970, we invited Dr. Aichroth's wife, Angela, and her son Mark to visit the Jones family at our Village Drive home, where we all celebrated Mark's seventh birthday and formed lasting family friendships.

Mark later graduated from Sandhurst, the British equivalent of West Point, and saw multiple deployments to Northern Ireland. When he married, our sons Dan, a Navy veteran, and Matt, a Marine, flew to England to be groomsmen in the wedding. Later, Mark invited Matt to join his Scots regiment for training, which included sliding down a rope 325 feet from a trestle. I knew nothing about that adventure until years later when Mark, standing on the porch of the Humana Building on a visit, estimated the distance to the ground at 325 feet—and then told me how he knew.

The Aichroth, Glasgow, and Jones families made several visits back and forth across the ocean, including one summer at Land's End, the southwestern-most point of England, where Paul and Malcolm proclaimed the water warm. So I dove in, and I've never been so cold in my life.

Aichroth and I played tennis on a grass court in Land's End—my first such experience—and later on the roof of a parking garage on a steep hill in Portofino, Italy.

Chapter Nine

FOCUS AND LIFT-OFF

"Walter Margulies had been in the branding business for more than three decades. One of the reasons we hired him was that he chewed us out the first time we met. Extendicare's tenth annual report had featured an attractive young woman in a swimsuit, sitting on a diving board in one of our mobile home parks, and a photo of Wendell and me in rugby shirts, drinking champagne. The hubris was too much for Margulies. He told us that our business was a serious one and that we must always, in everything we did, appear serious! He raised our consciousness about how we presented ourselves, not just with graphics and branding but the whole organization."

— DAVID JONES

Having made the decision to focus on hospitals, we focused.

I set ambitious goals for us. Goals are important; if you didn't have a goal line, how would you know how a game turned out? And I announced our goals publicly, which put pressure on the company. They were realistic goals, in the sense that I was pretty sure we could make them. But they did depend on rapid growth for a long period of time.

As Humana grew, Wendell and I continued to keep much of our team local. Why not? It worked. Another Louisville native, Bill Ballard, played a strong role in hospital acquisitions, although his path to our company was less than a straight line. "When I got out of college, I didn't know what I wanted to do," Ballard said. "But I was pretty sure I didn't want to be drafted into the Army and go to Vietnam. So I went to law school."

After graduating from the University of Louisville law school, he worked for the US Department of Justice in Washington. He went to night school at Georgetown University, earning his master's degree in taxation.

He represented the government in tax cases all over the country, working under attorneys general Ramsey Clark and John Mitchell. He met Bobby Kennedy several times, including an incident in which they tossed a football back and forth across his office, and Kennedy had called personally to offer Ballard a job. Ballard wasn't home at the time. His mother took the call and couldn't believe who was on the line.

"She could have died and gone to Ratterman's Funeral Home right then and been fine," said Ballard.

He eventually decided to leave Washington and take a job in Portland, Oregon. David Grissom found out and told Ballard that the Jones, Cherry, Grissom & Boone firm needed a tax lawyer. On his thirty-third birthday, in 1969, Ballard and I had lunch. We had never met before. My intuition kicked in. He seemed a perfect fit, and we hired him. Ballard began traveling with me, handling the acquisitions of sixteen hospitals in multiple states in 1969 and 1970. I was so impressed that I offered him the job of general counsel for Extendicare.

Ballard immediately said yes. Salary wasn't even discussed. Two weeks later, somebody in finance asked Ballard about his salary.

"I haven't a clue," he said.

He then learned we were paying him twice what the law firm had paid.

"I thought that was fair," Ballard said.

On his first trip to buy a hospital, Ballard got off the small plane in the middle of a grass field in Marksville, Louisiana. The pilot flew off. There was no one else there. He saw a farmer plowing a field and walked over in his suit carrying his briefcase to ask directions. The farmer seemed to be speaking in French.

It only got worse from there. "We finally communicated, I went back to the airport, and somebody came and got me and took me downtown, where I promptly got arrested. It was their 'Pioneer Day' or some such, and if you didn't have a beard, you were in trouble. So, finally, the hospital folks came and got me out."

Extendicare eventually did have a hospital there. More adventures would follow for Ballard. "I remember one time I bought a hospital in Kissimmee, Florida. Nobody had seen it. I thought somebody had seen it. They thought somebody else had seen it. I went out and bought it, and nobody had seen it. Turned out Disney World was built right next door. We made a pile of money."

My memory differed from Ballard's. All this effort in finding hospitals to acquire, or a location to build one, depended on a lot of research, often looking at five or ten sites for each one bought.

Ballard also traveled with me for analyst and fundraising presentations. We became good friends and donated to each other's causes over the years.

"Most of the time in buying hospitals, it's pretty much a gentleman's negotiation," said Ballard. "It's not loud. Occasionally people, when they think you're being disingenuous, tend to get a little vociferous. David is always good at putting everybody in the public at ease. But I've seen him lose his temper, especially when he thought somebody was trying to take advantage of the company."

Ballard had also been the target of one of my bursts of anger shortly after joining the firm. He had screwed up something—or at least got the blame for it—and the company culture was to admit to it, deal with it, and move on. I have very high expectations for the people I work with and hold people accountable.

During the early 1970s, Extendicare's learning curve required a little outside shaping. As the business expanded and changed from nursing homes to hospitals, Wendell and I sought a new, more fitting name for the company. Having sold all our nursing homes in 1972, we had clearly become a hospital company by early 1974—we owned and operated forty-nine hospitals with 4,847 licensed beds and would soon add another 2,785.

Extendicare—the name was based on "extended care facility," Medicare's term for a nursing home—no longer applied. Company leaders wanted a name that would be less limiting and still work if the corporation changed its strategy or entered a different business. In search of a name, Wendell and I visited major advertising agencies in New York.

We found no inspiring ad folks, and disappointed, we returned. Then as an afterthought, we sent Carl Pollard, now our CFO, back to New York to visit Lippincott and Margulies. Walter Margulies, who was Jewish, had escaped Paris just ahead of the Nazis during World War II. With Gordon Lippincott—an engineer—Margulies created a marketing and branding company in 1943. By the time of Pollard's visit, the company was world-famous, having created the logos for RCA, American Express, Chrysler, and Amtrak. Pollard returned from New York and insisted the company hire Margulies.

Wendell's and my first encounter with Margulies left us temporarily chastened and permanently changed. Extendicare's tenth annual report, in 1971, had featured an attractive young woman in a swimsuit sitting on a diving board in one of our mobile home parks. It also included a photograph of Wendell and me in rugby shirts, drinking champagne. The hubris—especially the model—was too much for Margulies, who strongly criticized it.

One of the reasons we hired Walter was that he chewed us out over that report. He didn't ever want us to have our pictures taken unless we were wearing dark suits. He raised our consciousness about how we presented ourselves, not just with graphics and branding but the whole organization. He told us that our business was a serious one and that we must always, in everything we did, appear serious!

By then, Margulies had been in the branding business for more than three decades. He was the best at what he did of anybody I ever met, head and shoulders above the rest. He was also the best at billing. He would call up and say he had read so-and-so in *The Wall Street Journal* and send us a copy of it. Then we'd get a bill for $15,000.

Margulies's primary contribution was coming up with the name

Humana—humanity being fitting for hospitals. The word had another virtue: It was not limiting. If the company went in another direction, "Humana" could still apply.

We loved the name. When Humana split into hospitals and health insurance, I chose to run the insurance side and kept the Humana name. The hospital division became Galen, named for the ancient Greek surgeon and philosopher.

By the early 1970s, I had learned that running a hospital business really wasn't much more complex than running nursing homes. We realized that new, state-of-the-art hospitals in underserved areas would have a great appeal to patients as well as physicians. We looked all over the country and found good locations, typically in fast-growing states. Florida is a good example. Its population was exploding, and the old non-profit hospital system wasn't keeping up.

But the pace of Humana's push into hospitals was also prompted in part by a government edict: the certificate-of-need legislation enacted in some states in the 1960s and early 1970s and then signed into federal law in 1973 by President Richard Nixon. The legislation grew out of a concern that the construction of excess hospital capacity would cause competitors in the areas that already had enough hospitals to overcharge or try to persuade patients who didn't really need hospitalization to accept it.

I had other feelings about it. That certificate was engineered by people who were already in the business, to keep competitors out. Monopolies can lower costs, but they never lower prices. Monopolists may have the lowest costs of anyone, but why should they share them? They don't. So it was beyond stupid, but you have to obey the law.

The law—which still applies in Kentucky but in none of its seven contiguous states—went into effect on January 1, 1974. We knew we'd have to get ahead of it and start fast on our plans to build hospitals. After the 1972 sale of our nursing home equity for $25 million, I made the rounds of many lending institutions trying to borrow more money to expand the hospital chain. Finally, Equitable Life & Casualty Insurance Company lent us $50 million.

Using that $75 million—and hurrying before the January 1, 1974 certificate-of-need deadline went into effect—the company quickly began building twelve large new hospitals. I estimated it would have taken the company ten years to get permission to build all those hospitals under a certificate of need. Our hospital locations were well chosen, so we didn't have any problem paying for them. But to give you an idea of their value, the one we built in Virginia Beach, Virginia, for $8 million we sold about ten years later to a competitor hospital group for $65 million. By then—somewhat ironically—the certificate-of-need legislation was protecting Humana from competing hospitals being built or expanded in that area. We didn't like the law, but it often protected us.

Wendell, who had a strong and sophisticated interest in buildings and architecture, was often involved in designing the hospitals. As the company grew, making its presence felt across Louisville, he would later become heavily involved in designing other structures, including the Humana Building and the Kentucky Center for the Performing Arts.

Eleven of the twelve new hospitals proved highly successful. One, in Springfield, Illinois, was problematic. Unhappy with their existing hospital, Springfield doctors had campaigned for a new one. After the hospital was completed, the older hospital changed its policies, luring back many of the original dissidents.

The situation illuminated the role local doctors could play in the success of a hospital. By this point, we had a lot of experience working with doctors as businesspeople. Many of the hospitals we bought were owned by doctors who were tired of running them—often because they were not very good at it, or the hospitals needed expanding or even replacing. But while we often bought out doctors, we would not partner with them in owning hospitals. Such situations would become more common in the future as doctors partnered with some hospitals—but never with a Humana hospital. I believe a doctor should never have a financial incentive to hospitalize a patient. We never partnered with doctors. We didn't believe we should ever be on both sides of a medical transaction.

✳

Wendell and I made a deliberate decision to make Humana the only hospital company to place its name in front of every hospital's name: Humana-Audubon, for example. We believed the only reason not to put the company name on a hospital was the fear that something wrong might happen. But there are many more good things that can happen than bad things, and we made a decision to always use our Humana name.

Long-term success in the transition from nursing homes to hospitals, and later into insurance, would be built on a single, consistent management philosophy: Everything that was critical—quality as well as productivity—must be measured and compared.

To me, these were two sides of the same coin; you couldn't get quality without productivity, and you couldn't get productivity without quality. Both required that you do the right thing, and that you do it right the first and every time. Measuring all critical elements allowed Extendicare's less successful facilities to catch up quickly with the others. The company held a management committee meeting every Tuesday morning, where managers were encouraged to bring new ideas—and defend their high costs.

If there was a legitimate reason, then it wasn't an issue. But measurement forces all that stuff out into the open. You can't hide it. Measuring and comparing was made easier as information technology improved, and we were early adopters. But it was more about management and focus than machines. We had clear performance standards for all critical functions, measured relentlessly, and held people accountable for acting on the insights.

I had earlier been surprised to learn that although nursing homes with the highest costs claimed better quality, the opposite was often true. If you spend money on the wrong things, you are going to have bad outcomes.

Nursing homes were a good business. We were good at it. We had attracted and trained lots of bright, capable nurses and administrators. Most of our best administrators stayed with us as we transitioned into hospitals.

Along the way, Wendell and I would occasionally have to fire people or at least transfer them to other areas because the job wasn't getting done. I rarely had second thoughts. What is it they say? "Often wrong but never in doubt." We didn't have to fire that many people, and I don't think we ever made a mistake in firing. I think the mistake people make is not firing.

Once you see that someone's either done something wrong or is not suited for the job, you have to make a move. We had many cases where we transferred people to work that was more suitable. They might not have appreciated that, but it gave them time to sort out whether they wanted to stay or go. To be on the team, you must be fully committed. It's really important that everybody on the team knows where the goal line is and what the game plan is.

Once that transition to hospitals started, the heads of specific hospital areas—such as dietitians, radiologists, and those in clinical diagnosis—would be invited to Louisville for annual meetings to compare notes, form friendships, and meet company specialists in their areas. That's how I got to know the people in the hospitals. I couldn't go out and visit one hundred hospitals all the time, so they felt good knowing there was a qualified executive at headquarters who had the time and responsibility to keep up with whatever was going on in their area.

I shared a book titled *Integrity Works* with top company executives, a slim volume offering a broad array of strategies and examples for becoming "a trusted, respected, and admired leader." Among the suggestions from authors Dana Telford and Adrian Gostick: "You mess up you 'fess up," "You keep your word" and "You stay the course."

Humana also created a Quality College of doctors and nurses who would immediately go to any hospital that had a special problem—an unexpected death or an above-average infection rate that could require more research or possibly result in litigation. We wanted to know exactly what happened and why. The Quality College immediately obtained all the facts. We tried to do whatever we could to make things right and prevent a recurrence.

I called this philosophy "Planning for Success." I would compare my ability to manage increasing complexity as the company grew and changed to a parent lifting a baby: When a baby's tiny, it's easy to lift. I know mothers who have twins, and before long those twins each weigh twenty to twenty-five pounds, and the mother can still lift both. Why? Because she has lifted them every single day, and her strength builds as their weight builds. Someone coming into a complex organization like Humana today will have a tougher job. But if you've been there every day along the way, it's like picking up that baby. You don't notice it because everything that's come before is in your head, and with every new piece of information the brain knows where to put it and how to connect.

Chapter Ten

Proudly Not Non-Profit

" 'You can't attain the moral high ground by assertion, only by performance.' I kept that quote on my home bulletin board and used it to answer media criticism about our hospitals making profits. If a non-tax-paying hospital can do a better job, do it. Nobody ever beat us on performance. There is simply no moral high ground in not paying taxes on profits from your business. Our costs were lower. So we saved Medicare and Medicaid tons of money."

— DAVID JONES

Getting into what I called the "soul" of the business, I said hospitals must create places where physicians can do their best work while giving loving care to all the people who come there, some for joyful purposes like having a baby, some because they're dying.

Competing with many established hospitals, including some much-loved non-tax-paying hospitals, was like shooting fish in a barrel. There were some good ones, but only those where the leaders created conditions that allowed doctors to do their best work. Even those rarely matched our relentless focus on measurable quality, productivity, and patient satisfaction.

One hospital that tested our values and processes early on was the ancient St. Joseph's Infirmary in Louisville, owned by the Sisters of Charity of Nazareth. Extendicare bought it in 1970. Built at Fourth and Broadway in 1830, it had been rebuilt in 1926 as a 509-bed facility at the corner of Eastern Parkway and Preston Street. Its features included a grotto at the rear of the building, giving patients and staff a place to enjoy the fresh air.

Inside, though, the old building was in dire need of change. It didn't have private bathrooms, and its air conditioning consisted of about 2,400 separate window units.

The sisters sold it to us because the building was obsolete and because they had an upside-down business pyramid with few working sisters compared to the number in retirement. They needed income to cover their retirees. They were wonderful to work with and went to great lengths to assure themselves we would operate the hospital in an honorable and effective manner. We paid for it with a note with a high rate of interest. And that interest rate was what they needed.

A very important partner in that transition—and later a strong Louisville leader and a role model in the development of Humana—was Kathy Mershon, a young nurse. Eleven years later, in 1981, Wendell and I appointed her as the first female vice president in Humana history.

Mershon's rise illustrated the growing opportunities available to women—and the personal, business, and public relations struggles involved in any hospital's transition from non-profit status into the corporate world. She had grown up in Charleston, South Carolina. Her mother was a nurse, as were many relatives. The career appealed to Mershon, echoed within her. She had a clear head and was a good problem-solver. She wanted to make a difference in people's lives.

Mershon started as a nurse at St. Joseph's. "I loved it," she said. "That may have been the most satisfying work I have ever done."

She—along with all the hospital staff and its patients, including aged priests and nuns—first learned about the sale of St. Joseph's to Extendicare in July 1970 on the eleven o'clock news. It was frightening to many. No one in the hospital knew anything about Extendicare. Many in the hospital field—and their patients, for that matter—were unaware of the growing trend toward tax-paying, investor-owned hospitals, often called "for profit" by critics. Those who were aware seemed wary at best.

140

Mershon's daily rounds had taken her to almost every floor of the eight-story hospital. She knew it had serious problems, but she also worried about the change. Her chief nursing officer struggled with it. The priests and nuns were unhappy. No one knew what to expect.

"The sisters were angry," said Mershon. "All of a sudden, they had complaints. And I told one of them, 'Sister, you know I understand. This is a change for all of us. But I'm the same person today that I was yesterday when I was taking care of you. That's no different.' "

The hospital became a target for employee collective bargaining. There was tension in every department. The director of nursing retired, and Mershon—one of two nurses in the hospital with a master's degree—was asked to take over temporarily. When a better candidate could not be found, Mershon's appointment became permanent. She was twenty-eight years old.

"I was scared to death," she said. "These other employees had been there forever and ever. It was a tense time."

But Extendicare offered a quick infusion of capital and corporate support. It upgraded all the rooms and modernized the bathrooms. Other things also changed. The crucifixes did not go back on the walls—bringing complaints from many quarters—and Extendicare installed its quality improvement program, measuring each step of the way.

"It was all very sophisticated compared to what we were doing," Mershon said.

The transition was painful—as it could and would be at other not-for-profit hospitals going through similar sales. "I couldn't sleep at night. It was horrible," said Mershon, "but in the end, the sale turned out to be a good decision."

We encountered resistance as we competed with or acquired non-profit hospitals owned by religious, community, or charitable organizations. The sale of even a crumbling facility like St. Joseph Infirmary to a "for-profit"

company like Humana inspired many questions, if not controversy. Was it right to make a profit on sick people, and where might that lead in terms of health care? People were afraid; they were attached to the idea that hospitals should be non-profit, so transforming even obsolete institutions presented challenging social and financial issues.

It also produced what I considered unfair, self-righteous criticism in the media and among the medical establishment, including close to home.

Most nursing homes were then tax-paying enterprises, unlike most hospitals, so the media's attention to the company was new when our business changed. At home, we took a lot of grief from the *Courier Journal*. We were always called "for-profit" this and "for-profit" that. When I wrote to them, I called them the "for-profit" newspaper and television organization, which for some reason they didn't like.

I am proud that our performance in understanding, and meeting, the needs and values of patients and their physicians made us profitable, allowing us to create more than 100,000 stable, well-paid jobs with dependable pension benefits. What you call "for-profit" I call "tax-paying." Profit is never an end; it's an absolute requirement. No enterprise, however worthy, can continue unless all costs, including the cost of capital, are covered.

I believe that profitable hospitals should pay taxes, regardless of ownership, and should compete on quality and affordability. The notion that a hospital that's profitable but doesn't pay taxes somehow has moral superiority over one that does pay taxes is ludicrous. That's a rather skewed way of thinking.

One of my remarks in a *Wall Street Journal* story best explained my philosophy: "You can't attain the moral high ground by assertion, only by performance." I kept that quote on my home bulletin board and used it to answer media criticism about our hospitals making profits. If a non-tax-paying hospital can do a better job, do it. Nobody ever beat us on performance. There is simply no moral high ground in not paying taxes on profits from your business. Our costs were lower. So we saved Medicare and Medicaid tons of money.

Because of its insistence on unexcelled, measurable quality and productivity, Humana's profits tended to be about four times higher than the "non-tax-paying" competition. We were making 12 percent pre-tax; they were making 3 percent pre-tax. When you're making 12 percent instead of 3 percent, you can spend more on quality and productivity and satisfying the values and needs of your customers. But while Humana hospitals were earning about 12 percent, some half of that went to local, state and federal governments while "non-tax-paying" competitors typically earned about 3 percent and contributed almost nothing to local, state, or federal governments. This was a distinction seldom, if ever, noted by critics.

Humana hospitals spent more on patient care and less on administration, and our prices were generally below the competition. Most "non-tax-paying" hospitals—such as those owned by religious and charitable organizations and colleges—lacked our level of management and failed to measure either quality or productivity.

An article in the July 3, 1983 *Courier Journal* headlined "Hospitals are debating what is the best method for making cost comparisons" went directly to that point. While acknowledging the difficulty in comparing costs across different hospitals, levels of patient care, cost-analysis indexes, and hospital specialties, the story by Robert Pierce said, "The *Courier Journal*'s study also showed three non-university hospitals—Humana Hospital-Southwest, Humana Hospital-Suburban, and Humana Hospital-Audubon—had larger earnings, last year, before taxes, than the nine [local] not-for-profit institutions combined."

Humana executives interviewed for the story also noted that lower costs benefited the federal Medicare program, which then based payments on what the services cost the hospitals, not the patients.

"The way we look at it," said Henry J. Werronen, one of Humana's senior vice presidents, "we have comparable charges, and we pay taxes. That's a helluva performance."

※

By 1976—eight years after opening its first hospital—Humana owned about forty. Soon we had 40 percent of the Louisville hospital market.

St. Joseph Hospital, an outdated building with many maintenance and medical facility needs, closed in 1980. The infirmary relocated to a new building a few miles away on Poplar Level Road, named Humana Hospital-Audubon.

Just as Humana Hospital-Audubon was opening, I invited Mershon to meet with Wendell and me at company headquarters. She knew me a little: While a nurse at St. Joseph's, she had cared for my mother after my mother lost her leg. Wendell and I offered Mershon a new company position, corporate vice president of nursing affairs. The job would give her the responsibility for developing quality, consistency, and cost-effectiveness for the company's thousands of nurses.

"I was shocked," said Mershon. "I'm having this conversation with them like it's the most normal thing in the world. I remember going back to my car and going back to work and thinking, 'Wow. Do you know what just happened?' "

In her new job, Mershon left behind the hospital pager and the crush of patients. She traveled the country, and the world, visiting Humana hospitals and implementing the programs she had seen St. Joseph's adopt. She gave talks and trained more nurses to take leadership roles, expanding her dream, and their dreams.

As a shortage of nurses became critical to the company's success in the 1980s, I pushed the idea that Humana should create its own schools of nursing. That led, in 1989, to the Humana Health Institutes and later the Galen College of Nursing, with campuses in Louisville, San Antonio, and Tampa Bay, three places where the company's nursing needs were most critical.

I chose Mershon to lead the Galen College of Nursing, which would lead to nursing and management careers for thousands of other nurses. Galen is still training many nurses every year. At one point, Humana employed 37,000 registered nurses, who became a tremendous resource for management-level positions across the country.

144

Along with Dr. Marjorie Perrin, who had a doctorate and extensive experience in education, Mershon wrote their starting curriculum on her kitchen table in two weeks. She got all three schools up and running in about ten months. Humana attorney Martha Clark led in securing regulatory approval in the three states.

They addressed the nursing shortage with a program that refunded one year of tuition for every year worked at Humana hospitals. Mershon retired from Humana in 1992, but remained involved in many local, state, and national health care issues—including as chair of the board of the independent Galen College of Nursing, spun off by Humana in 1994. The credo I suggested served her well in all venues: Remember names, treat everyone the same, never write a memo longer than one page.

Chapter Eleven

Peter's Principles

"The key points in Peter Drucker's book would become the foundation of Humana's growth: 'Organizations exist to create and satisfy customers. Marketing and innovation are the basic functions of an enterprise,' he wrote. 'Executives' effectiveness is more important than their efficiency.'

"Wendell and I waited until Monday morning, called Drucker at home, and asked to come see him. We spent two days in Drucker's modest home in Claremont, California, and I would go back there regularly for thirteen years for both friendship and advice on Humana. He was the greatest marketing guru that ever lived."

— DAVID JONES

A t the core of our management philosophy was what we learned in the nursing home days: Measure and compare everything that is critical, quality as well as productivity. But Wendell and I grew in our thinking under the teaching of Austrian-born author Peter Drucker, a wise and occasionally enigmatic consultant whose ideas revolutionized modern business management. His approach was based on clear objectives and meeting the needs and values of those being served: the customers.

I had never heard of Drucker when Wendell called me early one Saturday morning in 1974, all excited about a book he had just read—Drucker's *Management: Tasks, Responsibilities, Practices.* Wendell—who had never heard of Drucker before that weekend either—had been transfixed by the 861-page book he read in one long night at LaGuardia Airport in New York as he waited for a delayed Eastern Airlines flight. Humana had total revenue of $106.7 million in 1973, but Wendell knew there was a lot of room for growth and quality improvement. He had seen a path forward in Drucker's book.

"David, come on over," Wendell told me. "This guy Peter Drucker has written a book about us."

Wendell had underlined some passages so heavily I could barely read them. I had to buy my own copy.

Drucker had a fascinating family history. His mother was the first female surgeon in Austria; his great-grandfather had been surgeon general of Great Britain and served at the Battle of Waterloo. Born in 1909, Drucker grew up in a time when it was customary in well-to-do Central European families to send the eldest son into banking, the second into the military, and the third into the clergy, a generational attempt to cover all the bases. He was the eldest son.

Drucker's story was living history that read like inspirational fiction. When he was twelve, he lived in a garret above a bank while learning the trade. He also earned a law degree in Hamburg, got into journalism, and covered the tinder-box landscape of the Balkans for the *Manchester Guardian* between the two World Wars.

He wrote a book denouncing Hitler and then had to flee to London in 1933, barely escaping Germany with his life. In London, he met Doris Schmitz, his future wife, who was Jewish. She worked for a large retail firm, Marks & Spencer, and assisted her husband as he began writing his thirty-nine books on business practices. A mountain climber, memoirist, and inventor with degrees in physics and law, she started her own business at eighty-two and lived to 103.

The Druckers' friends got them to the United States, where he worked as a college professor, eventually joining the American War Production Board during World War II. His analysis of American business was highlighted in a 1946 book, *Concept of the Corporation*, which outlined the self-inflicted threats facing General Motors.

In the early 1950s, the far-seeing Drucker noted that computers were changing the entire business world. He warned American companies in the early 1960s of the rise of Japanese industry. In the 1990s, he introduced the concept of the "knowledge economy." An observation in one of Drucker's early books demonstrated his grasp of history: "The three most charismatic leaders in this century inflicted more suffering on the human race than almost any trio in history—Hitler, Stalin, and Mao. What matters is not a leader's charisma. What matters is a leader's mission."

When we read Drucker's book, the company was still relatively new to the hospital business. *Management: Tasks, Responsibility, Practices*, covered the challenge facing Wendell and me: How do we grow from here? At its heart, the book explains that good management must be part of a successful business and often leads to more success than just relying on economics, quantitative analysis, and behavioral science.

Drucker's key points would become the foundation of Humana's growth: "Organizations exist to create and satisfy customers. Marketing and innovation are the basic functions of an enterprise," he wrote. "Executives' effectiveness is more important than their efficiency."

Wendell and I waited until Monday morning, called Drucker at home, and asked to come see him. Drucker said, "Sure. I don't send bills; the charge will be $1,500 a day for two days."

We spent two days in Drucker's modest home in Claremont, California, and I would go back there regularly for thirteen years for both friendship and advice on Humana. He was the greatest marketing guru that ever lived. I and others successfully promoted Drucker's house for the National Register of Historic Places, not because of the structure but because of who lived in it.

In those two days in 1974, Drucker never answered a question. He asked us questions only about our business, forcing us to think about exactly what we were doing. Our takeaway: Building a business is all about understanding customers and meeting their needs and values while creating the conditions that allow people to do their best work.

Drucker also believed in concise, hand-written notes to thank people, a kindness I admired and would follow. We became friends over the years, and when Claremont Graduate School created the Drucker School of Management, I became its founding board chairman at Drucker's request.

That friendship extended to the Jones family. Once when Drucker caught an airplane ride with us, he, Betty, and Dan got caught up in a long discussion on the book *The Bridge on the Drina*, a look at the horrific history of suffering imposed on residents of Bosnia from the sixteenth century to the beginning of World War I. The atrocities included heads being cut off and placed on stakes on the bridge as both sides in the conflict went back and forth across it. Betty had read a lot about that area. Dan was finishing his PhD in history at Indiana University. Their deep discussion brought the families even closer together.

Drucker always studied history and leadership. He was an ongoing influence on Humana and me. One story has Drucker asking the top Humana executive team to sketch an organizational chart of the company as team members saw it. Carl Pollard drew three boxes vertically, each containing one name:

David Jones

David Jones

David Jones

Drucker preached that profits are never a goal or an end: They are a means to survival. Unprofitable enterprises do not survive, nor do their jobs or pensions. Good intentions are vital but never sufficient.

Performance and results are required and must be measured. It all goes back to the same thing—quality. You hear me talk about that all the time because quality is the cheapest thing there is. For example, we never allowed deferred maintenance on any building or equipment. We repaired everything as it was needed.

※

If asked to explain my business philosophy, I return to one of my observations from the 1981 Humana annual report, which remained relevant throughout my career: "The world is turning, the system is evolving, and those who do tomorrow what they did yesterday are likely to be caught short."

For example, market research had indicated that consumers' number one priority was a dependable emergency room. It showed that most people entering an emergency room were first met by a clerk who would determine how a patient would pay. Humana changed that. The first question—asked by a skilled triage nurse within sixty seconds of entering one of our hospitals—was, "Why are you here?" followed by, "What meds are you taking?"

The nurses had a hard time with that. They said, "What do you mean, you want us to be the first ones to meet someone? You always have to go to the desk."

We said, "You don't have to go to the desk. You don't want somebody dropping dead waiting to talk to a clerk." We turned the ER around, so you paid on the way out. We provided faster treatment, and we had better outcomes and more satisfied customers, and satisfied customers are more likely to pay than dead ones.

As a result, emergency room business increased—and with half of a hospital's admissions generally coming in through the emergency room, Humana's occupancy rate climbed while competitors' fell. With hospital costs largely fixed, the higher occupancy increased profits and allowed better treatment of patients.

I'm somewhat relentless in imposing my will on a situation, but that paid off for us big time because it met patients' needs.

Humana hospitals all had doctors on their boards, including those from OB/GYN, pediatrics, medicine, surgery, and ER, leading to a feeling their needs and opinions were respected, allowing them a voice.

Our emphasis on quality led us to assign a physician, Dr. David Rollo, to work full-time assessing medical technology. He observed developments in the medical field and always had someone on his staff keeping up with all advances in equipment and technology. By purchasing equipment in volume for one hundred hospitals, Humana held down costs. Along the way, Rollo learned of lithotripters, effective and non-invasive devices that pulverized kidney stones with shockwaves, thus replacing surgery. Humana had the first sixteen used in the United States.

We could afford to hire fully trained and capable professionals. We were always on top of things. As a CPA, I watched the numbers.

Humana created an organization called the Humana Club. It met annually and would reward successful hospital administrators with cash bonuses, stock options, and recognition. It was the company's premier social event of the year, and no administrator wanted to miss it, although many did, as standards were high.

Wendell and I tried to manage the event for a few years, then turned it over to Lindy Barber Street, who worked in our public affairs office. Street easily handled the complex effort, making it fun for everyone. She was given added responsibilities and soon became a vice president and valued member of senior management. When Humana split in 1993, she became vice president of the hospital firm, Galen.

Chapter Twelve

STOCK MARKET TROUBLE, BUSINESS SUCCESS

"Extendicare stock was $8 a share in the initial public offering in January 1968. It opened at $16 and ended the day at $20. It rose to $84 in December and was used to acquire nursing homes and hospitals. By 1974, however, the stock had fallen to $7.50.

"Betty and I had built a house; we'd bought a car. We bought a house for my parents and a car for both of our parents. So I'd borrowed maybe a million dollars on my stock, and my loans were called. Wendell had the same circumstances. We were nearly bankrupt."

— DAVID JONES

The 1973 oil crisis, a stock market crash, and a sharp economic downturn led to 1974 being the most difficult year in Humana's history, and it battered my personal finances—and Wendell's. Mortgage rates rose to 12 percent. Inflation climbed from 3.4 percent in 1972 to 12.3 percent in 1973. The American economy slowed from 7.2 percent GDP growth to minus 2.1 percent. Interest rates spiked in the 1970s to almost 23 percent.

Extendicare stock was $8 a share in the initial public offering on January 31, 1968. It opened at $16 and ended the day at $20. It rose to $84 that December and was used to acquire nursing homes and hospitals; it was soon split two for one. But by 1974—the year the company adopted the name

152

Humana—the stock had fallen to $7.50, or $3.75 for the post-split shares.

When the company went public, I had about 170,000 shares of stock, or 17 percent of the company. At $84 a share, it was worth about $14 million. At its 1974 value, it was worth $1.3 million—a drop of $12.7 million, or 91 percent, in value. The stock was selling at three times earnings. Both Wendell's and my bank loans were larger than our shares could support. So, by federal regulation, the banks had to call in the loans. It was particularly difficult for me because I was on the board of First National Bank, where I had borrowed the money.

Betty and I had built a house; we bought a car. We bought a house for my parents and a car for both of our parents. So I'd borrowed maybe a million dollars on my stock, and my loans were called. Wendell had the same circumstances.

We were nearly bankrupt. I could see it coming. It wasn't as if I didn't know it could happen, but it was embarrassing. I knew it was an issue that had to be dealt with. I obviously didn't know what strategy would work, but I didn't shoot myself or run around whining. I did something. I talked to Sam Klein.

Klein, who owned the Bank of Louisville with his brother Izzy, had rescued me in the company's early years, providing a $35,000 certified check on short notice, enabling the company to acquire its third nursing home, in Virginia, in 1963. Eleven years later, during one of the deepest financial downturns in American history, Klein was again ready to trust me. He told me he could not lend money against my devalued stock, but he was willing to give me and Wendell each a $1 million character loan.

Sam said, "Give me a second mortgage on your house, your car, your dog, whatever you've got, but you can't give me stock." So he loaned me money to pay the other bank.

Klein wasn't finished. He asked if I believed the Humana stock was a good value. The stock had tanked, but I said the company was financially in good shape with a bright future. With its stock selling at three times earnings, solid management, and my full understanding of the operation and its potential, I was totally confident of its future. So Sam asked me if

I wanted to borrow another million dollars. I told him "Yes," and bought another 250,000 shares. He made the same offer to Wendell, who also bought more shares. Sam Klein was the best banker I've ever known, and he remained Humana's main banker and best friend until his death in 1995.

A very significant change in Humana operations came in 1974 after company executives and I attended a presentation in White Plains, New York. There, IBM's Dewey Walker explained the IBM 360, an original mainframe computer system designed to cover the complete range of small to large, commercial and scientific applications. It also would allow its users to purchase a smaller system that could be enlarged as needed. Prior to its installation, Humana had been using punch cards to record all its data.

I was intrigued. Walker looked at Humana's business system and suggested the company have one central office in Louisville for all the hospitals. That setup would enable better monitoring of the entire system. It's an insight that seemed so simple, yet we hadn't thought of it.

We'd had modestly skilled and paid people negotiating with Medicare, Travelers, Aetna, and Blue Cross. All those companies were keeping our money for sixty days or longer because we didn't know better. Dewey suggested we hire bright, capable people and have one person manage our total relationship with Travelers and another who could manage our relationship with Medicare. It was wonderful. It changed our whole way of doing business.

So I hired Walker, who led Humana's pioneering use of the IBM 360 to improve productivity and administrative quality dramatically. The 360 allowed us to operate all our hospitals with one highly professional back office. Fifty hospitals with just one financial office! Productivity soared, and so did profits. We were called "the black box company" because all the financial functions and essential information ran through a computer in Louisville.

Despite the tough economy and market conditions, Humana saw an opportunity to buy American Medicorp, a hospital chain that was slightly larger than Humana but was also selling at three times earnings. Humana had about 5 million shares outstanding, which were selling for around four dollars a share, or about $20 million. American Medicorp had 10 million shares outstanding at about two dollars a share—also about $20 million. The two founders of American Medicorp were willing to sell the chain to Humana for about four dollars a share, or $40 million.

I saw the deal as an irresistible bargain. I went to banks all over the country, but none would lend me the money. I couldn't get a penny. They all thought the sky was falling just when amazing bargains were available. Any time when almost everybody agrees on something in the market, it's invariably wrong. Our investment bank, Salomon Brothers, told us to pull in our horns, not to make acquisitions at a time like that. It was ridiculous advice. Buying when prices are low was something that Wendell and I understood well—but our Wall Street experts didn't.

The federal government paid us on a cost-plus basis for both Medicare and Medicaid, which accounted for about half of our business, so our debt was similar to federal government bonds. For this reason, I was not hesitant to take on debt at that time, but few others understood.

About four years later, Humana would finally buy American Medicorp for $26.20 a share—a deal that was still a huge bargain. The push for the purchase came in September 1977 as Betty and I were having dinner with the Cherrys at the Oriental House on Shelbyville Road. We said we tried to buy Medicorp back in 1974, and it would still be a perfect fit. So we were eating Chinese food, then put together our plan the next morning.

The purchase was a "hostile takeover"—dealing directly with a company's shareholders because management was unwilling to agree to a merger or the takeover. Humana had little cash at that time, so it offered what today would be labeled "junk bonds" to complete the deal—junk bonds being defined as a high-yield, high-risk security sometimes offered by a company lacking a stellar credit rating. I think the term "junk bond" was coined about then. I was highly insulted that someone thought our bonds were junk. We were told there had never before been a successful hostile tender offer using bonds instead of cash or stock.

In the course of that deal, Humana was sued in numerous courts. I spent two days on the witness stand in the main case, an antitrust suit in Philadelphia. The American Medicorp attorney was a former federal judge. He asked me questions while demanding "yes" or "no" answers. Always a talker, I answered in full. The lawyer, who brought a cadre of other legal experts with him—a group I labeled a "Greek Chorus"—complained bitterly, still demanding I answer "yes" or "no." The judge, however, allowed me to respond to each question in detail.

I never worried much about that antitrust case. I thought American Medicorp made a mistake in spending so much effort on it. Humana won all the lawsuits, with Wendell, CFO Carl Pollard, senior vice president Bill Ballard, and general counsel Tom Flynn each handling separate cases. We never doubled up. We had a capable group of colleagues. I didn't worry a bit about each one handling a different lawsuit.

American Medicorp had large hospitals in Illinois, Nevada, and California, and about fifty in all. The deal doubled Humana's size to about one hundred hospitals. The biggest was the Sunrise Hospital in Las Vegas, making it the largest hospital in the entire system at a time when Las Vegas was the fastest-growing city in the United States.

Humana eventually paid $303 million for American Medicorp in cash and debt—a deal described in a Philadelphia paper as "the shark that swallowed the whale." Humana's stockholders strongly approved the deal. When it was completed, Wendell showed up at work with a surprise for everyone. Earl Reed, from Humana's accounting/reimbursement department, described the moment:

> I was walking down one of the hallways, and around the corner comes Wendell. He was dressed in jeans, a flannel shirt with one of those old leather vests with lamb's wool showing around the edges.
>
> I knew something was up when I saw what he had in his hands . . . four bottles of champagne. He put them in my

arms and simply said, "We won, go get everybody together and have some fun."

Between 1977 and 1978, Humana grew from 15,700 to 35,000 employees; revenue more than doubled to $764 million, with a net income of $22 million. As we combined these two organizations with many different procedures, accounting expertise and an intuitive sense of good business practices were vital. I always used the shortest depreciation on assets I could because, while longer depreciation would allow a company to report higher profits, a shorter depreciation write-off would provide more cash. It also presented a more realistic picture of a company's financial health.

The time value of money is always a critical element. I understood that in my bones because I'd been doing all this stuff for so long, and it meant we had much more money to use to grow faster. I recognized another thing: In both the hospital and nursing home business between 1966 and 1983—when the Medicaid and Medicare rules were changed—the company prospered while being paid on a "cost-plus basis." This allowed only a small profit, but the government was then paying the interest on half of our debt.

I looked at that and thought, "Well, half our business is coming from the government, so half our debt is like a government bond." I don't know why everybody didn't understand or look at that.

We were able to grow fast because I piled on debt that I was able to convince the lenders was not going to be a problem for them: The government was paying for 50 percent of it. In many of these things, like the decision to abandon yesterday's success, it was an easy decision for me because I was watching what was going on.

In a 2011 book commemorating Humana's fiftieth anniversary, business writer Laura Rowley pointed out that only a dozen years after Humana had leased its first hospital, the company owned ninety hospitals in twenty-three states and two European countries. By 1980, Humana's revenues had grown at an annual rate of 32 percent, exceeding all but two companies in *Financial World* magazine's annual ranking of ten-year performers.

After the acquisition, Humana closed the American Medicorp office in Philadelphia, interviewed its top executives, and hired five of them to strengthen our management team. The merger meant that Humana's centralized computer and administrative system and leadership team could now be used to run nearly a hundred hospitals.

One very good member of that team was Karen Sholtis Coughlin, a popular pediatric nurse who had risen to executive vice president. Always a nurse at heart, Coughlin went to Chicago under Humana to take charge of the Michael Reese Hospital, a facility in such poor shape its owner paid Humana $40 million to take it over.

It was an important teaching hospital, and they didn't want it to go broke on their watch. Karen went up there and sat down with the doctors and asked them what it would take to enable them to do their best work, and before you know it, the hospital was profitable again.

She left Humana after eighteen years, in 1998, eventually becoming chief executive of PHS Health Plans in Connecticut while also being named one of the hundred most influential women in business by *Crain's New York Business* magazine. When she died of leukemia two years later— fit and active at the age of fifty-two—it was a very personal loss for all of us at Humana.

Humana stock would rise from its $3¾ to $4 figure in 1974 to a year-ending $22⅞ in 1978. It rose to $41⅞ in 1979 and $96.1667 in 1980. Humana's formula for success was working. Our unit costs declined, and our profit margins expanded. It's an easy business to scale. Many businesses are. When you try to do something different, though, as we did with the trailer parks, it's a different story. You have to learn the whole business. We knew the hospital business.

But I also knew how agile our company had to be.

※

Proof of that agility would come in 1982 as a new University Hospital was built on Preston Street in downtown Louisville. It replaced the old

General Hospital, an inefficient medical dinosaur being operated by the University of Louisville as its medical school teaching hospital. With 90 percent of its patients indigent, the hospital lost $5 million in 1982, with that money coming from the university's modest $25 million endowment.

With that loss, University Hospital began to turn away indigent patients, and U of L president Donald Swain began a futile seven-month search for a hospital willing to take over its operation. I had once served briefly on the U of L board of trustees and, as an alum, cared about the university, so I assessed the situation and made a proposal to Louisville Mayor Harvey Sloane, Jefferson County Judge-Executive Mitch McConnell, and Kentucky Governor John Y. Brown.

Humana took on what became Humana Hospital-University under a contract that stipulated it would accept all responsibility and risk, provided it had full authority. Second, the city, county, and state would continue their subsidies to the hospital in 1983 exactly as they had been in 1982— when the hospital had lost $5 million. For each year after that, the city, county, and state would have to increase their payments by the lesser of the percentage increase in its tax revenues or the consumer price index. Third, Humana would pay to lease the facility and give the University medical school an interest in any profits.

The various government groups loved the deal. It capped their liability, which had previously been open-ended. The U of L trustees voted for it. The medical school faculty approved it by a 74-26 percent margin, with the surgical staff voting against it.

That occurred when the head of the surgical staff told me he was a tenured professor, and I could not have a say on whether he was on the staff. I told him, "Congratulations! Humana is not involved with your relationship with the university. If you are a tenured professor, I'm sure you earned it, but if you don't follow the rules and regulations of the hospital, then I have the power to refuse membership on the hospital staff."

I also got strong feedback from Humana stockholders who called to tell me I was crazy; nobody ever made money on a charity hospital responsible for treating indigent patients. In the 1983 transaction, Humana leased the hospital for $6.5 million a year for four years, with options to renew at $6 million a year thereafter. The move was initially controversial. It meant Humana would guarantee care for all adult indigents in the city and county, as well as many poor from neighboring counties. The contract also provided that Humana would donate 20 percent of hospital profits to the University of Louisville School of Medicine.

The medical school would still oversee teaching and research at the new hospital, and Humana would be required to give the teaching program a $4 million grant by the fifth year, plus interest on the $4 million each year before that, in addition to 20 percent of pre-tax profits.

Kentucky Medicaid costs were rising more than 25 percent a year at the time, and shareholders continued to criticize me for taking on what they believed to be a sure loser. Humana and I made three immediate changes that turned a tired, dispirited, money-losing hospital into a smoothly functioning facility loved by its staff. As a result, the hospital soon became the nation's first charity hospital accredited with distinction by the Joint Commission, an independent organization that accredits more than 21,000 health organizations and programs.

First, at my insistence, the old regime of city, county, board of health, and the U of L medical school as owner/boss was instantly replaced with Humana's clear management authority. Next, an experienced, capable management team, headed by Gary Sherlock, was installed. Third, the team met with medical staff to learn what the doctors needed in the way of staff, supplies, equipment, organization, and clarity to excel. The team met those needs, and the doctors responded with their very best work.

In both cases, we listened and responded, and so did the physicians and staff. Overnight the hospital census improved, enabling it to cover the costs of doing things that led to our universal goals: unexcelled, measurable quality and productivity in meeting the needs and values of patients and their physicians. The city appointed an ombudsman, who was granted the non-appealable power to rule on whether a potential patient qualified as an indigent adult. In our ten years operating the hospital, no ruling was ever required.

The easiest change—and the most efficient—was to set up a Medicaid office in the hospital itself, something that hadn't been done before.

When we took over, the hospital had bad debts of 28 percent. After we took over, if somebody came in and said they couldn't pay, we helped them qualify for Medicaid (meaning that government insurance would pay the hospital and physicians). Our bad debts dropped to 3 percent. We operated it like our local Suburban and Audubon hospitals.

Despite predictions that the hospital could lose as much as $10 million the first year, it broke even. It earned $1 million in the second year, and $40 million in its tenth year, with the U of L medical school receiving 20 percent of the profits, or $8 million. That was the last year of Humana management, as it was among the hospitals spun off to shareholders as Galen, Inc., in 1993. The decade (1983–93) of Humana's management was the best period in that hospital's history.

Not everything we tried worked. Wendell and I launched another health care business in the late 1970s. Called MedFirst, this was among the first of the urgent care centers that would come to be known as "Doc in a Box." MedFirst's business reasoning was logical. Many people needed to see a doctor right away when sick but were unable to do so. MedFirst became a successful business but mostly a "break-even" enterprise. Although the facility might see fifty patients a day, there wasn't much profit by the time the company paid the doctors and all expenses. But, if one of those patients was admitted to our hospital, our revenue doubled.

What we learned was that many private doctors disliked urgent-care centers because they had worked for years building up a practice, and urgent-care centers made it easier for younger doctors to compete, costing the older doctors business. Doctors' goodwill was essential to our hospital business, so we sold MedFirst. It had been a good idea in general but not for us at the time. So we exited, taking some losses but drawing on the lesson of the mobile home business: Focus on what fits your skills and context, and eliminate distraction.

Adding it all up, about seventeen years after Wendell and I had each borrowed $1,000 to build a nursing home, we were the two principal stockholders of the largest hospital chain in the United States. Good patient care was always central to its operation, as were disciplined business practices, described this way in a company profile:

> Some of the features that distinguished Humana from the other hospital chains early on were its non-conforming management decisions, the refusal to overpay in buying hospitals, the refusal to manage hospitals it did not own, and rigid cost-control measures well-enforced through the company's centralized management. These methods became much discussed because they seemed remarkable in the industry. . . .
>
> The cost controls eventually became one of Humana's greatest assets. Between 1975 and 1980, Humana grew quickly and achieved economies of scale, like other hospital chains, by making bulk purchases of supplies and equipment. Unlike some competitors, however, Humana remained very centralized, operating all patient billing and data collection out of its home office. Freed from the distraction of managing hospitals it did not own—also unlike most competitors— Humana concentrated on strict quality, productivity, and profitability goals.

In the early 1980s, Humana began designating some of its hospitals Centers of Excellence in providing specific kinds of care, such as Humana Sunrise Hospital in Las Vegas for kidney disease, Humana Lucerne General Hospital in Orlando for spinal cord and open-heart surgery, and Humana Women's Hospital in Tampa for obstetrics and gynecology.

※

Wendell was legendary at Humana for demanding high quality. He visited a hospital one day and noticed a hole in the wall from a repair panel. When he returned to the same hospital about a month later, the hole was still there. He fired the administrator on the spot.

I could be equally demanding. My approach was generally a little softer, but the word got out. If I saw a cigarette butt in the hospital parking lot, I would pick it up and put it on the administrator's desk. I wouldn't say we were harsh. I would say we were knowledgeable, experienced, and very exacting. Such stories make the rounds.

Other stories about Wendell came with a little humor around the edges, particularly when Humana began buying hospitals overseas. The first purchase was in 1975, of the brand-new Wellington Hospital in St. John's Wood, London. It was a private hospital, not part of the British National Health Service system. It was also a hospital in chaos. Humana sent Bill Heburn, age thirty, to manage it.

He was soon having difficulties with the hospital's founding CEO, a doctor who had basically built the hospital and was the personal physician to the CEO and chairman of the board of the huge British & Commonwealth Shipping Company Ltd., from which Humana had bought the hospital. The doctor, in fact, had persuaded the shipping company to build the hospital in the first place, on the theory that anyone who got sick on its ships anywhere in the world could be treated at a company-owned hospital in London—despite the fact the illness could occur thousands of miles away.

Humana's purchase contract required this doctor be given a seven-year contract, and he was undermining Heburn at every turn. Wendell cured that; he hopped on a plane, flew over there, and called a meeting of all department heads, including the doctor. He said,

> I'm Wendell Cherry, president of Humana. This is Bill Heburn, executive director of the hospital. Doctor, as we're speaking, your furniture is in the hands of the removal agents.
>
> And I want you to tell me now if you'd like it carried to the

back of the hospital, where there's a doctors' building, or to Harley Street, where many doctors have offices. We've rented space over there, but I want you to tell me now. Make your choice.

Once the doctor knew who was boss, he turned out to be one of the best employees Humana ever had. You can imagine the capabilities of a guy who could talk the CEO of the British & Commonwealth Shipping Company Ltd. into building a beautiful hospital in downtown London. So we would ask the doctors what they needed to do their best work. They would come up with lists, and a lot of times the stuff would show up in a day or two.

When my mother had her accident in London, I had learned the benefits of the British National Health Service hospitals, which at the time offered free service to anyone who entered. Neither she nor I had ever paid a penny in British taxes, yet my mother received free care for two and a half months. My father, in England with her, had a prescription filled—for 55 cents. We sent a generous gift to the hospital.

The downside was that the National Health Service used "rationing by scarcity," which meant it had a certain appropriation, and if it didn't stretch to meet all the needs, people had to wait, as did doctors who needed equipment.

In our hospital, the surgeries were soon running twenty-four hours a day because some of the finest surgeons in the world lacked access to the facilities and equipment to meet private demand. Many patients were from the former British colonies and were aware of the high quality of the London-based physicians. And the private system in London was entirely free of much of the bureaucracy and paperwork associated with America's unnecessarily complex health care system.

Many of the patients in the Humana-London hospital had insurance, but for those without, its London prices were comparable to those in our US hospitals. With such demand, Humana quickly built a second private hospital for women and children, just two buildings down from its first.

Wendell was involved in another incident at the Wellington Hospital—one that involved royalty and pigeons. Soon after Humana acquired Wellington, Wendell received a phone call from Lady Astor, who asked him if he was president of the company that owned the hospital.

"Yes, ma'am, that's true."

"Well, they don't bring me enough toast."

"Lady Astor, leave it to me. I'll take care of it."

Wendell then called the hospital manager, David Laird, and asked why Lady Astor wasn't getting enough toast.

"Because she was trying to feed every pigeon in London," Laird replied, adding that her room had a balcony with sliding doors.

In another notable incident involving royalty at the hospital, King Saud of Saudi Arabia had rented the entire top floor while having a hip replacement, with members of Scotland Yard on guard. Middle Eastern tradition had it that if you touch the hem of the garment of the king, he must give you money. At the king's request, a man was stationed outside the hospital with a basket of £20 notes—then worth about $40 each—to compensate the supplicants for being denied the chance to touch the royal raiment. When it became apparent the same people were returning for more—and the line soon stretched around the block—the gift was reduced to £10 notes.

Laird also had a hand in Humana purchasing a hospital in Geneva, Switzerland. It began with a Thursday call from Fred Frank of Lehman Brothers—who had also found the Wellington Hospital in London for us. Frank told me that a non-profit group in Geneva had built a large new hospital there to replace a smaller one. Three Swiss banks had financed it, but it was going broke, and another medical company, National Medical Enterprises, Inc. (NME), had been negotiating for it.

I quickly called Laird and told him to fly to Geneva—only an hour away by air—to check it out. Meanwhile, Wendell and I would fly over Friday and meet with the bankers on Saturday to discuss a sale. Laird called back from Geneva a few hours later and reported the hospital had more concrete in it than the whole Humana system; the war-conscious

Swiss had duplicated the entire hospital underground.

Wendell and I flew to Geneva Friday night, met with the bankers on Saturday, and bought the hospital. When the NME representatives showed up Monday morning, it was game over.

Wendell went back for the actual closing. Neither one of us spoke French. Property closings in Switzerland use a notary who reads the contract.

Wendell sat through it. He said he could barely stay awake because he didn't understand a word of what was said. The long and the short of it is the notary charges one percent. Ours was a $30 million deal. We paid the $300,000 fee. But we acquired a gorgeous new hospital, and it soon became successful.

Chapter Thirteen

Roots and Wings

"Betty is an absolutely amazing person. She turned out five unspoiled, engaged, capable kids. I was there and was part of that, but she was the main part. The luckiest thing in my life was the person I married. We've been a team."

— DAVID JONES

Betty and I had five children in thirteen years, between 1958 and 1971. David, Jr. was the first; after him came Sue, Dan, Matt, and Carol. Dave and Sue were born when we were at Yale. Their first home was half of a Quonset hut, a corrugated metal home. A year later, after I graduated from law school in 1960, we came back to Louisville. We lived with Betty's parents for a short time and then moved into our $15,000 home on Lowell Avenue. It was a wonderful neighborhood, where I played football and baseball in the street with the neighbors and their kids. The Englert family across from us had seven children, so Dave and Sue had friends, and the older Englert kids babysat for them. Dan was born while we lived there.

Matt and Carol's first home was on Village Drive, close to Cherokee Park, one of many Louisville parks designed by Frederick Law Olmsted. In the woods behind our yard was a meandering stream we could follow down to Beargrass Creek in the iconic Big Rock area of the park.

Dave, Sue, Dan, and Matt attended Louisville public schools for many years until the school system became so crowded it required double sessions. Eventually, the four of them would have four separate schedules while Betty was home with Carol, our newborn. We then switched all the kids to Kentucky Country Day.

With the success of Humana, we knew our family had advantages as we moved the children into the private KCD, but we worked hard to avoid giving them a sense of family exceptionalism. Once old enough, all our kids had part-time jobs. We were a big, close-knit bunch, with all four grandparents still living and a lot of togetherness on weekends. Betty and I are very proud that all our children and grandchildren have been scholarly, and we helped with their educations. But we would not leave our grandchildren any inheritance, and I never bought any of my children or grandchildren a car.

When you grow up in humble circumstances, as I did, it's easy to learn to value money and to value a job. I'd say the hardest thing for Betty and me in our married life was raising kids with good values. That was very intentional with us.

Dave, our eldest, was born in January 1958. I was timing Betty's contractions and reading *Prosser on Torts* at the same time. Dave's inspiration, like so many in our family, came in his early school years when he fell in love with books. His second-grade teacher, Laura Schumann, challenged him to read more. After that, he made A's or the equivalent all the way through law school. He was also a good athlete, competing on the Lakeside Swim Team until age sixteen and playing football and soccer at KCD. With Dan as a teammate, KCD won the state soccer tournament in 1975. Dave was named football captain and most valuable player in his senior year. He has continued his swimming, hiking and bike riding, even competing in triathlons long into his adult years.

He had the family gift of languages and a curiosity about the world. In 1974, he and four other KCD students spent the summer traveling with Paul Hagenau, their German and Latin teacher and a true Renaissance man. They went to Middle Eastern, Asian, African, and Mediterranean countries. The journey occasionally meant living on the edge, taking chances. They took the last overcrowded train out of Greece as it was about to go to war with Turkey over Cyprus, sleeping in the corridors. They also went to Calcutta and visited Mother Teresa. As Dave remembers, "It was before she was a global figure. The mission was a humble shelter for the dying poor. She and her sisters went out and collected people who were otherwise going to die in the street and brought them into the mission we visited to die with dignity. That was a shocking interaction with poverty and death for a sixteen-year-old high school kid from Louisville."

In his senior year, after immersing himself in German, Dave moved to Germany for four months to study at the St. Anna Gymnasium, an almost 500-year-old school in Augsburg. He lived with the Freislederer family, whose five children were about the same ages as the Jones children. In time, all five of the Freislederer siblings would come to live with us in Louisville, and all of the Jones siblings would live or travel in Germany, as would Betty and I. The Freislederer parents did not speak English, so I took both undergraduate and graduate German courses at U of L, plus some private tutoring to be able to visit them. Mrs. Freislederer and Betty spoke French together, so she carried the conversational load until I caught up with my German.

Dave was accepted at both Princeton and Yale, but I never pushed him or any of our children toward Yale. He was attracted to New Haven itself, a grittier place that seemed closer to the real problems of the world. He met his wife, Mary Gwen Wheeler, in a freshman English class. They started dating their senior year. After graduating in 1980, both received two-year Yale-China teaching fellowships. Dave taught English at Hunan Medical College in Changsha, Hunan Province, and Mary Gwen taught at the Chinese University of Hong Kong—a distance they described as a "ten-day round-trip letter away"—after graduating in 1980.

It was a great time to be a young American in China. The country was just reopening to the world after Chairman Mao's Cultural Revolution and a thirty-year freeze in relations with the United States. One summer, he and Mary Gwen traveled for six weeks in China by rail and bus, and after finishing their teaching contracts, they backpacked for six months through southeast and south Asia. Returning to the United States at the end of 1982, they went their separate ways for a while, with Dave joining the First National Bank of Boston—with assignments in Hong Kong, Taiwan, and New York—followed by a short stint in Louisville helping in my misguided attempt to modernize Belknap. Mary Gwen worked in New York's Chinatown on job training and education. In 1985, they got engaged and reunited in New Haven, where Dave went to Yale Law School and Mary Gwen to the Yale School of Management.

From there, they moved to Washington to continue their international interests, with Dave joining the US Department of State's general counsel's office as they started their family. They thrived there, and we loved visiting as grandparents until Humana's board recruited Dave back to Louisville to work more closely with me—a story for another chapter.

Sue was born just fourteen and a half months after Dave, in April 1959. It had been a busy day in the maternity area of the hospital. The resident doctor had fallen asleep, and no one could wake him. With hospital staff in short supply, I helped push my wife's bed down the hall to the delivery room, where a second doctor took over.

Sue is single, independent, and a more private person than her siblings. At KCD, she excelled at field hockey and displayed her mother's knack for languages, earning 800s on her college placement exams in both French and German. Her score on a French examination put her among the top ten students in the nation.

Sue applied to several colleges and also chose Yale, partly because our old law school friends, the Duffys, still lived there. She studied Russian and Swahili and worked toward a degree in comparative literature. Her French greatly improved after she spent two semesters in Paris, one at the Sorbonne and one working in a bank. She also proved to be a gifted writer. Sue graduated from Yale, then later attended college in North Carolina, where she became an expert in children's literature, and where she now works in a public library. She writes poetry, and her poems have been published in several magazines under a pseudonym. She also works with the Jones family foundation in Louisville, helping with its wide variety of cultural and academic initiatives. She's a good cook and has become very handy at home repair. Her friends include "The Neighborettes," a group of single women, mothers, and widows who help each other.

Dan was born in July 1961, about a year before our first nursing home opened. He was placed in the middle of our five children, a position he says he would use to try to help everybody get along.

As a child, he, like our other kids, would walk over to nearby Cherokee Park and play in Beargrass Creek. These experiences ignited his interest in the diverse Louisville Metro Parks system. "It was a nice childhood," he remembers, "and the Highlands is still my favorite part of the city."

Dan was an all-state soccer player at KCD, leading the state in assists his junior year when KCD won another championship. He went backpacking in the Red River Gorge in east-central Kentucky in summers and on breaks.

He felt no pressure to go to Yale, but on a visit to New Haven found Yale "magical." He had no idea what his major would be, but he also loved languages, and with Dave in Changsha, he focused on Chinese. In the summer between his sophomore and junior years, he took the nine-week total immersion course at the Middlebury College Summer Language School in Vermont, prompting him to recommend the school to his mother, who later became a student there.

Dan spent his junior year abroad in Taiwan, then met up with Dave for a six-week trip across northwest China by bus, train, and foot. They were strangers in a strange land, pushing into places they probably shouldn't have—and often getting away with it. "In the cities that weren't open, where we didn't have a travel stamp, they'd just put us back on the train," Dan said. "But sometimes they'd say, 'Well, you're already here.'" He took off the next semester to teach English to department store employees in Taiwan and to hang out in a nearby apartment complex, enjoying Taiwanese beer with other visitors from Germany and Canada.

Returning to Yale the next fall, he took a course that sparked an interest in geology, a passion that would come into play later, followed by another course at the Yale Forestry School called Local Flora. After graduating with a major in Chinese language and literature, he taught English for a while in New York's Chinatown. Still unsure what he really wanted to do with his life, he enlisted in the Navy. Afterward, he returned to Louisville to work with me on some development projects, including designing the Mockingbird Gardens subdivision, where he built his first small park. Then his interest in travel, geology, and nature led him to Utah State University, near the Bear River Mountains in the Wasatch Range north of Salt Lake City. He earned a master's degree in history but spent his free time walking trails and studying native plants.

In 1991, he married Lisa Petrilli, his Yale classmate whom he'd known in Louisville since kindergarten. Their honeymoon included walking an 18,000-foot-high pass in Nepal. While Lisa did her medical residency in Indianapolis, Dan got his PhD in history at Indiana University in Bloomington. He taught at Franklin College and then the University of Louisville. But his lifelong passions for history, geology, parks, and preserving the environment all came together in the early 2000s when he led the creation of The Parklands of Floyds Fork.

Matt, the fourth of our five children, born in February of 1967, always wanted to be in the military. When he was only three years old, one of the electricians working on our house began calling him "Little Sarge" because he was always wearing a uniform. Matt could also be a little adventurous. Although he was never in serious trouble in school, he was—as one of his siblings described him—"a kid who knew his way to the principal's office." He was the only Boy Scout in the Jones family. He joined Troop 315, a very active group whose trips included camps in New Mexico, walks in the Red River Gorge, and an infamous trip into the Daniel Boone National Forest in eastern Kentucky when Matt was about twelve.

On that trip, the troop was due back at 4 p.m. on Sunday but didn't show up. I wasn't too alarmed since five or six adults were with the scouts. But when we had still heard nothing from them the next morning, I decided to get involved, along with Frank Lambert, the father of another scout and later a Belknap Hardware executive. We picked up Humana pilot John

Landrum, drove to London, Kentucky, borrowed a single-engine plane, and began flying patterns in very foggy conditions over the area where the scouts should have been. The scouts heard the plane and, true to their training, started a smoky fire. With the aid of local residents, Lambert and I hiked back into the woods to find the lost campers, who were a little bit nervous and very annoyed that they had to be rescued.

While at KCD, Matt was a good athlete and student. He played football, wrestled, ran the half-mile in track, and got a perfect 800 score on the verbal portion of his college SAT exams. He also began taking fencing lessons at the Jewish Community Center with the renowned Francis Wolff, which led him to the Kentucky state championships in both epee and foil. He was epee captain of the Yale team that won the Ivy League championship, and he qualified for the national Junior Olympics after his sophomore year. Matt had considered going to the US Naval Academy but decided on Yale because of family precedent and because he wanted a more mainstream college experience. Fate stepped in. A random meeting with a worker at Yale's physical plant led to his being contacted by a Marine Corps selection officer who told Matt about a summer platoon leader's class at Quantico, Virginia. "It was basically a boot camp," Matt said, "and if you didn't like it, you didn't have to come back. So I guess I liked it because I went back."

After graduating from Yale, he took his commission as a Marine, then completed the Basic School and Infantry Officer Course in Quantico. His graduation from Quantico coincided with Iraq's 1990 invasion of Kuwait, and his platoon was assigned to Al-Jubail in Saudi Arabia, then to Kuwait for Operation Desert Storm. On the second day of the ground offensive, Matt's platoon caught heavy fire, and Matt was wounded. He was flown to Saudi Arabia, then Germany, and Walter Reed Army Medical Center for treatment. It was a traumatic time for our family, but he made a full recovery.

He met his wife, Nancy Poirier, while stationed at his next post: Camp Pendleton, California. She was in law school at the University of San Diego and would later earn a CPA and work pro bono with military clients on estate planning and service-related benefits. As with all career military families, Nancy became adept at helping her husband and children cope with new assignments and long absences. Matt frequently was gone for long periods of time, often unable to tell them much about where he was or what he was doing.

In the early portion of his twenty-seven years of service, Matt commanded a Marine detachment on the nuclear aircraft carrier *USS Theodore Roosevelt*. He was deployed to Okinawa with the 3rd Light Armored Reconnaissance Battalion and ran a Marine Corp Reserve Training Center in Terre Haute, Indiana, which he said was the only good family time they had while he was in the service. After 9/11, his life got considerably busier, with deployments to Iraq with the 13th Marine Expeditionary Unit and again as commander of the 3rd Light Armored Reconnaissance Battalion operating in western Al-Anbar province. Ten Marines under his command were killed during this second deployment in 2006. He wrote each family a letter—a Marine custom—and would later visit several of the families. Afterward, Matt was selected to attend the National War College, where being number one in his class led to him becoming a junior aide to Secretary of Defense Robert Gates.

Matt was then assigned to a thirteen-month tour of Afghanistan, conducting operational assessments for the International Security Assistance Forces Joint Command. Promoted to Colonel in 2010, he spent some time in the Pentagon before being selected in 2012 for command of the Marine Corps Tactics and Operations Group in Twentynine Palms, California. After that, he served as operations officer and chief of staff of I Marine Expeditionary Force, a unit of about 57,000 troops. His many awards included the Defense Superior Service Medal, Legion of Merit, Bronze Star, and Purple Heart. He retired as a Colonel on December 31, 2016.

Four years after Matt was born and thirteen years after Dave, along came Carol in January 1971. She would learn that being the youngest of five children would have some advantages but also create some tough acts to follow. Matt was the sibling she really grew up with, and the two of them remain very close—although one family story recalls four-year-old Matt, no longer the youngest in the family, going to his mother soon after Carol was born and suggesting she "throw that baby away."

"That baby" would grow into a great athlete who was given the same freedom as her siblings to find what she enjoyed most and then be in a place to give back to family, friends, and community. Carol is a lot like me. She's an activist; she's passionate. And she's a wonderful mother. She also takes good care of her mom and dad. She would feed us every night if we let her.

Carol was the only one of the five Jones children to attend Kentucky Country Day School for all twelve years. She would walk down the hill from our house to catch the bus with Matt and any other kids still at home, then perch herself in a tree to look for its arrival. She also spent some time thinking about having to follow the academic and athletic successes of the four siblings ahead of her in one of Louisville's very successful families.

"Being the youngest child," she said, "you want to be different. I spent a lot of time trying to be different from what I thought the perception was of me. And then I realized I didn't really know what that perception was."

She started playing the piano and violin at a young age but then discovered sports, especially basketball. She was the starting point guard on the KCD team as a freshman, set a school record for assists, and helped her team beat every larger city school it played except mighty Ballard, which won by one point. She was named most valuable player on the basketball, volleyball, and softball teams, competed in the hurdles, long jump, and sprints in track, ran cross-country, and played golf.

Carol's first college choice was American University in Washington, DC, primarily because she had enjoyed Washington on her junior class trip. She also liked the idea that Dave and Mary Gwen were living there, and Matt would be close by in Quantico. "When I got to American, though, I realized it was probably not going to be the right fit," she remembers. In the spring, she visited a friend at The University of the South—often called Sewanee University—in Sewanee, Tennessee, way up in the Appalachian Mountains, with hiking, mountain biking, and rock-climbing adventures nearby. She fell in love with the school, its honor code, liberal arts curriculum, and mountain environment. I encouraged her to apply. She switched to Sewanee, where she played basketball and got a degree in philosophy.

While at KCD, she had been recruited by Transylvania University women's basketball coach Mark Turner. After Carol graduated from Sewanee, he hired her as his assistant coach at $2,500 a year, with her family adding another $9,500 a year to help. She also coached soccer and golf. After a year, she took an assistant basketball coaching position at Murray State University in far western Kentucky. It was not a good experience—the federal Title IX mandates, intended to bring parity to men's and women's sports, hadn't yet reached Murray—so she returned to Transylvania the next year as assistant athletics director. While there, Carol, then twenty-eight, earned her MBA from Xavier University in Ohio by attending classes two nights a week at Midway College, west of Lexington. Following in family footsteps, she also went to Middlebury College for several months to study German.

She met Paul Levitch, who had graduated from KCD three years ahead of her and was working in college admissions at Transylvania. They married and moved to Louisville, where he began a college counseling service, and Carol worked on the business side. They later divorced. Carol had converted to Judaism, Paul's religion, although he had not asked her to. Betty and I, and sometimes other family members, would go by her house on Friday evenings to observe Shabbat with her and her children. Carol has coached girls' basketball and soccer at KCD; has been very involved with the Boys & Girls Clubs of Kentuckiana, where she became board president; and has served on the boards of Middlebury College and of Louisville's Virginia Chance School, which focuses on progressive, hands-on, often outdoor education for children from preschool through fifth grades. Most recently, she became a vice president of Main Street Realty, where she has learned from two masters, Ken Payne and Bryan Johnson.

※

The family was always busy. Education, travel, and athletics of all kinds were a constant focus—not just for the kids but also for Betty and me. Before having children, Betty and I took four-day driving trips to far western Kentucky, to Wickliffe and Reelfoot Lake, where the Mississippi offers some Civil War history, and where the New Madrid Fault and earthquakes of 1811–12 temporarily sent the Great River flowing backward. Other times we would drive to the eastern Kentucky mountains, places of great natural beauty marred by discarded refrigerators and such being tossed in the hollows to rust.

The early trips with the children, through the 1960s, were classic Americana, the Joneses tightly packed into five- to ten-year-old station wagons, with local and national parks our only affordable destinations, and modest motels with swimming pools along the way. They included Spring Mill Park in Paoli, Indiana, with its restored grist mill, caves, and lakes, and Clifty Falls near Madison, Indiana, with its Ice Age waterfalls and canyons, almost incongruous when outsiders picture Indiana. We sang songs, told stories, and did some reading. We packed food and found roadside places to picnic. We changed diapers along the way.

In later years, family trips sometimes took us to more far-flung places with a more historical bent. Co-conspirators in those travels would be three University of Louisville professors and friends: Stephanie Maloney, chairman of the fine arts department; her husband, Tom Maloney, a professor of philosophy; and John Hale, chairman of liberal studies. We treasured their friendship.

Stephanie was a noted archaeologist. In the 1980s, she was just beginning what became a nineteen-year archaeological excavation in Torre de Palma, Portugal, with John as her chief assistant and Tom buying groceries and telling funny stories. Matt and Carol spent a summer in Portugal, digging with a spoon! Roman coins from around 400 AD were found there, along with many objects and building remains of great interest. We supported the project throughout its life and made multiple visits to the site, often traveling with the professors at the season's end. On one trip, Betty (by then a French professor herself) and I joined them for the pilgrimage journey on the Camino de Santiago: Dijon, France, to Saint-Jean-Pied-de-Port, then across the Pyrenees to Santiago, Spain. We drove rather than walked, but it was still an adventure.

Stephanie and John often team-taught graduate courses, and Betty and I completed two of them: The Vikings and Celtic Art and Architecture.

Beginning in the '70s, we took the kids on annual skiing vacations in Europe or the Rockies. We took some of them to Greece one year and Turkey the next. I never worried if Wendell was in charge. If he wasn't there, Carl Pollard was in charge.

I don't take stuff home with me at night. It might be in my head, but I'm not obsessive about controlling. Maybe some people say I am, but it enabled me to go to the kids' ball games, to go home and be a good father and husband, and to have a life. I don't work long hours. I never did.

It's a whole lot more about doing the right thing and being effective. It's not a matter of how much time you spend; it's how you get from here to there.

※

Our family's long relationship with Middlebury College in Vermont started with Dan, who, in the summer of 1981, had taken an immersion course in Chinese there in preparation for his semester abroad in Taiwan. He proclaimed that—even after taking a year of conventional Chinese-language courses at Yale—it was the hardest thing he had ever done.

Dan suggested to his mother that she should continue her French studies at Middlebury. He also kidded her that if she went to the French school at Middlebury, she ought to buy a new wardrobe because those students were so chic. The summer school idea—but not the wardrobe—appealed to Betty.

Middlebury, which would be part of Jones family life for thirty-five years, had long blended American history with academic success, especially in foreign languages. It was the first American institution of higher education to grant a bachelor's degree to an African American, in 1823. It was also the first formerly all-male liberal arts college to become a coeducational institution, in 1883.

Betty had audited several humanities classes at U of L in the early 1960s while I was teaching nights and working as an attorney. She had also been taking some graduate courses in French at U of L. The idea of summer courses at Middlebury was appealing.

Beginning in 1982, she would attend Middlebury for five consecutive summers, earning an MA in French language and literature. From the mid-1990s, we would fund the Betty and David Jones Language Scholarships, in seven languages, for up to fifty graduate students at Middlebury each year.

Betty joined the board in 1993 and served as the school acquired the Monterey (now Middlebury) Institute of International Studies in Monterey, California, in 2005. She served on the committee that recommended the acquisition, and I spent ten years on the Monterey board.

Betty and I were always a team. We had always supported each other through my years in the Navy, law school, her graduate studies at Middlebury, and then in business. In our early years in Louisville, we often talked about my business plans. She could calm me down as needed. When the *Courier Journal* wrote stories or editorials critical of me for something Humana was doing with its "for-profit" hospitals and making money off the sick, I sat down and wrote fiery letters in reply. Betty then edited them.

"Dave says I took out all the adjectives and adverbs," she would say of her input, "and by the time he brought it home and I edited it, he said it was too boring to send."

She also had thoughts on the business. For the first three nursing homes, Wendell, Bass, Weisberg, and I had personally guaranteed twenty-year mortgage loans and later demand notes for working capital loans prior to the 1968 initial public offering. Betty would sometimes worry about the money being borrowed to build the company. She told me she didn't really want to know if we were in bad financial shape. I would remind her the banks had more to worry about than she did.

"It was a little scary," said Betty. "My dad was very conservative about finances, and I think Daddy was shaking his head until the day he died about the things we did. But that's the way the young are. The old are always more conservative, but my parents had a lot of confidence in Dave."

She praised Sam Klein and Charlie Will, the bankers who helped us buy larger homes as our family grew, as they had helped get the company started and keep it going.

"A lot of others didn't want to bet on these young guys," she said. "They were lawyers, and the bankers were people who didn't understand why they were leaving law to start a business."

We enjoyed being with Wendell and his wife, Liz. Neither Betty nor Liz participated in the company's business meetings, but they shared a common belief about the importance of the company's efforts. Luck was a part of it, too.

"Dave always felt that way," Betty said. "Carey Thompson, who was Dave's good, good friend, always said, 'The harder I work, the luckier I get.' I think that's true."

Although I often brought my spreadsheets home as the company expanded, Betty says I never showed any real anxiety: "He is totally optimistic. He just knows things are going to work out," she remembers. "We'd talk about it, and I'd ask some questions, but it was really a separation of labor, and I pretty much dealt with the house and the children."

My optimism came from my mother and my older brother, Logan. Given our financial situation in 2019, few people would have suspected that we once lived in half a Quonset hut while I was a law student at Yale or that I earned living expenses for our growing family by working three jobs in New Haven.

When you add it all up, the GI Bill payment of $110 per month covered only the Yale Law annual tuition of $1,350. My college costs at the University of Louisville had been paid by a Navy ROTC scholarship, so the family had government assistance for seven years. Betty and I were grateful and relished the memories—but we were still broke.

Betty says, "We're basically unchanged in any way from the day we married and are grateful for the opportunities to give back. Dave is a very happy person, and I think that must be his Irish background. They had a lot of tussles in their household, and I think things were not always easy when he grew up, but he's always been a very happy, optimistic person. His mind is lightning quick, and he can focus, so he can balance a lot of things."

The balancing act included a night class in German I took at the University of Louisville. I was the fifty-year-old college student who was also building Humana, but I always kept a low profile in class.

One of my classmates, Victoria Slone, married with two sons and eventually seeking a doctorate in molecular biology and immunology toward a career in medical research, remembers chatting with me in class. She asked if I worked in downtown Louisville.

"Yes," I answered, leaving out any mention of my resumé.

When we decided to move from our home in Louisville's Highlands— an area Betty and the children loved—we purchased land on Poplar Hill Road near the Ohio River. We worked together on the design for our new house in 1970, preserving that Highlands feel by adding a Tudor look. Thinking ahead to old age, we put our bedroom on the ground floor, where it would be accessible, with the five kids' bedrooms upstairs.

In keeping with tradition, when the children grew up, they and the grandchildren would visit on many Sundays, sharing a pancake brunch. Other Sundays, Betty and I were invited over to one of our children's homes for a bagel breakfast or dinner. During the week, we welcomed babysitting jobs for our eleven grandchildren.

Socially, I might drink a beer or a glass of wine, but I never have a second glass: I never want to lose control. I've got a whole lot going on.

With two other couples in 1986, Betty and I started the Joy Luck Book

Club, a couples' club that meets to discuss about eight books a year. Our meetings begin with some socializing while the hosts serve dessert. Then the hosts offer an often-provocative review, and the others jump in on discussions that usually last three or four hours. Because we are totally familiar with each other, no one holds back on an opinion. I have never been treated with any deference—other members of the book club are accomplished and have had interesting life experiences, too. No one ever misses, and no one would ever think of coming without reading the book. It's a serious book club.

Judy Waterman and her husband, Norton, a surgeon, were neighbors and book club members who became good friends, as did their children with our children. Club members are politically diverse, with many religions represented: Catholic, Jewish, and Protestant. We have had many differences of opinion but always respect each other's views and get along.

"I'd read a lot," says Judy, "but I think the variety and thoughtfulness that members put into their reading was new to me." I was so very proud of Betty's literary knowledge and insights.

By 2018 our group had discussed, praised, parsed, or eviscerated 264 books, with Betty, the club historian, keeping track of all our books and discussions. Betty would always give me books for Christmas. She belonged to two other book clubs, one dedicated to French works. I am a constant reader. I might be reading two or three books at the same time, moving from book to book, even while watching a U of L basketball game. If the commercials get to be too much or the game is boring, I will mute the sound and keep reading.

Family always came first. While building Humana, I traveled extensively but was able to attend most of our children's and grandchildren's events, never missing a birthday or ball game. I was on the board of a major company in Chicago when a conflict arose over a very important issue, with a company meeting on the same date as the rehearsal dinner for our son Dave's wedding. I was at the dinner—Betty insisted on it.

Our household had no pretensions. When I came home for dinner, I would whistle to signal my arrival. Betty, who often cooked dinner, would greet me with a kiss.

"It was out of *Leave It to Beaver,* " daughter Carol remembers.

There was some old-school discipline. Children who broke the house rules or missed curfew were grounded. There was no alcohol in the house. We decorated the Christmas tree together, with the annual stress of trying to untangle the lights.

All of us were well-read and opinionated. We would engage in discussions, debates, and the occasional arguments. While at work, I left instructions that whenever any of my children called, even if I was in a meeting, I wanted to take the call. Carol said, "Dad would love to talk to us. He'd get on the phone chipper, in a great mood, and I'd have no idea if the stock had just lost 80 percent of its value. One time in college, I just called to chit-chat and when that became apparent, he said, 'You know I'd love to talk to you, but I'm in a meeting. Would you mind if I called you back in a little bit?' I think it was a board meeting."

But nobody raises five very active children without serious problems and disagreements. Carol remembers a less-than-idyllic moment—as a teenager—spouting off, cursing her father under her breath, and locking herself in the bathroom. She had never heard her father swear. "He got very upset," she recalled, "and understandably so. I remember thinking I wish I'd never said that."

All the things I was able to do were made possible by Betty. She was always there, maintaining discipline and transportation and the calendar and providing love and nourishment and all those things. Betty is an absolutely amazing person. She turned out five unspoiled, engaged, capable kids. I was there and was part of that, but she was the main part. The luckiest thing in my life was the person I married.

There were also family medical issues mothers have to deal with while the husband is away. When Dave was about three years old, he stuffed finger-painted newsprint into a kitchen garbage can, accidentally snagging an electric cord connected to a coffee pot. The pot fell, spilling hot coffee all over his back. He suffered second-degree burns. His mother loaded him into the car and took him to the hospital. For a month after, he walked around with a salve-coated diaper tied to his neck like a cape, unable to be dressed.

As the family was vacationing on Cape Cod, Dan fell off a bridge into a stream, and his mother leaped in after him. Another time at Lakeside Swim Club, Matt, who was too young to swim, got dragged into the water. Betty, a good swimmer, went right in after him, too.

But generally, life at home was low-key. We ate breakfast together almost every day; I was rarely in a suit and tie unless I had a formal meeting to attend. When one of the children would ask me about the suit, I would often say something like, "I'm meeting with bankers today, and when you meet with bankers, you've got to be on your 'A' game."

When Betty hurt her back in later years, I would cook her breakfast, and we would sit and talk at the table for an hour or so, catching up on local and world events and family activities. We were—as our children called us—"old-fashioned" parents, strict disciplinarians, with Betty taking the lead when I was away. The occasional spanking was a possibility. As they grew older, the children would be put on home "probation" or grounded when necessary. They were given non-negotiable curfews. If they were too late or didn't call, I would get out of bed, climb into my car, and go looking for them.

We never bought a car for our children. Meanwhile, they could use the family car, with curfew rules strictly enforced. I taught all the grandchildren how to play poker. The game stakes came from a bag of pennies. Do the grandkids ever beat Grandpa at poker? Not too often.

Like my mother, Betty and I have always tithed 10 percent of our earnings regardless of our financial situation. That later increased significantly. We have helped many organizations and individuals over the years, but in later years our time, energy, and money have focused on public education, Kentucky's greatest need.

I tell the kids, and anybody who wants to know, the best thing about being wealthy, besides the independence it can give you—and I was independent before I was wealthy—is helping other people. You just go on and do what seems to be the right thing to do. It's more about your head and your heart and your family and how you were raised.

Neither Betty nor I allow the Jones name to be attached to any of our gifts. A plaque on the wall in our house reads:

There are only two lasting bequests
we can hope to give our children.
One of these is roots, the other wings.

Betty and I always planned for the time when neither of us would be here. We aimed our personal C.E.&S. Foundation, with its educational and environmental programs, far into the future. All five Jones children share those goals. We encouraged them to earn their own way, and that required a good education, which we provided.

Part III

ATTENTION AND
ENGAGEMENT IN RIVER CITY

Previous page:
Celebrating the announcement that the Presbyterians would be moving their national headquarters to Louisville, 1987. John Mulder, president of the Louisville Presbyterian Theological Seminary, left.

Chapter Fourteen

David Jones 1, Ben-Hur 0

"The original Kentucky Center for the Performing Arts design was a big white elephant. It was going to cost twice as much money as the original Houston designers had proposed. Governor John Y. Brown had been elected, and he slimmed it down. He was a leader and a gutsy person, and he turned it over to Wendell and said, 'See if you can fix it.'"

— DAVID JONES

Charlton Heston, the movie icon who had impersonated Ben-Hur and Moses onscreen, was coming to Louisville to lend Hollywood star power to the opening of the gleaming new Kentucky Center for the Performing Arts in November 1983. He would arrive early, with time to kill. So he asked his agent to find a good player for a tennis match. It turned out to be me, one of the two civic leaders most responsible for turning the new arts center from an idea into reality, the other being my best friend and arts champion Wendell Cherry.

Humana's strong connection to—and financial support of—the Louisville arts community was already well established by 1979, when Penelope Morton, an Actors Theatre of Louisville board member, asked to meet with me. She wanted to discuss artistic director Jon Jory's vision for the theater.

Jory had taken over leadership of Actors, then a small regional theater, in 1969 when it was only five years old. In 1977, it staged *The Gin Game,*

191

which won the Pulitzer Prize for drama. Jory wanted to transform the two-year-old Festival of New American Plays into an incubator—and a national showcase—for playwrights' best new work.

In a two-page request, Jory noted there was no professional, effective, or affordable venue for new plays in the United States. He requested $100,000 a year for a three-year commitment. He would just go on and do what seemed to be the right thing to do. I thought Jory's thoughts were clear, his passion evident, and his talent already well established. Besides, he had said it all in two pages. I talked it over with Wendell, and we agreed to the proposal.

In 1982, Wendell and I renewed the $100,000 grant for another three years. Without our asking for it, the name "Humana" was added to the annual showcase: the Humana Festival of New American Plays. The concept—and the name—stuck. In its ongoing seasons of sponsorship, Humana would donate more than $20 million to the festival. During annual five-week runs over that time, the festival introduced more than 450 plays to national and international audiences. Under Humana's sponsorship, two won Pulitzers: *Crimes of the Heart* (1981) and *Dinner with Friends* (2000).

The Kentucky Center for the Performing Arts took root in 1980 when the Kentucky General Assembly created a public/private partnership to build a center designed by the Houston firm of Caudill Rowlett Scott, with the Humana Inc. Design and Construction Department in charge of construction.

The original Kentucky Center for the Performing Arts design was a big white elephant. It was going to cost twice as much money as the original Houston designers had proposed. Gov. John Y. Brown had been elected, and he slimmed it down. He was a leader and a gutsy person, and he turned it over to Wendell and said, "See if you can fix it."

Wendell relished the job. He had already been involved in building many Humana buildings across the country, including hospitals and office buildings, at the cost of several billion dollars. Working with Humana executive Lin McLellan and architects Robert Harris and Jim Walters,

Wendell told the men, "Straighten this out. Get us a building that is functional."

The building would cost $33.75 million, with the state paying $20 million; I committed to raise $14 million in private donations. In addition, the City of Louisville built part of an adjacent parking garage.

Wendell became involved in fundraising, too, securing money for the Louisville Fund for the Arts. Stuart Jay, an old friend, Wendell's next-door neighbor, and our former partner in the Kentucky Colonels basketball team, said Wendell's mercurial personality was on display in that fundraising phase, too.

He dropped by Wendell's office one day just to talk. Smoking a cigar, Wendell was on the phone, loudly complaining in a one-sided, profanity-laced conversation, telling someone that the $10,000 he had donated was "peanuts compared to what you should be giving to the Fund for the Arts, and I'm sending your f—king check back."

Wendell then hung up. Jay remembered that I, who had been standing at the door, leaned in and said, "Wendell, if you don't tell people how you feel, they will never know."

Wendell's passion for the arts center was also noted by Rose Lenihan Rubel, who served with him on the center's first board of directors. In a book honoring him after his death, she wrote,

> He presented pages of details about the building and the people who would be employed. He enlisted the help of arts groups and schools, which brought together the community's interests through involvement in the project.
>
> He often became so engrossed in the project he would lose track of time. It was not unusual to receive a call at midnight or 2 a.m. from Wendell, telling me to be prepared to fly out of town at dawn to view furnishings for the center.

Wendell would donate and arrange donations from others for works by artists including Alexander Calder, John Chamberlain, Jean Dubuffet, Louise Nevelson, Joan Miró, Malcolm Morley, and Tony Smith.

The center was completed on schedule—and on budget. Its performance areas were named for Robert S. Whitney, founding conductor of the Louisville Orchestra, and Moritz von Bomhard, founder of the Kentucky Opera.

Another name also would go on a plaque of donors in the center— Logan Jones. My older brother, who I idolized and who had been such a strong part of my life, had died the year before, and I dedicated my support in his honor.

The center's official opening night, on November 19, 1983, was a sold-out, $750-a-ticket gala organized by Dotti Cherry, Wendell's wife. Heart surgeon Allan Lansing helped sell hundreds of tickets to doctor friends. Distinguished guests included Heston, soprano Jessye Norman, Lily Tomlin, Florence Henderson, Diane Sawyer, Douglas Fairbanks, Jr., and eighty-four-year-old Lillian Gish.

To thank the men and women who built the center, we held a party for 2,000 construction workers and their families at a "hard hat" event a week earlier—a tradition of honoring workers at many of our new buildings.

After the Kentucky Center opening, the guests—in one of the most joyous moments in Louisville arts history—all happily marched down the street to the Commonwealth Convention Center for a reception, with local arts groups performing along the way. It was a marvelous picture: hundreds of celebrants smiling, strutting, and dancing across downtown Louisville as we introduced a whole new era in its arts.

A few days before the arts center's premiere, Heston's agent called the center's executive director, Marlow Burt. He was trying to find an opponent for a tennis match. Burt called Wendell, and then Wendell passed the word on to me.

"Wendell," I said, "what have you gotten me into? The guy's Ben-Hur."

I played tennis most of my life—finally retiring from a Monday night league in 2015 at age eighty-four. Playing twenty years in that league, I became legendary—and not in a favorable way—for my attire. Play began at 6:30 p.m., making it difficult for me to get home and change into my tennis regalia, so I always wore my black work socks on the court. At the end-of-the-year banquet, the other players presented me with three pairs of white socks.

I played Saturday doubles tennis matches for thirty-four years with three men who became very good friends, Bill Stodghill, John Speed, and Phil Lanier. Stodghill was a lawyer and Yale graduate. Speed was a Princeton and Harvard Business School graduate and insurance executive. Lanier, a lawyer and CSX Corporation executive, was twice president of the Louisville Orchestra board.

We played outside in the summer and inside all winter. Betty described them as three "very gentlemanly people," and I thought, "How can those guys stand playing with me?"

Just as I was competitive in basketball, I was pretty competitive in tennis. I could really cover the court (as a younger man), and when I ran out of speed, I relied on guile. They're both helpful. Speed's better than guile, but guile is better than nothing.

Betty also would play tennis for a time, taking lessons and then playing mixed doubles with me, even winning a tournament with her competitive partner, who would occasionally "poach"—running in front of her to make a winning shot.

I also played handball and squash, my favorite sport, for many years. My squash attire also bottomed out with black socks. I played on courts I had built in Humana-Suburban Hospital in 1972 and the Humana Building fitness center in 1984.

When I retired from squash following a double-knee replacement, about twenty friends and fellow players gave me a retirement roast. They listed ten reasons why I always won. Among them: I wore dark socks, I had more experience, I was older, I didn't like to play softball, I kept score, and I owned the place. The gifts included knee braces, a softball, an oxygen tank, a football helmet, glasses—and black socks.

Picking up from my days at Yale, I also had a brief fling with golf, winning a Pendennis Club outing in 1967 at Hurstbourne Country Club when a seven-iron shot dropped into the cup on the 18th hole, giving me an eagle and a final score of 78. I won a dozen golf balls for low net and a handsome silver bowl for low gross. I took the bowl home, where Betty planted a flower in it.

With nothing at stake, I played the same course a week later and shot a 95. So, I could sometimes elevate my game to meet the level of competition.

After I agreed to play the tennis match with Heston, we met at the Mockingbird Valley courts on Zorn Avenue. I arranged to have the Mockingbird Valley pro on hand just in case Heston needed better competition. Heston won the first two games, but I won twelve straight games to prevail 6–2, 6–0.

He had a strong serve, but the courts were clay, and I don't think he was accustomed to playing on clay. So, he said, "Dave, I want you to come out to California. I want to have a rematch—and we're going to play on concrete."

Heston wrote me a note with an invitation, but we were never able to get together on a tennis court again.

Chapter Fifteen

ARTIFICIAL HEART, REAL DRAMA

"The heart program itself created results no one had expected: We financed the artificial heart program largely because Dr. Lansing knew that the heart worked mechanically and needed human testing. The worldwide publicity and 'halo effect' creating a favorable impression of Humana overall were unintended consequences of thoughtful decisions made intentionally by Wendell and me.

"The story continued around the world for 620 days and longer. People thought, 'If Humana hospitals can handle artificial hearts, what can't they handle?' "

— DAVID JONES

T wo neighbors having a backyard conversation over a beer is commonplace. But one such talk in Louisville in 1983 led to a $25 million experiment that captured the attention of the world for nearly two years and resounds today. It occurred when Dr. Allan Lansing, a renowned Louisville heart surgeon newly recruited to Humana's Audubon Hospital, invited me over for that beer.

We had only recently become neighbors, but our relationship had some history. On a flight from New York to Louisville, I read about a program to help children with heart defects living in countries unable to treat them. A Rotary International program would fly the child to America for treatment, along with a doctor from the same country. The child would be treated, and the doctor would be trained to perform such surgeries back home.

The Rotary Club would find a doctor and a hospital that would donate services or would find donors to pay. I told Lansing, who was already performing pioneering pediatric heart surgery at Humana Hospital-Audubon, that if he donated his services, Humana would pay all hospital expenses.

Lansing had trained in Houston, where famed heart surgeons Denton Cooley and Michael DeBakey had worked. He agreed to my request and, over a period of four years, performed more than 200 surgeries at no charge in Eastern Europe, Central America, and Louisville. As a result, Lansing was named a "Point of Light" by President George H. W. Bush in 1991.

Lansing made follow-up trips to those countries to work with the doctors and the young patients—a precursor to many Humana Foundation-sponsored trips to Romania. In time, he and I would receive Romania's highest civilian award.

Before the backyard conversation, Lansing and I had discussed his work with the University of Utah, implanting artificial hearts in calves. It worked well until the calves grew too large to be kept alive with an artificial heart.

Lansing and I discussed Dr. William C. DeVries implanting an artificial heart into Seattle dental surgeon Barney Clark. I eventually invited DeVries to Louisville, promising that as long as the heart project was making scientific progress, there wouldn't be any hospital charge. I pledged that Humana would support up to one hundred artificial heart transplants. DeVries was very much intrigued.

I thought about the implications of heart transplants beyond the medical procedures—the social, legal, and ethical considerations. I asked Dr. Walter Hume, a Harvard-educated surgeon at Humana Hospital-Audubon, to help guide the process. Uncharted medical research waters require informed patient consent. We created a committee of unassailable experts to counsel us and prepare the critical consent document.

Hume assembled a three-person advisory panel to oversee the program to be sure all phases were legally, morally, and medically sound. The panel also would ensure that every patient fully understood the medical issues.

The committee was chaired by Dr. Dwight Emary Harken, Harvard University's legendary chief of thoracic surgery. Hume had studied under Harken years earlier. Harken's pioneering work in heart surgery had begun during World War II; while stationed in London, he was the first to remove shrapnel by cutting into the wall of a beating heart, then inserting a finger to locate and remove the metal pieces. He removed shrapnel from 130 hearts without a fatality.

The second panel member was Albert R. Jonsen, a bioethicist and an author. A former Roman Catholic priest with a doctorate in religious studies from Yale, he was one of the first bioethicists to be appointed to a medical faculty. A pioneer in clinical ethics, Dr. Jonsen was selected by the National Heart, Lung, and Blood Institute to help formulate regulations governing the use of humans in research (which was the status of artificial hearts at that point).

The third panel member was a leading scholar in family law and medicine, Walter J. Wadlington, the James Madison Professor of Law at the University of Virginia. His career included being a member of the Institute of Medicine of the National Academy of Sciences and director of the Robert Wood Johnson Foundation medical malpractice program. He also served on the board of the American Society of Law and Medicine.

The three men considered every aspect of the procedure. Humana paid for Lansing to train under DeVries in Utah. Lansing promised to build a dedicated Humana Heart Institute International program in Louisville that would perform both artificial heart implants and human heart transplants, the latter beginning in 1987 and expanding nationwide to include other organs.

Lansing and I had a very strong relationship, but his day-to-day work with Humana intersected with Bruce Perkins, another working-class Louisville native and U of L graduate. Perkins worked for Humana in many executive capacities over thirty-eight years and was chief operating officer at Audubon when Lansing became involved in the heart program.

Lansing had his methods. Perkins remembers that when Lansing thought he wasn't getting all the medical equipment or support he needed, "he would call downtown," i.e., David Jones.

"So Lansing called downtown, and David just showed up out at Audubon Hospital one day," Perkins said. "He walked into my office, and from the window at the far end of my office you could see downtown Louisville."

I remembered the surprise visit, too: I walked over to the window and mentioned I could see the Humana Building from there. I then turned, pointed at Perkins, and said: "Al Lansing tells me he needs a few things to prepare for the artificial heart operation. I told him that I'm sure you will obtain them promptly."

I paused, then added, "Have a good day," and left.

The equipment was there the next day.

The first Humana-sponsored artificial heart patient would be William Schroeder, a fifty-two-year-old retired Army civilian employee from Jasper, Indiana. The surgery was performed by DeVries on November 25, 1984.

To accommodate the 300 reporters covering the event, Humana had to rent the bottom floor of the Commonwealth Convention Center, with thirty-seven television vans parked outside. Even after the media swarm left town, the *New York Times* medical reporter, Dr. Lawrence Altman, stayed in Louisville for months.

With such massive press coverage, a complete patient-privacy policy was put into effect—a policy one photographer tried to subvert by hiding in a laundry hamper and then popping out in the coronary care unit.

This worldwide coverage was handled by Tom Noland, later Humana's senior vice president for corporate communications, who—incredibly enough—started with the company the day after Mr. Schroeder's operation. His success at handling the event said a lot about timing, good luck, his serendipity, and our ability to find and keep talent.

Noland was another find with a Kentucky connection. His father, who served on a Navy destroyer escort in the South Pacific in World War II—including the battle of Okinawa—had grown up on a family tobacco farm on Poosey Ridge, near Richmond, Kentucky. After the war, he worked more than thirty years for the R. T. Vanderbilt Company in Connecticut, a chemical-and-mineral giant.

Noland's ambition was to be a writer. He attended Duke University, then transferred to Yale, where he majored in history—an eventual connecting point to the Jones family. He began working summers at the *Anniston Star* in Alabama, and then the *St. Petersburg Times* in Florida. His wanderlust also led him to backpack in Europe, particularly France, where he learned the language.

He worked three years in Alabama for the *Anniston Star*, returned to France in June 1979, did some teaching, and became the first European bureau chief for the *Atlanta Constitution*, traveling Europe for stories. He was in London for the wedding of Prince Charles and Lady Diana Spencer in 1981. He also began writing stories for *Horizon* magazine, covering art events. Noland began exchanging letters with its American editor, Vivian Ruth Sawyer. They married in 1982.

"We ended up kind of falling in love by letter," said Noland.

Vivian joined him in Paris. Tom expanded his freelance work, but they began to feel a little too comfortable.

"We loved living there," said Tom. "We wanted to have kids, but we really didn't want kids who didn't know what baseball was—and who spoke better French than we did."

Yet their lives in Paris did immerse them in a journalistic story they would forever remember: the death of Princess Grace of Monaco. While covering the G7 Summit in Paris in 1982, Noland met Don Kirk, then with the *Los Angeles Times* but soon to become foreign editor for a new publication named *USA Today*.

The two men became fast friends. Kirk asked Noland if he might have any interest in becoming Paris correspondent for *USA Today*. Noland said sure, then forgot about it as the men moved on with their lives.

Around one o'clock in the morning on September 15—about three months after the summit meeting—Noland got a frantic call from Kirk, who told him to catch a plane and get to Monaco; Princess Grace had been killed when her car went over a cliff.

There were no flights at that hour. Kirk needed a story in two hours; *USA*

Today was being launched that day. Noland had only two communication devices: his phone and a combination radio-toilet-paper dispenser he'd gotten as a joke wedding present.

Noland went to a bathroom, sat down, and tuned in the radio, but there was no news. Vivian wandered in and suggested he just look up the Monaco telephone prefix and call people at random. The news had been carefully guarded in Monaco, and few knew about it.

With the phone cradled against his ear, Noland started calling complete strangers, taking notes, writing responses of anguish over the death of their beloved fairy-tale princess. At 3 a.m., Noland called Kirk with the story. It ran on the front page of the first edition of *USA Today*.

But eventually, Noland and his wife decided to leave Paris. They wanted an American city that was a "metropolis, not a megalopolis," with a strong arts culture. The only American city that fit—and Noland had been in the city a few times while visiting folks in Poosey Ridge—was Louisville.

They knew no one in Louisville. Vivian did some research and came up with the name "Wendell Cherry" because he was an art collector. Noland, who had never met Wendell, wrote him a letter, basically saying he and Vivian were thinking of moving back to America, that Louisville seemed like a nice place—and they also were interested in the arts.

"We're going to be in Louisville in November," Noland wrote. "Would you have time to see us?"

The letter ended up on the desk of Wendell's assistant, Joan Hester, who read all his mail. Wendell rarely responded to such letters but noticed it on the desk because of the foreign address and postage. He read the letter and asked Hester to set up a November appointment. Tom and Vivian had purchased one-way tickets home from Paris. They met with Wendell for an hour, talking art, France, and their future.

"You want to move from Paris to Louisville?" asked Wendell, a little more than curious. "I think that's great."

I briefly poked my head into that meeting, then left, not knowing Noland or Sawyer. Meanwhile, Wendell promised to help the couple find jobs at places like the *Courier Journal* or the J. B. Speed Art Museum. There were no offers. The morning they were getting ready to fly to Connecticut to stay with Noland's family, I called them. Serendipity. I had a Yale meeting in New Haven soon and invited Tom and Vivian to join me for breakfast. I knew only of the Yale connection, and their French connection, Betty's favorite language.

Noland had never thought about working for Humana. He was a journalist with an interest in the arts. But I knew the company needed someone with a journalism background to handle the media coverage of the artificial heart program.

"I'd never heard of it," said Noland later.

Noland and Sawyer flew to Connecticut. I met them for breakfast two days later. I offered him a job. Noland answered that he knew nothing about health care.

"That doesn't matter," I responded. "We really need somebody like you right now. I think we're going to have a lot of media come to Louisville. Can you start in a week?"

Noland later revealed he was thinking: "Wow, I got a job. This is great. It's PR. I wonder what that is?"

Noland went to work for Humana on November 26, 1984, the day after William Schroeder's artificial heart implant. His PR office was to be in the National City Tower. That Monday, he found no one there. A janitor told him everyone was over at the Commonwealth Convention Center, including the reporters he was to brief with details of the operation.

"I mean, there were literally hundreds of reporters, some from foreign countries," Noland recalled. "Everybody was in a giant room. I worked from 8 a.m. until one in the morning. I didn't care. It was wonderful."

Noland, Sawyer, and the Jones family became fast friends. Noland was the only person Betty trusted to speak for me in my absence. The couples have been together in the Joy Luck Book Club for thirty-two years and counting. When Noland was interviewed once in Tennessee, he talked about our work together beyond the heart transplant. He said he watched me intuitively pick the right people for jobs, then allow them to flourish, inspiring them by always expecting success. Noland also remembered trying to thank Wendell for his opportunity at a grand party at Wendell's house, but Wendell, greeting guests outside, wouldn't accept it.

"Ah, hell," he said, "I was just trying to add some class to the joint. Get on inside."

✳

The artificial heart surgery had its critics. Humana received many passionate letters about the procedure, some in praise and some from angry people motivated by religious beliefs: They didn't believe an artificial heart should be placed in a human. They contended once the original heart was cut out, the soul was lost. The Louisville police became involved in sorting out the mail, wearing gloves while placing letters in one pile or another to check for threats.

Schroeder, DeVries, Wendell, and I were the subjects of long articles in the December 10, 1984 *Time* magazine, with a very focused-looking DeVries on the cover, holding pieces of an artificial heart. One story detailed Humana's cost-effective management and its new insurance plans, citing the artificial heart program as an example of how a corporation can use its resources to develop a new field of medicine.

Its profile on Schroeder included photos of the operating room as he was given an artificial heart, with about a dozen green-clad doctors and nurses assisting DeVries during the procedure. Schroeder suffered a relapse an hour after the surgery when he began hemorrhaging along stitches connecting the artificial heart to his aorta but soon recovered.

Schroeder, an outgoing father of six and a retired quality control inspector, was shown sipping a Coors beer a few days after the procedure, which resulted in a few cases of the brew being forwarded to the hospital from Denver.

One humorous incident involved President Ronald Reagan, who was set up to call Schroeder after the operation. Pat Davis, Audubon Hospital CEO, accepted the call, believing Reagan was on the line. He wasn't. But she—and then Schroeder—went through several "Hold for President

Reagan" moments before the president finally came on the line. Schroeder and Reagan talked for some time, and then Reagan asked him, "Is there anything I can do for you?"

"Yes," Schroeder answered. "My Social Security check is late."

Schroeder's check arrived soon afterward.

Schroeder and his family, well aware of the possible dangers involved with his procedure, had signed a seventeen-page consent form before the operation. He would suffer a series of strokes, the first only two weeks after the surgery, greatly affecting his speech. One reason given was that the solid titanium valves in the experimental artificial heart had caused his blood to thicken.

Hospital officials did all they could to make him feel comfortable, including staging a wedding at the hospital for his son, as his father could not leave the hospital for the scheduled event.

Partly incapacitated, Schroeder lived for 620 days, which was longer than four other Jarvik-7 recipients. Improvements in the artificial heart allow it to be used today as a life-prolonging "bridge" for patients awaiting a heart transplant.

In 1987, the federal government withdrew support for its program to develop a permanent artificial heart, saying the human body just didn't seem to be able to tolerate it. There were also increasing ethical concerns. Lives were prolonged, yes, but patients then had to deal with other serious medical issues. Some doctors—including Robert Jarvik, who invented the artificial heart—continued to try to develop more sustainable models, and some are still used in hospitals in emergency situations.

Humana stopped supporting such surgeries. It had supplied Schroeder with an apartment across from the hospital because he had to carry his battery to power the artificial heart. I estimated the program probably cost Humana $25 or $30 million, but the effort required it.

I wouldn't say he had a good life, but death was imminent; the surgery extended his life for a time. What we learned was that the materials in the artificial heart didn't react perfectly with materials in the body, creating the strokes, and the doctors learned a whole lot from those strokes.

The heart program itself created results no one had expected. We financed the artificial heart program largely because Dr. Lansing knew that the heart worked mechanically and needed human testing. The worldwide publicity and "halo effect" creating a favorable impression of Humana overall were unintended consequences of thoughtful decisions made intentionally by Wendell and me.

The story continued around the world for 620 days and longer. People thought, "If Humana hospitals can handle artificial hearts, what can't they handle?"

Chapter Sixteen

Architecture, Poetry, Civic Progress

"In all great art and architecture, there is one thing that must be present: a sense of poetry. We believe this building, designed by Michael Graves, creates this sense of poetry. Its quiet beauty presents a form grounded in past architectural tradition yet moving vibrantly into the future."

— DAVID JONES and WENDELL CHERRY, at the
1985 dedication of the Humana Building

Even as we were helping create the Kentucky Center for the Performing Arts, Wendell and I were making plans for a new company headquarters just across Main Street to enable all of Humana's far-flung Louisville employees to be in one place. We wanted a unique design—a building that would be environmentally friendly yet reach well beyond anything the Louisville skyline had to offer—setting a new standard for buildings in relation to their surroundings and the city.

We decided it was something you get to do only once in your lifetime, and we wanted to do it right. Wendell and I held a design competition that attracted five of the world's most eminent architects, Norman Foster, Ulrich Franzen, Michael Graves, Helmut Jahn, and César Pelli. Each architect was paid to create a design, something I believe hadn't been done since the design competition for Chicago's Wrigley Building or Tribune Tower in the 1920s. We wrote in a preface to a book about the building,

Our desire was for the participants to focus on its location: the nineteenth-century architecture, the mixture of other buildings in the immediate area, the imposing geographic prominence in the city, and most important, the Ohio River— where the city's life began. We further desired that the building enhance the overall visual impression of the Louisville skyline.

Of the five architects, Graves was probably the least known. He was added to the list only after another very famous designer, Philip Johnson, declined to enter and suggested Graves. We challenged them to design a building that would cause anyone who wanted to build in Louisville thereafter to think about it. There were a lot of nice buildings, but not in terms of really thoughtful architecture.

The candidates were carefully examined. I hired Tom Owen, a University of Louisville archivist, Metro Council member, and historian, to take each candidate on a walking tour of Louisville to get a feel for the city, the riverfront, and the building site. Wendell flew to Portland, Oregon to inspect a Michael Graves building.

The competition produced models of five very different structures, all now on display in the Humana Building. Wendell and I examined each, writing back and forth to the architects for more details. We made a final decision only after I suggested we both sit down and rank our favorites from one to five.

We called that the Delphi Method. We were not going to talk about it. We were just going to do it. And then we just put our lists out, as you do in high-low poker. And we both had Graves's building ranked number one.

The building Graves designed was twenty-seven stories high. It included 525,000 square feet of space with an open colonnade, a fifty-foot entrance waterfall reminiscent of the nearby Falls of the Ohio, and an open-air observation deck overlooking the river. Metal trusses projecting from the building paid homage to the river bridges. An innovative energy system, drawing and circulating constant-temperature water from the Ohio River's aquifer, was expected to reduce heating and cooling costs by 30 percent.

Twelve different shades of granite and marble were used, all selected by Graves. He sourced them from all over the world and had them sent to Carrara, Italy, where they were cut and shipped to Louisville. Humana architect Jim Walters went to Italy to oversee that process. I call him the "Cosmic Architect" because I've never given him a job that he didn't do well.

Construction began in October 1982. It was completed in May 1985, on time and on budget, rising 417 feet into the sky. The total cost was $60 million, which included about 80 percent of the finished interior spaces, the rest to be finished as needed. The American Institute of Architects gave the building its National Honor Award, and *Time* magazine named it one of the ten best buildings of the decade.

Wendell and I wrote of the building at its dedication:

> In all great art and architecture there is one thing that must be present: a sense of poetry. We believe this building, designed by Michael Graves, creates this sense of poetry. Its quiet beauty presents a form grounded in past architectural tradition yet moving vibrantly into the future.

In *The New York Times*, architecture critic Paul Goldberger struck a hopeful note:

> Most pleasing of all is how neatly this building works into the streetscape and skyline of Louisville, a city that has been wrenched apart by wretched architecture and poor urban renewal decisions over the last generation. Humana seems the only downtown building whose design is devoted to knitting this town back together, not to tearing it further apart—this is a tower built to sit on a city street, not behind an empty plaza, and it relates easily to its neighbors.

※

The 1980s were good years not just for Humana but for the city of Louisville. The Humana hospitals, the artificial heart program, Actors Theatre and its Humana Festival of New American Plays, the Kentucky Center for the Performing Arts, and then the Humana Building had given the city and the company a glow it never had.

The great surge in civic pride and national attention extended to sports, too. Hometown hero Darrell Griffith led the "Doctors of Dunk" to the University of Louisville's first NCAA basketball championship in 1980. Six years later, "Never Nervous" Pervis Ellison and his teammates gave coach Denny Crum a second national title.

A year earlier, the Humana Building had been completed, symbolizing a city—and company—on the rise.

Looking back three decades later, I see that for the first time in the history of the company, Humana was taken seriously in its hometown, not because of the things we had done that were truly helpful, but because of our new building. There's something about architecture, the solidity of it.

Other growth would follow. I had always loved airplanes and, in the late 1980s, played a part in the revitalization of Louisville International Airport.

United Parcel Service, the airport's chief user—especially at night, when UPS planes from all over the world fly in and out—was growing rapidly. The airport lacked parallel runways and needed improvements to the terminal as well. There had even been discussions over the years of building a new airport in a county just east of Louisville.

J. D. Nichols, an Airport Authority member, business leader, and experienced pilot, came up with a workable plan to add a parallel runway to the existing airport. The estimated cost was $50 million. If it could be financed and built, UPS would remain in Louisville. If not, UPS would leave, along with thousands of jobs.

Nichols recruited me to help find the money. We first asked Mayor Jerry Abramson, who said no. We then climbed into Nichols's helicopter, flew to Frankfort, and landed right beside the office of Governor Wallace Wilkinson. We asked him to find the $50 million needed to build the

210

parallel runway and keep UPS in Louisville. He said yes. Thanks to him and J. D. Nichols, we have the necessary parallel runway and Louisville's vibrant, largest employer.

In 2019, Louisville's UPS operation was the company's biggest in the world, with almost 18,000 employees. It normally handled two million packages per day and four million near Christmas, with 378 daily flights in and out of the city, eventually connecting to 220 countries and territories.

Education had always been an important issue to me. My ongoing work with improving it included a role in the passage of the Kentucky Education Reform Act (KERA) during the Wallace Wilkinson administration in 1990. KERA's genesis was with the Prichard Committee for Academic Excellence, which had been organized in 1983 to improve Kentucky's very poor investment in education.

At the time, Kentucky was last among the states in high school graduations, third from the last in educational funding, and was deemed a failure, especially by the poorer rural districts, who sued the state in the late 1980s in an attempt to force change. In 1989, the Kentucky Supreme Court ruled the state's public school system was unconstitutional, inefficient, and inequitable because tax revenue per student was much lower in poor districts than in wealthy ones.

I worked with John Hall, the CEO of Ashland Oil, and Oz Nelson, CEO of UPS, to organize the business and labor communities to support ambitious reform and the tax increases that would be necessary for meaningful education improvement. In the end, KERA included some of the most sweeping changes of any educational reform law in US history. Its first goal was to reduce economic disparity among those districts, but it also changed the governance of schools and set up an accountability system where all schools were judged on the performance of all students. KERA has worked well for the most part, but more changes were needed later to maintain that progress.

My involvement in the public arena was also evident in the summer and fall of 1995 when Mayor Abramson proposed to close Third Street, in the center of downtown Louisville, to expand the Commonwealth Convention Center.

I had been out of town with Betty, on vacation. We first heard of the proposal after attending a movie at the old Vogue Theater in St. Matthews. We bumped into two couples who owned buildings or businesses downtown and were worried about the closing's impact on them. The plan had been heavily lobbied by the Kentucky State Fair Board, the public agency that owned the convention center. But it still had to be approved by the Louisville planning commission and board of aldermen.

I was surprised to learn that closing an essential artery was being seriously considered for already congested downtown Louisville streets. The reason given was that the convention center would draw more national events if it had two levels of contiguous floor space, so Third Street would have to be closed to make that possible. However, no data were offered as to benefits versus costs. It was just, "Trust us."

I very much opposed the idea. Most incoming traffic to downtown Louisville from Interstates 64 and 71 entered on Third Street. Furthermore, Fourth Street had already been shut down to make way for a major restaurant and entertainment destination. The plan, in effect, to build a wall across Third Street was a terrible idea.

I scheduled a meeting with Abramson. As I waited outside the mayor's office, Sally Brown, a longtime friend and the widow of W. L. Lyons Brown, late president and chairman of the Brown-Forman distilling company, came out with her son. They had been on the same mission.

"I hope you have better luck than we did," Brown told me.

At the meeting with Abramson and Deputy Mayor Joan Riehm, Riehm quickly told me that the street closing was a done deal. If I didn't like it, I could sue.

Deciding that a done deal was not a good way to conduct city business—and not wanting to sue the mayor—I asked Ken Payne, the president of my Main Street Realty company, to investigate what other cities had done to expand downtown convention centers. I also asked PricewaterhouseCoopers to help with cost projections and ways to finance alternative solutions.

Payne reported that both Indianapolis and Albuquerque had kept important downtown streets open by "bridging" the new buildings over those streets—as was eventually done in Louisville. Taking the matter personally, I eventually met with eleven of the twelve aldermen to explain how the city could affordably expand the center while preserving the Third Street throughway. I also had plans for meeting the twelfth alderman.

Before that meeting, I got a call from Abramson, a man I liked, greatly admired, and worked with as a progressive mayor. He told me, "Dave, I only have one vote left, so you win."

I replied, "Jerry, I haven't met with that alderman yet, so you may have no votes."

Rather than publicly claiming victory, I suggested that Abramson call a press conference and announce that he had found an affordable solution that met the needs of the convention center and saved Third Street.

Not all changes I inspired made such headlines. One serious issue with almost comic overtones occurred in the early 1970s, when I was briefly a member of the Jefferson County Air Board. Historically, men and women at both Bowman Field and Standiford Field (now called Louisville Muhammad Ali International Airport) had to place a dime in a slot to use the enclosed toilets, but the men had free use of urinals. A woman might have $50 in cash but no dimes.

I went to a board meeting and challenged its members, including the airport manager. "Look, show me how much money we're getting from those dimes, and let's see if we can't take those slots off and make them free," I said.

The majority of the board agreed with me: The coin slots were removed from all toilets. The manager was soon gone, too.

✳

Forever interested in improving Louisville—and the way outsiders view it—I hired Louisville native Rowan Claypool, a 1980 Yale graduate, to work with my embryonic Main Street Realty development company. Claypool later created a program called Bulldogs in the Bluegrass, which placed Yale students in internships in businesses and non-profits in the Louisville area. The program brought young people into the city and later bloomed into Bulldogs Across America in nine cities.

Claypool would explain in a Yale alumni magazine article:

> There was not a Yale College graduate younger than thirty-five living in Louisville in the summer of 1999. There had been fourteen years of zero in-migration.
>
> The topic of brain-drain in Kentucky was something that caused everybody to sort of sit up and ask how we were going to be a thriving economic engine if we were losing a significant portion of bright young folks. I just dreamed up something to address it.

He calculates that at least 400 Yale students have since spent time in Louisville, with forty-five graduates moving to town and employed for at least a year. Claypool has also created a successful teacher-recruitment program called Teach Kentucky that has reached across the nation to recruit high-level college graduates or seniors interested in teaching. They work in Louisville public schools with a full-time salary and the opportunity to earn a master's degree.

"Seventy percent of the teachers are staying beyond their two-year commitment," Claypool wrote in a 2015 *Insider Louisville* essay, "and 60 percent are making Louisville their lifetime home."

Chapter Seventeen

Hardware and Hard Lessons

"If Belknap had been sold, its corporate soul would not be in Louisville, it would be in Chicago. The company was on the verge of going broke. What is it they say? Fools rush in where angels fear to tread. Well, I was the fool that rushed in. I told myself I'm going to save this longtime Louisville company from these corporate raiders."

— DAVID JONES

I lost $60 million by buying Belknap Hardware and Manufacturing, a company with roots in Louisville then going back 144 years. This turned out to be another case of straying too far from what I knew best, as with the earlier investment in mobile home parks. Even so, downtown Louisville became better for it.

Part of my reason for the 1984 purchase of Belknap was that it was a hometown company providing many jobs that needed saving; that was reason enough for me to buy it. But the company's grim financial realities soon overwhelmed any good intentions.

Belknap was special, a Main Street Louisville icon titled "The World's Largest Hardware Plant." But its facilities were aging and badly in need of upgrading and repair.

The company sprawled over a fourteen-building complex between Main Street and the Ohio River and Second and Jackson Streets, an area five blocks long and from two to three blocks deep. Those red brick buildings, most built between 1890 and 1929, included thirty-seven acres of floor space, much of it connected by underground passageways and covered bridges that enabled workers to unload merchandise and move it from one warehouse to the next, albeit in a clumsy, awkward fashion.

Its future in Louisville seemed uncertain in 1984 when a group from Chicago made a hostile offer to buy the company, which was publicly traded, although not very often. At the time, I was certain that if Belknap were sold, its corporate soul would not be in Louisville; it would be in Chicago.

I believe that if the Chicago group—led by Clyde Engle—had been successful, the new owners could have liquidated Belknap's assets at near full purchase price and still have left the out-of-town raider in full possession of potentially valuable downtown Louisville real estate. They were the same buildings and property that would later become, with my help, part of the critical revitalization of downtown, drawing in the Presbyterian Church USA headquarters and creating a massive Humana presence.

Belknap's winding history in Louisville began well before the Civil War. Just before his twenty-ninth birthday, William Burke Belknap opened an iron store at Third and Main Streets on April 1, 1840, mainly to sell nails, horse and mule shoes, spikes, and other forged items.

On May 30, 1843, Belknap married Mary Richardson, whose father was president of a Louisville bank. As the company evolved, Belknap created an immense network of salespeople stretching across the entire South. The Belknap family mansion would become the first home of Louisville's Pendennis Club, a traditional, segregated men's club that became the gathering place for the wealthy's parties, social events, and billiards.

In the beginning, the company had big teams of horse-drawn wagons to deliver goods. Its hardware operation expanded from 1,274 wholesale items in 1880 to 75,000 items in 1940, many featured in a ten-inch-thick catalog almost 4,000 pages long.

By 1957, the company was selling 90,000 items, many under the

216

"Blue Grass" label. In 1960, Belknap had become the largest hardware wholesaler in the nation in sales, net worth, and floor space while selling to customers in thirty states.

Its catalog was considered a competitor of the retail sales giants Sears, Roebuck and Montgomery Ward. A cornucopia for anything a home builder or hardware store would need, it offered items from building materials and furniture to rugs, toys, furs and jewelry, pocketknives, cutlery, hammers, saws, hatchets, saw blades, chisels, tin snips, nuts, bolts, and shears.

The line grew to include more diverse, if not somewhat incongruous products, including revolvers, rifles, ammunition, hunter's clothing, croquet sets, radios, and church bells. At one point, the catalog listed more than 110,000 items, requiring hours—if not days—of armchair browsing. All that required a sales network plus hundreds of people in Louisville to warehouse and distribute it all.

All stories about Belknap stressed its family-like atmosphere and loyal employees, a work ethic that I could appreciate. I remembered a time when Betty's father, who owned a pharmacy, could order many of the non-medical items he needed from Belknap wholesale and then go pick them up.

The company's training program included starting new executives on the floor filling stock orders or unloading boxcars full of coal stoves. Many Belknap employees worked there for forty or fifty years. One man, Frank Strohm, worked there for seventy years and, in 1950, was named company president for one hour as a reward. In later years, some employees sought union representation, leading to a 1978 strike.

The larger problem was that in an increasingly competitive market, Belknap had unwisely continued to operate in antiquated brick buildings with old elevators to shuttle all the goods up and down, pneumatic message tubes in the ceilings, and old black phones on desks.

The company also had a policy of not charging customers for freight delivery, and, illustrative of old-school staffing policies, forty of its executives had personal secretaries. Consequently, it had a weak profit line, showing only $2 million in profit on sales of $170 million in 1983.

For all that, the company stock, according to financial experts, was undervalued, making it potentially ripe for a takeover. The Engle group controlled 304,666 shares, or 21.2 percent, of Belknap. I had purchased 108,100 shares or 7.54 percent. Many other Kentuckians bought shares, keeping an estimated 50 percent of the company at home. Meanwhile, Belknap stock had risen to $24.50.

I was to be Belknap's salvation—its "white knight." After speaking with some very welcoming Belknap company directors, and Louisville stockbrokers, I led the leveraged buyout. I purchased the company for $35 million, paying $24 a share. A group of investors, including a few members of Belknap management, had bid $20 a share, and Engle, the corporate raider, had bid $22 a share. Belknap had, at that time, about 1,700 vendors, 12,000 retail accounts, and about 50,000 retail items.

Belknap was on the verge of going broke. The Belknap stock seemed to be selling at a really low price, and I rushed in. What is it they say? Fools rush in where angels fear to tread. Well, I was the fool that rushed in.

I brought in former Humana executive Frank Lambert as president. Lambert, trying to streamline operations, quickly eliminated one-third of the company's workforce and much of its former management team. He cut product lines and shifted distribution to new Louisville and Jefferson County Riverport sites along the Ohio River south of town, as well as sites in Dallas and Charlotte.

The moves, criticized by many in the Louisville community and by longtime Belknap employees, lowered company profits and reduced its cash flow. A declining market did the rest. Unable to pay suppliers, Belknap filed for bankruptcy protection on December 4, 1985, and closed on February 4, 1986.

The Belknap experience came at a very busy time in my life. I was running Humana as it expanded and was an active member of other corporate boards while keeping up with our very busy family. But I accepted full blame for the bankruptcy.

I hadn't done any due diligence. I hadn't looked at it. Of course I thought I could save it. I wouldn't have gone into it if I hadn't. I told myself I'm going to save this longtime Louisville company from these corporate raiders. I thought I was protecting jobs. I also was intrigued by the company's enormous old warehouse buildings and thought they and the location would someday be valuable.

I didn't know anything about the business, and I just made a big mistake. And I paid for it. So, while people think I'm some kind of business genius, I'm not. I'm just a guy who's had some successes and some failures.

To ease the financial pain for others, I did something I didn't have to do in the bankruptcy proceeding. I put up $25 million of my own money to pay the creditors and the pensions of employees who lost their jobs. That took my total financial loss in the Belknap venture to $60 million. I didn't have to do it, but much of my concern about the bankruptcy left when I agreed to pay the unpaid debts. I think I did the best I could.

My son Dave left his job as an international banker to return to Louisville in early 1985 to help with Belknap. As the company spiraled down, he commuted back and forth during his first semester of law school to help me sort through the limited options, which converged into the decision to file for bankruptcy in December of that year. As I had learned from Humana's misguided effort in the mobile home business, when you're in a hole, stop digging. "Belknap was a huge mess," Dave said later. "It had been sucked dry by the former owners of every nickel they could get out of it. It had been underinvested."

Meanwhile, Clyde Engle, who had led the Chicago group, did not fare well in his future deals—a strong indication Louisville would have been the complete loser had that Belknap deal gone through. In 2010, Engle was ordered to pay a $53 million judgment to a group of Tennesseans for his part in a faulty land deal. He also saw his Coronet Insurance Company shut down in Illinois on claims he looted it for personal gain. State regulators also shut down his Bank of Lincolnwood for making bad construction loans to real-estate developers.

※

The Belknap experience proved optimism doesn't always equal success. Yet in 1986, my financial loss with Belknap was somewhat balanced out because I was also a director and large shareholder of Royal Crown Cola Company, whose stock I had been buying for two years.

I became involved in the company through W. T. Young, an old friend, very successful business partner, Humana board member, and chairman of Royal Crown. Together, Young and I controlled about 25 percent of the company stock. A financier and corporate raider named Victor Posner owned about 25 percent, and other owners had the rest.

Along with the possible financial rewards, I had a very personal interest in Royal Crown. My mother and I had always loved RC Cola—the taste-bud connection going back to my childhood.

For fun, I would put its flavor to a test for Betty. I would pour three glasses of drinks—Coke, Pepsi, and RC Cola—and put their names on the bottom. Betty chose RC Cola as the best tasting every time, but she always swore that it was Coke—that I had mislabeled—because she thought she preferred Coke!

Royal Crown stock was about $7 a share when Young and I began buying it in the early 1980s; its shares rose to $33 by January 1984. As we began competing with Posner for control of the company, we visited him in Miami on the top floor of an old apartment hotel with armed guards at the door.

When we got to the top floor, we had to pass through two sets of sliding steel doors. Obviously, Posner had enemies. We were not his enemies.

Young and I had reached a mutual agreement. We would sell our shares to Posner for $37 a share, or we would buy his for $37. Posner lectured us incessantly, as if we were business novices, then offered to buy only *our* RC Cola shares for about $45.

We refused. We told him he had to buy everybody's shares at that price. We were not going to leave the rest of the shareholders to his good wishes. Posner refused. The next morning—believing we knew something about Royal Crown that he didn't—Posner made a public hostile tender offer for $40 a share.

I can't imagine what kind of mind would think that way, but we said, "You could have had it for $37 yesterday, but if you're going to pay $40 today ... fine."

Thus, much of my financial pain from the Belknap bankruptcy was soothed by the RC Cola stock sale. I made almost as much money on my RC success as I had lost on Belknap. And then, I ultimately ended up with the Belknap property.

Victor Posner—who had lectured Young and me on our business shortcomings before making a very bad deal all his own—would later face legal issues. While being described in *Forbes* magazine as "having the arrogance of a banana republic dictator" and "master of the hostile takeover," he would plead guilty in 1988 to tax evasion and fraud for inflating the value of land he had donated to Miami Christian College.

He paid $6 million in fines and was ordered to devote twenty hours a week for five years working with the homeless. It was one of several such charges he would face that ultimately had him barred from any activity in securities.

Meanwhile, back in Louisville, John Mulder, longtime president of the Louisville Presbyterian Theological Seminary, paid a visit to me in 1987 to talk about the possibility of some of the old Belknap buildings becoming a new national Presbyterian headquarters in Louisville.

The Presbyterians had split over slavery before the Civil War, with the northern branch headquartered in what was called "The God Box" on Riverside Drive in New York and the southern group headquartered in Atlanta.

Seeking reconciliation, the church's general assembly met in Biloxi, Mississippi, in June 1987 to choose a central headquarters site in a border state, such as Missouri or Kentucky. A church relocation committee had recommended moving to Kansas City in a real-estate deal promoted by former Dallas Cowboys quarterback Roger Staubach, with an old hotel to be converted to the new headquarters.

Louisville had supposedly been eliminated from the discussion because of its inadequate air service; Kansas City was a big favorite. But I had a plan to bring Louisville back into the picture: I offered to donate two of the old Belknap buildings to the Presbyterians. I took Jim Walters to inspect the buildings. Jim was Humana's chief architect and longtime vice president of design and construction. We both immediately saw the potential in the 275,000 square feet of eighty-year-old brick and mortar.

It took some imagination. There was a railroad track in between the two buildings, and the place looked like a garbage dump. The two buildings had different levels. One had six floors, and one had five floors. That empty space made it possible to create ramps and steps, and other needed features.

Walters was not deterred. He said, "Oh, this is wonderful. This will be an atrium." Sure enough, if you go over there now, they have a beautiful ninety-seven-foot atrium joining the two buildings with a stained-glass cross letting in light. It would become symbolic of the two sides coming together in a church with about 1.5 million members in 9,600 congregations.

To lure the Presbyterians to Louisville in the 1987 convention vote in Biloxi, Mulder had taken along miniature Louisville Slugger bats with delegates' names on them. I flew Mayor Jerry Abramson to Biloxi to deliver a rousing speech. Louisville was chosen by a narrow vote of 332–309, a decision that would irritate members who favored Kansas City.

They say no good deed goes unpunished, and, as a result of giving those two buildings to the Presbyterians, I was given the task of being fundraiser for the renovation. Which I was happy to do.

The buildings were gutted, renovated, and joined together with the atrium. I also saw to it that a parking garage was built nearby. About 300 white-collar church employees, most transfers from New York and Atlanta, began moving into the building on August 3, 1988, with another 225 workers hired locally—a big step in the rejuvenation of Louisville's then bleak Ohio River waterfront.

The Belknap building upgrades did not stop there. When Humana also needed more space, I agreed to sell what would become the eleven-story Humana Waterside Building at my cost, much less than it was worth. It provides office space for thousands of Humana employees just a block off the Ohio River and Waterfront Park.

Combining theatrics with a need for more open space, two of the old Belknap buildings were imploded in October 1993 as part of a Hollywood promotion for the movie *Demolition Man*, with Sylvester Stallone, Wesley Snipes, and Sandra Bullock in town for the event. The televised demolition created room for an enchanting small park in front of the Humana Waterside Building—and an inviting addition to the restoration of the Louisville waterfront.

Chapter Eighteen

Main Street Realty

"Main Street Realty officially began during the Belknap bankruptcy. Ken Payne was dealing with the complex bankruptcy proceedings when, on a phone call with several attorneys, they needed to form an entity through which I would take title to the Belknap buildings. The entity had no name. Payne was sitting in a chair at 101 East Main Street. That was it. Main Street Realty was born."

— DAVID JONES

I have always loved real estate. The passion arose, in a sense, when my brother Logan and I began rehabbing houses in our old Louisville neighborhood. While in our late teens and early twenties, with Logan in the lead, we worked with Liberty National Bank borrowing money for the projects. Thus, I learned the finance game early, which was essential to financing Humana's first nursing homes and so much more.

As my Humana stock began paying dividends, I used them to invest in land. I knew I should diversify beyond Humana stock—then my only asset—but didn't want to sell any because I always had great confidence in the company. I also knew that whatever I invested in beyond Humana should be something I didn't need to monitor closely. Raw land seemed just the thing.

My purchases were based on principles I had learned in a real estate course I had taken at the University of Louisville. An excellent instructor taught me there are two things to be most aware of: transportation arteries and the direction of the city's growth.

Heeding that message, I first purchased farms totaling about four hundred acres at four intersections of the not-yet-completed Gene Snyder Freeway, which started construction back in the 1950s and finished in the late1980s, looping around the southern and eastern edge of Louisville. Eventually, I would own a dozen farms in that same Jefferson-Oldham County area. I bought them with the help of Louisville realtor Carol Hebel, whose husband, Charlie—a descendant of a five-generation Louisville family—had been a classmate of mine at Male High School and the University of Louisville.

From the early 1980s into the 1990s, Carol found all those farms for me, and three or four others that I would kick myself for not buying. I invested in them as farms—basically vacant land. It was a no-brainer to buy them. And farm values kept going up and up.

I think a lot of people probably understood that if they had the capital and the patience to wait while that land developed, it would be a good buy. But they'd have to pay taxes on it and keep the grass cut. There are some moderate expenses associated with holding land for a long time.

Carol had gone into real estate after graduating from Sacred Heart Academy and Spalding University. She gravitated to buying and selling farms. She had a classic realtor mindset—the money is fine, but the real fun is putting together a deal. Like me, she was community-oriented, had a strong focus, understood time management, and was raising children. While running an office with sixteen agents, she was president of the Kentucky Derby Festival and a leader in the arts community.

She estimates she sold me more than ten pieces of investment property. Most were in Jefferson and Oldham counties. I always paid cash. She says land that was selling for $1,000 an acre in the 1960s and 1970s is now worth at least $30,000 an acre.

If the farms I bought had outbuildings or cattle, Carol would manage the farms for me and sharecrop the land, sometimes tearing down buildings that could be dangerous if left empty. Betty and I would check out the properties occasionally, but most of the time, my trust in Carol was so strong that I would buy the property sight unseen.

"He knew where to come get me if I made a mistake," said Hebel.

※

Main Street Realty would evolve from those experiences, but it officially began during the Belknap bankruptcy. Ken Payne, an accountant at Coopers & Lybrand who had long done my family business and personal tax returns, was dealing with the complex bankruptcy proceedings when, on a phone call with several attorneys, they needed to form an entity through which I would take title to the Belknap buildings. The entity had no name. Payne was sitting in a chair at 101 East Main Street. That was it. Main Street Realty was born on December 23, 1986.

Jim Walters, Humana's vice president of design and construction, who helped create the Humana Building, the Kentucky Center for the Arts, and so many other projects, helped get Main Street started. He helped with the renovation of the former Belknap buildings for the Presbyterian Church and for Humana, each a wonderful adaptive reuse of historical space.

But soon after that, Jim left to pursue his dream of an independent architecture and design firm. That firm, Bravura, would go on to play a leading role in other major Louisville projects, including Waterfront Park, Fourth Street Live, the Iroquois Amphitheater upgrade, and Old Forester Distillery, along with always helping with our Parklands of Floyds Fork projects. I continued to work with the "Cosmic Architect" as he built a wonderful business, and I never stopped marveling at his creativity and effectiveness.

Main Street Realty would go on to become a successful real estate development company and much more. The organization did a lot of the planning, analysis, and construction work on my non-profit and volunteer community projects, including building affordable housing in West Louisville. We also successfully advocated against public plans to close Third Street for the Commonwealth Convention Center and overcome

226

elite opposition to new bridges across the Ohio River. Its largest civic task was helping with the almost 4,000-acre Parklands of Floyds Fork. We handled a lot of the planning, engineering, and construction work at cost.

Main Street was effective in this wide range of work because of its fine staff. My administrative team followed me there when I retired from Humana in 2005, but long before that, in 1989, Ken Payne left Coopers to join Main Street. My trust in Ken started when he was a young accountant working on my personal matters and grew during the complex, often frustrating Belknap bankruptcy. He eventually rose to president of Main Street.

Like so many of the people I trusted to lead my businesses over the years, his hometown was Louisville. His parents and grandparents, however, had been farmers in Barren County, Kentucky, near Glasgow. His father, Ray, left the farm at age sixteen, lied about his age, became a US Army Ranger, and went ashore in the D-Day Normandy invasion at age nineteen. His unit of two hundred men was cut down to twenty-three.

After the war, Ray, who never finished high school, launched a successful career in insurance in Louisville. His life's philosophy, adopted by his son, was to always listen carefully to anyone you are talking to—bank president or ditch digger—and you will learn something. He also believed in never saying anything bad about anyone.

After leaving insurance, he started a successful construction company. Ken did construction jobs for his father in the summers, working with painters, hod carriers, and drywallers. He endured the inevitable guff from other laborers as "the boss's son" until he worked his way into their respect. "I would always get the crappiest job to do," he said.

In the late 1970s, he began working inside the company office, first as a junior payroll clerk, eventually becoming comptroller. He earned his business degree in 1981 at age twenty-one by attending night classes at U of L. He had watched as his father struggled to keep his business going during the very difficult late 1970s and vowed he would never get into the development and construction business.

With a GPA of "only" about 3.6 and fearing the accounting firms would want a 4.0, he called the recruiter at Coopers & Lybrand and introduced himself. He said he was already the comptroller of a business and was ready to work. He was hired on the spot.

I first met Payne when he was twenty-two, assisting with my tax returns. He sat there at the big conference table and just watched and listened. At age twenty-four, Coopers gave him the Jones family's personal and business tax accounts.

During the Belknap bankruptcy proceeding in 1986, Payne saw my irritation as the process wore on. The company had filed for bankruptcy protection, meaning I did not have to add any more of my money to the millions I had already invested in a misguided attempt to salvage a poorly run hometown company. He knew I didn't have to pay the $25 million for pensions and to creditors. I said it was the right thing to do; I wanted to help.

Payne says I have mellowed over the years but remain a man of little patience. He remembers one meeting at the original office at 111 West Washington Street. I was unable to find a parking spot, so I just parked on the sidewalk.

He also talks about a time I offered to fly him and his wife, Lynda, to a Florida vacation in my plane. Before they left, I called Payne to ask if he would mind taking along a suitcase for one of my children. I took the suitcase over to the Paynes' house. They were surprised to see it was an ancient number held together with duct tape.

My old-school frugality showed in other ways. One day I dropped by Payne's office wanting to go to lunch. A senior vice president joined us. We ended up at one of my favorite places, a White Castle, each of us ordering a plate of five White Castle sandwiches. Another of my favorite lunch spots is Cunningham's Creekside on Harrods Creek, where the three-dollar grilled cheese sandwich is my usual choice.

As we worked together on projects through the years, Payne said his main goal was to finish the Parklands quickly enough to allow Betty and me to tour it from one end to the other. He succeeded.

❋

We were joined in that Parklands success by eastern Kentucky native Bryan Johnson, Main Street's senior vice president, who was born and grew up in South Williamson, Kentucky, barely a three-point jump shot from West Virginia.

His father worked in a local bank. His mother was a coal miner's daughter whose father first went down into the mines at age twelve with barely a third-grade education. She attended Alice Lloyd College in Pippa Passes, Kentucky and the University of Kentucky and received a medical degree from the University of Louisville in 1957. She then returned to the eastern Kentucky mountains and practiced there for forty years.

Of Bryan Johnson's three brothers, one became a doctor, one a CPA, and the other a lawyer and a CPA. Bryan played on the Belfry High School football team that lost the state championship game to Franklin-Simpson. While in high school and barely in his teens, he and his older brother sold bottled Cokes in his mother's medical clinic and at the local Appalachian Regional Hospital. They would unload the Cokes off a delivery truck before going to school, at one point in the mid-1970s earning more than $100 a week.

With his father's help, Bryan began dabbling in stocks, options, and CDs with the Coke profits. He invested $1,000 in five gold Krugerrands and sold them for $3,000 about a year later. He earned an accounting degree from the University of Kentucky, then a UK law degree in 1988, always with the thought of working in business. His law school degree comes with a David Jones story.

On his birthday in March 1984, Johnson was recognized by the Beta Gamma Sigma honorary society for being in the top 10 percent of students in the UK business school. I was the guest speaker at the event, and all Bryan knew was the speaker was some guy named Jones who was a CPA and an attorney and started this company called Humana.

"I didn't know what Humana was," Johnson would say. "My mother was there, and we talked about what I wanted to do next. I said I didn't know. She said why don't you go to law school like this fellow."

Law school it was. He and his wife, Rhonda, a native of Matewan, West

Virginia, were married in 1986, during his first year. In 1988 he was hired by Coopers & Lybrand, primarily as a corporate tax attorney. Rhonda taught kindergarten.

At twenty-five, Johnson began working with another accountant, Ronnie Abrams, on my personal and business accounts. At our first meeting, I looked at Johnson, then Abrams, and asked, "Where are you getting them from, high school?"

As we worked together, Johnson asked me a lot about my business and how to create and sustain its growth. In 1996, after working with me for about eight years, I hired him to work for Main Street Realty as vice president, with Ken Payne as senior vice president. The two made a perfect pair, with Johnson having a more mellow approach than Payne.

A few years later, Johnson and Payne, after talking the matter over between themselves, met with me about their futures. Payne suggested they both be promoted.

Promotions granted.

Chapter Nineteen

SUFFER THE CHILDREN

"In a Romanian orphanage and in the AIDS hospital, we found infants and small children lying or standing in tiny cribs, row upon row, rocking back and forth in a heart-rending display of what we learned is called 'unloved child syndrome.'

"In each institution, Boone Powell and I lifted some of the children from their cribs and held them in our arms, a simple act that seemed to provide comfort, but which was rarely performed in the overcrowded and understaffed locations. We resolved to use our knowledge, contacts, and resources to improve these unbearably sad conditions."

— DAVID JONES

Our ability to help others greatly expanded in early 1990. The Iron Curtain had fallen, revealing the still-sprawling ruins of World War II, depressed economies, and the intimidating, murderous shadows of regimes of dictators such as Romania's Nicolae Ceaușescu.

President George H. W. Bush wanted to help nations desperate for doctors and medical care. He called me. I was floored that the president was on the line. The president's call came following a sudden and welcome surge of history. Although the twenty-eight-mile-long Berlin Wall separating communist East Germany and democratic West Germany had fallen on November 9, 1989, the nations emerging from behind the Iron

Curtain remained in a dangerous and turbulent area in need of strong leadership, direction, and surgical supplies.

Would I help?

I promised I would go to inspect the situation; I had felt a commitment to national service for nearly four decades, stretching back to my days as a young Navy officer in the 1950s. When President Bush called, I already had a national and international connection: Humana owned hospitals across the United States, and in England, Switzerland, and Mexico. We had ninety-one hospitals with about 75,000 employees, half of whom were registered nurses.

I had already established a reputation in business. I was less known for my philanthropy and liked it that way. Betty and I always gave quietly. But obviously, President Bush knew about my credentials on both fronts and entrusted me with the daunting relief project. Reviving Romania was beyond any challenge Humana or I had ever taken on. I asked my friend Boone Powell, Jr., CEO of the Baylor Medical Center in Dallas, to help.

This would be two private US medical companies—with the help of volunteer doctors and nurses—resuscitating the medical care system for 23 million people, 5,000 miles away in a country where doctors might earn $30 a month. The project summoned us to apply the ancient and sacred Hippocratic Oath to modern medical practice: Treat the ill to the best of one's ability; respect a patient's privacy; teach the secrets of medicine to the next generation. Even on another continent—*especially* on another continent.

There isn't anything I've ever wanted to do that I haven't been able to try to get done. And I can't think of anything that makes me happier than succeeding in helping others with something that needs doing.

The president's call eventually inspired an innovative sixteen-year commitment involving hundreds of volunteer American medical professionals in an exchange program with Romanian nurses and doctors. Humana would donate about $11 million over that time. (The Romanian Assistance Project also ended up bringing its Neonatal Resuscitation Program to Poland for five years because of that country's high infant mortality rate. Medical professionals delivered new technology, policies, and procedures throughout Poland to save the lives of critically ill newborns.)

The American doctors and nurses would work in all thirteen Romanian medical schools. They would lift a nation devastated by war, greed, and lethal politics into the world of twenty-first century medicine. Initially, we had no idea which nations we might assist or what their needs might be, but how often do you get a call from the president of the United States?

During that call, President Bush offered me a seat on a government plane leaving soon for Poland. I promised him I would help—and would provide my own transportation.

I soon received a visit from an official with the US Department of Commerce, who explained that the program created by President Bush—and patterned after the Peace Corps—was called the Citizens Democracy Corps. It already had representatives in newly accessible countries such as Poland, Hungary, Czechoslovakia, and Romania.

The original plans to land my American volunteers and me in Bucharest in June 1990 were canceled by the US State Department following violent protests by coal miners in the still dangerous and unsettled country. The protests erupted after the country's first free elections, in the wake of the bloody 1989 revolt that felled Ceauşescu, the general secretary of Romania's Communist party.

Ceauşescu and his wife, Elena—who led a brutal regime of fear, poverty, and deprivation—were executed by firing squad on Christmas Day 1989, only six months before my scheduled arrival in June.

Because of that delay, Betty and I made a preliminary European trip to Berlin, arriving on July 1, 1990. We hopped into a taxi, traveled past the famed "Checkpoint Charlie," which had just recently opened, and through the Wall into East Berlin, chipping off a piece as a souvenir along the way. The road further into East Berlin led past piles of World War II rubble, and eager East Germans set up in dozens of trailers exchanging money.

Betty left that day to meet our old friend Lucy Duffy in France. I traveled alone through several newly accessible East European nations to assess the medical conditions in those countries. Most of my twists and turns were made at the spur of the moment, to learn what I could before deciding where to help.

The economic and cultural deprivation of Communist rule was evident everywhere—the decrepit housing, the pitted streets, the lack of industry, the sour quality of life. The encouraging sign was the optimism of those looking forward to the future because the Wall had finally come down.

I was struck by the Eastern European architecture, particularly as it related to the central public building in every country's capital. Each had an unbelievably huge, ugly building built from the same Russian plan. Everything was handed down. There was no initiative or innovation.

I did not get into Romania on that mission but heard much about the dire condition of the country. I learned Ceauşescu had virtually emptied the country's treasury to build a personal palace he planned to be larger and grander than France's 700-room Palace of Versailles. Romania—a sad and demoralized country—seemed most in need of help and perhaps the most open to it.

I returned to the United States and immediately turned to my old friend Powell, a fellow board member of Abbott Laboratories. He confirmed my thoughts about Romania.

Powell and I were co-founders of the influential Healthcare Leadership Council, made up of CEOs from all sectors of the health care industry to help guide federal health care policy. We were also the initial funders of the Courage in Journalism Awards program in 1990. The International Women's Media Foundation honors female journalists working in dangerous places around the world. More than one hundred women from fifty-four countries have received the award, which I continue to support.

Powell said he recommended Romania as the place we should help because of an experience he and his wife, Peggy, had shared. He had learned of a Catholic charity that had helped a family with two girls, nine and eleven years old, escape from Romania. The Powells invited them over to their home for Christmas Eve dinner and took them to their church, Park City Baptist. The girls' story led Powell to suggest to me that we also visit Romania. I quickly agreed.

Under the jurisdiction of the Healthcare Leadership Council, we assembled an assessment team of eleven people, including three doctors from Baylor University and four from Humana, a nurse, and a hospital executive. Baylor executive Bill Denton was especially helpful in developing and coordinating the mission. The team landed in Bucharest on September 6, 1990. We stayed at the Intercontinental Hotel on University Square, where many protesters had been killed in the 1989 uprising.

"When I went in with our team," Powell said, "my observation was that I had walked back in history, that we were seeing facilities and equipment we saw back in the Depression. Their medical people had been locked out of current scientific information because their government would not allow it to come in."

Later, I wrote of a dingy, unkempt hotel that looked as if it hadn't been painted in forty years. The town's residents seemed undernourished, friendly but suspicious, in a world where Ceauşescu hadn't allowed any public gatherings larger than two people. Powell and I made all the obligatory stops, meeting with the Romanian president and the health minister.

They all seemed happy to see us. I think they thought we'd be there only one time because a lot of visitors at that time were just looking for business deals. Powell and I visited an AIDS hospital, an orphanage, and the city's largest general and pediatric hospitals. We saw children with birth defects, AIDS, injury, and diseases that caused them to be hidden away for life. Many of their problems could have been easily solved in the United States.

We also found many excellent and caring doctors, men and women who could perform a medical diagnosis as well as anyone but didn't have the resources or medicines to heal their patients. Powell met with one doctor who had developed a way to create heart valves for patients from their own tissue—because he had no access to other solutions. Doctors from Louisville and Baylor were flown to Romania to teach, and Romanian doctors were trained in Dallas and Louisville as well.

"We fell in love with those people," said Powell. "We realized that they were not only very lovely people but very appreciative as well."

One particular moment Powell remembered was the day he and I toured a cancer center with an uncompleted room that was to become a chapel in a city and country where religious practice had not been tolerated. Powell and his wife had suggested the chapel, but there wasn't enough money to finish it. The visiting medical team donated a few thousand dollars to finish it. As Powell and I left the building, an Orthodox priest came running up to thank us and give us a Bible.

"I'll never forget it," said Powell. "We all stood in a big circle right there, tears running down our faces, and sang 'Amazing Grace.' "

Later, I wrote:

> In a Romanian orphanage and in the AIDS hospital, we found infants and small children lying or standing in tiny cribs, row upon row, rocking back and forth in a heart-rending display of what we learned is called "unloved child syndrome."

In each institution, Boone Powell and I lifted some of the children from their cribs and held them in our arms, a simple act that seemed to provide comfort, but which was rarely performed in the overcrowded and understaffed locations. We resolved to use our knowledge, contacts, and resources to improve these unbearably sad conditions.

In the city's largest general hospital, I found extensive cracks in the walls, produced years earlier by an earthquake. As we made the rounds of the hospital, light bulbs were removed from the room we were leaving and installed in the room just ahead so we could see.

Not only was the hospital short of light bulbs, but it was also short of aspirin, antibiotics, cleaning supplies, and staff. What we saw was unbelievable. They had absolutely nothing.

Reports from other members of the research team showed an antiquated, mostly broken health system in which all nursing education had been underfunded for sixteen years. It was also apparent that after long years of socialist rule, the old adage was true: The workers pretended to work, and the state pretended to pay them.

Even more debilitating, Elena Ceauşescu had imposed two medical edicts that created more heartbreak. One denied access to birth control to women unless they had already borne four children. The result: thousands of unwanted pregnancies and overcrowded orphanages. The second mandated that all newborns receive a blood transfusion through the umbilical cord at birth. Lack of accurate blood-analyzing equipment caused about 13,000 infants to receive HIV-tainted blood and develop AIDS. About half of them died.

As Powell and I made our visits and were hosted by the local leaders at obligatory meetings and dinners, the rest of the research team met their local counterparts. The idea: identify Romania's forbidding challenges and find the best medical partners to solve those problems.

All of us flew home together on Humana's plane. I explained that each must write a complete report prior to our landing in Louisville as a condition to being allowed to deplane. I'm told that some of the eminent doctors were unaccustomed to that management style, but they all wanted to get home, so they all complied. Their reports formed the building blocks of our recovery program.

A later member of that support team was Dr. W. Ann Reynolds, whose broad resume would eventually include fourteen years at the University of Illinois Medical Center. She was chancellor of the California State University system, chancellor of the City University of New York, and president of the University of Alabama at Birmingham. She was also the first female member of the boards of Abbott Laboratories and Humana and was helpful in the Romanian adventure, along with her husband, Dr. Tom Kirschbaum.

To help address the country's medical problems—especially babies born with AIDS—I flew some Abbott Laboratories equipment to Romania, along with teams of doctors from American medical centers to train the Romanians. I had no idea of the power of volunteerism. I can't tell you how much I love those volunteer doctors and nurses.

Joining me on one Romanian trip was Dr. Frank Austen, whom I had first met while serving on the Abbott board. Austen, who had contracted polio as a child when there were no treatments except hot packs, was motivated to become a doctor by that experience. He attended Harvard Medical School and dedicated the rest of his life to the research and treatment of polio, immunology, and the biology of asthma. I asked him to join the Humana board to widen its expertise.

Austen's broad-based knowledge was also very important in the Romanian mission, although he joked that I had other reasons to invite him along.

"He needed somebody he could trounce at tennis," Austen said. "No matter how much I practiced, or how many lessons I took, every time I thought I was going to win he simply talked me out of it."

Austen did find some solace. I was later approached by the Harvard Medical School to fund a tenured professorship. It was named the K. Frank Austen Chair, with an emphasis on immunology, and was funded by the Humana Foundation.

Project medical director George Rodgers and I formed teams to help with "blue babies"—infants born with heart issues easily repaired with surgery not available in Romania. Doctors and nurses from both countries were flown back and forth between Louisville and Romania to train and learn.

Cataract surgery—then very rare in Romania—was implemented in Bucharest, helping thousands who had their sight restored. A general heart surgery program was established by teams from the University of Alabama at Birmingham.

The visiting doctors and nurses grew very close in mission and spirit. Reynolds had grown up on a Native American reservation and a small farm in Kansas, the daughter of Presbyterian missionaries. She went on several Romanian trips with Betty and me, traveling between cities by bus. The band of bus travelers often had a collective sense of joy and accomplishment, even with the long days, marginal food, and work-related issues.

The bus passengers would break out in songs on these trips; knowing the lyrics to practically every song, I led the way. I knew "Down by the Riverside," "Old Man River," and "I Could Have Danced All Night." I also knew all the lyrics of all the verses to many Christian songs, including

238

all five verses of "Jesus Christ Is Risen Today."

On one bus tour of Cluj, Romania's second-largest city—with the Humana board along—we planned to have a picnic supper out in the country. As the bus pulled into a small town, a little band appeared seemingly from nowhere to greet us, playing something akin to polka music. As the sun set, the driver turned on the bus lights, and all the participants began dancing in the bright light and shadows. Reynolds said,

> David and Betty love to dance. My husband liked to dance, too. So we're all out there, dancing with each other to Romanian accordion music. And then, kind of in the midst of all this, appears this elderly woman, with one cow, with great big horns on the cow. She is obviously thinking we are all nuts, and that we are impeding the highway.
>
> She clearly walked that cow every evening about that time, and that cow walked steadily right down the middle of where we were dancing. And the woman was right behind, carrying a switch.
>
> We all stood back and smiled and let that cow through.

On a trip in October 2004, Louisville photographer John Nation joined us. On Halloween weekend, he expressed an interest in seeing Dracula's castle, the site of Bram Stoker's Gothic horror novel, known as Bran Castle in Romania. A big van load of us, including Betty, the Lansings, and Virginia Kelly Judd, was on the way to a conference when the driver heard us discussing the castle and said it was only a half-hour away.

We stopped by the conference, I made a brief talk, and off we went down back roads, reaching the castle at dusk. The castle managers said they were closing, no more tours, so we bought fake vampire teeth at the gift shop and shot silly pictures as darkness draped the looming castle. It made for a memorable Halloween.

✳

George Rodgers, division chief of international pediatrics at the University of Louisville School of Medicine and the Romanian project's medical director, made forty-five trips to the country.

He spoke of his first visit to an HIV/AIDS unit in a Romanian hospital when AIDS had only just been acknowledged there as a disease. Looking around the room, he could easily identify children with other diseases such as chicken pox, hepatitis, or pneumonia—all presumably in addition to AIDS—but no effort had been made to separate them.

"They could only offer these children a place to die and some nutrition along the way, without adequate staff to offer them any significant attention," he wrote in a Humana book about the project. Rodgers would later write of the experience, the sixteen years of shared knowledge and medical kinship: "I have really no way to describe the many impacts that the Humana/University of Louisville Romania Pediatric Project has had on my life. It has broadened my knowledge and perspectives in ways I never could have imagined. It has given me hosts of new and wonderful friends both in Louisville and Romania."

It would also bring him a wife, Dr. Tania Condurache. They met in Romania, and she would later work with him on the project there and on trips I funded to Ghana and South America.

President Bush could know only part of the impact our efforts would have on the wider worlds of medicine and education. But Bush wrote a foreword to *The Dacian Chronicles: Transforming Romanian Healthcare, 1990–2006*, Humana's compilation of stories written by many of the hundreds of American and Romanian doctors, nurses, and others who joined in the venture, with a special salute to Boone Powell and me:

> The fall of the Iron Curtain in 1989 brought enormous opportunities for Eastern Europe and its millions of citizens—opportunities to think and act freely that hadn't been enjoyed for two generations. At the same time, it brought daunting challenges. The economies of the former Communist countries had been stagnant since World War II. Enormous

progress had to be made, first for these nations to get back on their feet, and second to become competitive with their neighbors to the west.

... In contemplating new ways to accelerate the process, I formed the Citizens Democracy Corps to assist the newly emerging democracies of Eastern Europe in their transition to market economies. I reached out to the American business community and contacted many leaders, including David A. Jones. He agreed to help, and recruited his friend Boone Powell, Jr., president and chief executive officer of the Baylor Health Care System in Dallas. They chose to help Romania.

In these pages, through the accounts of those who served, you will encounter a remarkable "before" and "after" story. What had been in 1990 a country whose health care system was both dispirited and dispiriting, was by 2006 transformed into a place of achievement, innovation, and hope....

In addition to the president's gratitude were the poignant words sent to me in handwritten letters from Professor Dr. Mircea Maiorescu, the Romanian minister of health. He first met Powell and me in 1990 and offered praise for the whole American team.

How could we thank Professor Rodgers for the openness of his heart, the enthusiasm, the competence, and the wisdom necessary to outline the perspective of a long-lasting program ... in a moment when—after long years of dictatorship—we nearly had lost every hope.

The encouragement and the restoration of our hope have been the spiritual present of the Humana/Baylor program for Romania.

Our visits to Louisville have had another outstanding impact: Nobody returned home with the same mentality he or she had before leaving, and everyone has been stimulated to a better conception and activity in pediatrics.

We have experienced another superb effect: warm sentiments of sympathy friendships have been ardent between the American and Romanian specialists.

It is said to save a life is to heal a whole community. The Humana programs have changed the destiny of a whole generation of children.

In another letter, Maiorescu would write of their initial expectations for our visit and his joy with the results.

But we don't know anything definite. Who are these gentlemen? Will they keep their promises?

After forty-five years of economic and social ruin, we are a little mistrustful. However, we must hope. . . .

In short time we are astonished. In the fall of 1991, the first pediatrician team from Louisville arrives, a team of admirable professors directed by Dr. George Rodgers. . . who are dedicating their time and capacity to Romanian pediatrics. In Bucharest? No, all over the country.

They are visiting the main pediatric hospitals in the country. They are evaluating the situation, making great rounds, lecturing, teaching, getting to know the Romanian pediatricians.

Look. They are doing a lot of things despite the language barrier. We are dumbfounded.

Chapter Twenty

With the Help of My Friends

" The company would evolve and change. It reinvented itself several times while I was there. But David never reinvented himself. He was always the same."

— PAUL URBAHNS

A s the Humana mission grew around the country and the world—particularly in life-saving missions to Romania and other countries—our extended family always included our Humana pilots, who flew the medical teams back and forth into the country. I'd always had a strong interest in airplanes and took great pride and interest in our pilots who flew them, many with life stories similar to mine.

One of the real veterans was "Captain" Bob Dearing, who rose from Louisville neighborhoods to trips across the United States and Europe.

Dearing's family had its roots in rural Lebanon and Leitchfield, Kentucky. His father, William, was a pharmacist, and his mother, Virgil, was a seamstress at Fleischer's clothing store on Louisville's historic Fourth Street.

Dearing was born on July 4, 1929, just before the stock market crash that signaled the beginning of the Great Depression. His family moved around from Old Louisville to Camp Taylor. He attended Manual High School, joined the Civil Air Patrol as a cadet during World War II when he was only fifteen, and would never again be very far from airplanes.

243

He would catch a ride or hitchhike out to Bowman Field—then Louisville's commercial airport—to hang out and help sell two-dollar tickets for ten-minute rides over the city.

"I'd get 20 cents for each ticket," he would say. "Hell, I didn't have any money. That got me car fare back and forth to the airport." The clientele proved to be very interesting: "Most of them had never flown before. They'd come out in their jeans and overalls."

In those early days, Bowman had seventeen flying services. One owner, Ruey Wade, often saw Dearing at the airport. He asked him if he wanted a job washing and fueling airplanes. Dearing didn't have a driver's license yet, so he had to pull the planes around to the gas truck by hand, fuel them up, and tie them back down.

He was a natural pilot—careful, diligent, and unafraid. Working with the plane owners, and catching free rides whenever possible, he soloed at sixteen, the year he was finally old enough to drive a gas truck to parked planes. He got his private license at seventeen, commercial license at twenty-one, and flight instructor certification at twenty-two. College was never even a consideration.

"I was hooked," he explained.

It was an inventive world. With no radio communication between pilot and tower in those days, a pilot had to wiggle the plane's wings to signal his intentions. Over the years, Dearing would work at Kentucky Flying Service and then seventeen years with the Brown-Forman Corporation, where he would fly Sally Brown, her husband, W. L. Lyons Brown, and his brother Garvin all over the country. Two of Sally's King Charles spaniels, Mercury and Venus, were often on board. Dearing was always sure to have doughnuts on hand for the flights.

"I didn't even know who Brown-Forman was when I started," he said, "but it almost tripled my salary."

The side benefits included access to any activities the Browns cared to partake in—Muhammad Ali fights, fishing at Cabo San Lucas, and nights at the famed Mark Hopkins Hotel in San Francisco. Sally Brown, a nationally known environmentalist, lived to be a hundred and was a generous donor to my projects. When she and I were on a flight, she yelled up to the cockpit, "Bob, where's the doughnuts?"

He flew for Plainview Partners, a development company, and the Dairymen's milk co-operative before being invited to test fly a new Citation 5 jet I had purchased.

"I flew it for about a week," he said, "and stayed ten years."

Dearing was assigned to Main Street Realty, my development company, but began flying my family and me quite often. He also used his photography skills to capture those moments, including the Joneses' fiftieth wedding anniversary and Christmas at our house with all the family there.

I began calling him "Captain Bob," a nickname that stuck so well it went on his license plates. He was always courteous to airplane passengers, a trait both Betty and I noticed, along with his pilot skills. The Jones family enjoyed skiing in Aspen, Colorado, a very difficult place to land because of the mountains and winds. It challenged even skilled veterans with many hours in the air.

As Dearing and I talked about our families and our parallel early-life experiences, we became close and developed a mutual trust. He helped take me to rehab appointments following my double knee replacements. One day after Dearing had given me some family pictures he had taken, he got a thank-you note and a check in the mail. He called me afterward to ask a question.

"Mr. Jones," he said, "I really appreciate what you do for me, but what I would appreciate most of all is if I can call you my friend."

"Friends we will be for life," I responded.

Dearing, after he retired, recalled one other memory of his flights. He was riding as a passenger in the company plane, with Betty and me up front, facing forward. I was on the left, Betty on the right. As the plane leveled off after takeoff, I rose and got Betty a cup of tea; I often served as a flight attendant for everyone on company flights.

I sat back down and began reading a newspaper as Betty read a book. I saw something interesting in the paper, made a comment, and handed it to Betty. We talked for a while. Growing tired, I pulled down the shade and leaned my chair back. Then I reached over to hold Betty's hand.

"And I sat there," said Dearing, "and watched that, and tears came to my eyes."

✳

Another Jones family and Humana pilot was Gene Van Meter, a native of Salem, Indiana, and a US Navy veteran of the Vietnam era. He served on the *USS Princeton*, an aircraft carrier so old it had a wooden flight deck. His upward path in aviation also came with a lot of twists, turns, and serendipity. With an early interest in aviation, he found a job for $1.40 an hour pushing airplanes in and out of the Louisville Flying Service hangars at Bowman Field.

Later, he was a utility lineman for Southern Bell, and he would take advantage of the situation to seek other employment by making calls to arrange job interviews while perched on top of a utility pole. He earned his pilot's license courtesy of the GI Bill. He worked for several companies across the country as an instructor and charter pilot. One flight, in the service of a funeral home, included an embalmed woman in the back seat, with her head propped up.

He began flying for Humana in July 1973 and flew often with me and others.

Van Meter also flew on the first and last company trips to Romania. On the first trip, the airport runway in Bucharest was a World War II relic—deteriorating concrete slabs that shook the plane. The airplane was cleaned by old women with homemade straw brooms. In time the pilots would take cartons of cigarettes to give the women in appreciation. They accepted the gifts with tears in their eyes.

On the first trip over, the hotel was dark and gloomy, with a gift shop featuring a can of motor oil and a Mexican T-shirt. Armed men escorted him everywhere. On his final trip over, sixteen years later, he stayed in a brand new, full-service Marriott Hotel.

Continuing the sense of family at Humana, Van Meter's grandson, Matt Van Meter, became a pilot for the company.

✳

Paul Urbahns was another Humana pilot who became part of Humana's "Romanian family." He would make many trips with us, including a flight to a hospital in Landstuhl, Germany, after our son Matt was wounded in 1991 in Operation Desert Storm.

Urbahns was born in Valparaiso, Indiana, the son of a steel-mill crane operator and a mother who stayed home to care for her three children. As a twelve-year-old, he began working for a farmer who owned an airplane, which led to a job at the county airport at age fifteen. He soloed on his sixteenth birthday.

"Flying just seemed so natural to me," he said. "I felt very comfortable."

He went to Ball State University for about a year, dropped out, took part-time jobs at gas stations, then worked at Sears, in a steel mill as a welder, then in construction. In a department store in Valparaiso, he met—by sheer coincidence—a pilot he had known while working back in the farm-field airport. The pilot, Herb Longnecker, then with American Airlines, said he was starting a flight school. Urbahns said he was still very much interested in aviation but didn't have any money for lessons to work on his ratings.

"I didn't say anything about money, did I?" Longnecker responded, remembering Urbahns's interest and abilities as a teenager. "We'll work out the payments."

Still working construction, Urbahns upgraded his ratings, then became an instructor himself. In 1969, on a trip with a northern Indiana friend to Kentucky's Mammoth Cave, he stopped by Bowman Field. On a whim, he went into Louisville Flying Service and said he was looking for a job as a flight instructor. Two weeks later, he was hired and was soon working fifty to sixty hours a week for $138.

After flying charter for several companies and having made contact along the way with pilots John Landrum, Ken Machtolff, Jerry Tillman, Bob Dearing, and Gene Van Meter, he was hired by Humana in November 1982. He soon began flying me on business trips with the artificial heart program and flew me and others to Romania.

He took notice of my knowledge of the company airplanes, how much I researched their capabilities, my ability to discuss those needs with salespeople and manufacturers.

"That is really unusual for most CEOs," he said.

Like several of the pilots, he joined me on the ski slopes and tennis courts. He regarded me, rightly, as a fierce competitor on the court but a more reserved presence when it came to business.

"The thing I admire about him the most," Urbahns would say "is the fact the company would evolve and change. It reinvented itself several times while I was there. But David never reinvented himself. He was always the same."

Urbahns made about a dozen trips to Romania. He became disgusted at all the money dictator Nicolae Ceauşescu had poured into his palace. He felt the same way when he saw the streets where the government officials lived, lined with expensive shops and apartments, while people were starving in the villages.

"We'd go into these towns, and people would be lined up to go to the meat market," he said, "and the meat market would run out of meat. So they'd shut the door, and people would walk away."

The pilots were invited to go on tours of Romania, including the famed Ploieşti oil fields of World War II and the Carpathian Mountains, where welcoming officials greeted them with trays of bread, salt, and brandy. Then would come lunch—with gypsy dancers and singers.

These wonderful pilots took me to amazing places and made it possible for Humana to act in emergencies when others didn't. In 1992, when Hurricane Andrew devastated South Florida, including all our health care clinics, we were the first medical team to respond. At the time, Humana was still operating in both the insurance and hospital fields. I hopped on our company plane, which was the first private aircraft to land there.

Bruce Perkins, then second in command of that Humana hospital region, said our first priority was to get the senior citizen clinics back up and running. The responsibilities were split between Joe Berding, head of the South Florida district, my brother Clarence, who was Humana's vice president of real estate, Perkins, and myself. Perkins concentrated on finding double-wide trailers to serve as temporary offices. Clarence worked on finding generators and water. Tanker trucks normally used to haul milk were cleaned out and used to carry water to the damaged areas.

Humana doctors and nurses from the Daytona Beach area loaded up a Winnebago and headed to the devastation. They worked around the clock, free of the paperwork that normally came with their jobs.

"David Jones was on the scene very quickly," Perkins recalled. "He got in his plane, and he flew down. He was all over the place, finding ways to help people—money to the Red Cross, medications, whatever. We were up and running in less than forty-eight hours."

For a whole month, we provided just about all the medical care in the area. Then the Army came in and brought clinics. But we were able to get there fast and make a difference.

I have often said this sixteen-year Romanian experience got off to such a good start because of Virginia Kelly Judd, who was on her second day on the job when the Romania project fell into her lap. I joked that Judd got the job because the Romanians couldn't understand the western Kentucky accent of her boss, former University of Kentucky basketball player George Atkins, who was from Hopkinsville.

Perhaps a little more important, Judd was fluent in French, a common language with Romanian officials. Judd was thirty-eight at the time; her path to French proficiency had come because of a little help from Betty and me many years earlier. Her life, too, was filled with game-changing events and serendipity. She was born in Louisville. Her father, Charlie Shuck, a salesman, was a former Army Air Forces pilot who had been shot down over Italy in World War II. He ended up in a prison camp in Germany, where his assignment in the camp kitchen helped keep him alive. Her mother, Kitty Kelly Shuck, had a year of college.

Virginia always aspired to go to college, but money was an issue. Her life's goal was to be involved someday in international travel and education, to work for the World Health Organization in Geneva, Switzerland, and speak French every day—a dream that seemed impossible. She had fallen in love with the French language in a freshman-level class at Waggener High School in Louisville, but her parents had divorced, and there was no money for college. Her grandfather, Edwin Kelly, president of the Peaslee-Gaulbert Paint & Varnish Company, would pay her way.

"I told him I very much wanted to go to college," she said, "and he answered, yes, he wanted to invest in my future."

She went to the University of Kentucky for two years, majoring in French, and found she was looking for a little more rigorous language training and skills. With her grandfather's approval and support, she spent a year in an international study program in Aix-en-Provence in the South of France. She and another UK student lived with a young French couple. Two girlfriends from Louisville's Sacred Heart Academy came over, and they toured much of Europe in a Volkswagen van—part of her dream realized.

She returned to UK, added some economics courses, and earned a master's degree with a fellowship at UK's Patterson School of Diplomacy. Still searching, she tried banking and real estate, then kept the dream alive, eventually teaching French part-time at Jefferson Community College and the University of Louisville.

Along the way, she met Betty in a graduate French class at U of L. They became friends and eventually taught French together at U of L. With Betty's encouragement, Judd enrolled in and graduated from the French School at Middlebury College in Vermont, the very intensive summer language school where Betty had received her MA in French a few years before.

I first met Virginia when Betty and I made a surprise visit to her very small dorm room at Middlebury. We sat on her tiny bed. Judd sat in her only chair. I listened as Betty and Virginia spoke in French. Betty offered encouragement. As we left, I looked her in the eye and told her, "Virginia, you can do anything you set your mind to. I believe in you."

She took the message to heart.

That moment of truth came in the summer of 1990 when Judd had lunch with Betty, who suggested she apply for a Humana management intern program. She had the credentials—the degrees, the work ethic. The Humana program was to include six-month rotations in four areas of the company. Her first assignment was in the public affairs department. She was placed in the library on the sixth floor.

Her second day on the job, George Atkins came by and said, "So I understand you speak French, and you've got this international degree. I need you to call the Ministry of Health in Romania, where we learned they speak French. They certainly don't speak English. We're getting our CEO ready to go on a fact-finding mission to Romania in a month, and we need somebody to help communicate, to set up these meetings."

"Sign me up," Judd replied.

There she was, her second day on the job, a dream job in her hometown as an intern for the booming Humana company. It would require 2 a.m. phone calls to catch a particular woman in the Romanian Ministry of Health. She set up site meetings and visits and prepared a briefing book for the delegation. She didn't join the first eleven-person group; she didn't feel qualified anyway. But when that group returned, I thanked Atkins for organizing such a great trip. Atkins responded, "Well, I didn't do it. Virginia did."

Judd was asked to come to the plane so I could thank her in person. I also handed her the eleven reports that had been written in flight and asked her to consolidate them into a two-page executive summary for me.

"I pretty quickly realized I do have what they need," she said. "I was kind of blown away by the serendipity of it all. But he has a saying, 'When preparation meets opportunity . . .' "

Judd prepared the report. She also visited some of the team members, asking what could be done to help, working on a volunteer train-the-trainer model. Humana's visitors to Romania could not rebuild and refurbish orphanages; that would be too daunting and expensive. The solution— along with helping provide new equipment and medical supplies—would

251

be to fill in the information gaps, bring some Romanian doctors and nurses to the United States, and have volunteers go to Romania.

"Can we bring them here so they can see what's possible?" Judd asked in her report. "And can they return with newfound hope and ideas on how to bridge that gap?"

The Romanian mission was always totally humanitarian. Neither Humana nor any other company involved has ever made any money from the program. Judd quickly became the Romania Assistance Project leader, making twenty-five trips to the country between 1990 and 2006 and helping when its doctors and nurses came to the United States.

In 1996, Betty and I donated a large building in Bucharest for a new National School of Nursing; Hillary Clinton flew in to give the dedication speech. I estimated the building would have cost about $6 million in Louisville, but it was only $60,000 in Bucharest because its ownership was in question. It had passed through German, Russian, and local Communist hands during and after World War II. Romanian laws covering ownership were unclear. Fortunately, in twenty-two years no one has surfaced to reclaim the National School of Nursing property.

In one of her more memorable trips, Judd had a room in an antiquated hotel in Iasi, a city in the historic region of Moldova. The hotel was run by monks from the Eastern Orthodox Church. Seeking to relax, she filled a large antique bathtub with warm water. When she pulled the plug afterward, she learned the opening was not connected to a drain; the water ran out onto the floor and down the nearby steps.

In all, 131 teams composed of 249 volunteer medical and technical professionals traveled from Louisville to Romania, joining sixty-four teams from Dallas and smaller teams from Mount Sinai Hospital in New York City, the University of Alabama at Birmingham, and several other states and nations. All expenses were paid by Humana Inc. and its foundation and the Baylor Health Care System. All labor was donated.

During the same time, 266 professionals from Romania traveled to Louisville for training that was focused on previously determined needs, with their programs lasting one to two months.

With valuable support from the Baylor School of Nursing, Romania reopened its school of nursing. Some thirty-five American nurses trained more than 4,500 Romanian nurses in infectious diseases. Humana's work included new pediatric diagnostic and therapeutic techniques in areas such as neonatology, oncology, and rheumatology. A clinical psychology program was begun. Cardiac mortality dropped as the American volunteers introduced coronary bypass procedures. Infant mortality rates dropped 29 percent over a decade. I was overwhelmed by the care and generosity of the volunteers, the absolute difference they made in so many lives.

Every participant was a volunteer. We had many doctors earning $10,000 per week who gave up several weeks to go train Romanian doctors, often making multiple visits. Their remarkable generosity has given me the clearest understanding of the desire of American people to help other people.

In 2006, when it was clear a new generation of Romanian doctors had been empowered to sustain the change and build on it, the program was ended. Around the same time, the Humana Foundation made a million-dollar gift to the University of Louisville Department of Pediatrics. Betty and I matched it to set up a state program. "Bucks for Brains" matched both gifts so that $4 million supports a program modeled on the Romania Assistance Project in developing countries in Africa and South America.

Heart surgeon Allan Lansing and I were honored by the Romanian government, each of us receiving the nation's highest civilian award. Lansing had directed the project's cardiovascular surgery program, which developed two state-of-the-art heart surgery centers and significantly improved surgical techniques and outcomes. I was also given an honorary doctorate from Ovidius University in Constanţa, Romania. The college and the award were named for Ovid, the famous Roman poet who died about two thousand years ago. George Rodgers received an honorary doctorate from each of Romania's eleven medical schools.

Betty, who made many trips with me, wrote in *The Dacian Chronicles:*

> One only has to look into the tear-filled eyes of a young Romanian mother, whose newborn is alive because of a life-saving procedure introduced by one of the teams, to understand what is being done in this country.

One moment we both shared involved Dr. Dan Stewart, chief of neonatology at the University of Louisville School of Medicine. While touring a hospital in Moldavia, he was quickly escorted by a frightened staff to an infant whose face was turning blue. Stewart took the baby in his arms, removed a tube that had been improperly inserted, and carefully inserted it in the right place. The baby immediately recovered. A tiny life was saved.

The thing about the Romanian trip for these doctors was that every single one of them wanted to go again.

Circa 1936

"The Fighting Jones Brothers," as featured in the *Courier Journal.* Logan, left.

Logan Jones, Sr. and the "brilliant and fearless" Elsie Thurman Jones. "We had a strong religious upbringing. I don't know how well it took, but knowing right from wrong was crystal clear in my family and our neighborhood."

Senior midshipman cruise to Norway and Denmark on the *USS Worcester*, summer of 1953.

"I would describe Betty as not just my wife, but my pal."

"The luckiest thing in my life was the person I married. Betty and I have been a team."

Home sweet home at Yale: Betty, Sue, and David, Jr. in front of their metal Quonset hut, 1960.

BUILDING HUMANA

WHERE IT ALL BEGAN

Heritage House, 1962

"Wendell Cherry was a steady, thoughtful presence in my life as we built Humana. In some ways, it was an attraction of opposites. I can be on top of ten things at once. Wendell was like a laser." 1986.

Celebrating Extendicare's initial public offering with J. David Grissom, Carl Pollard, Stephen Mann, William Ballard, Jr., and Charles Teeple, 1968.

"Wendell and I held a design competition that attracted five of the world's most eminent architects. Michael Graves (center, on the porch off the 25th floor, 1985) was probably the least known."

The American Institute of Architects gave the Humana building its National Honor Award. *Time* magazine named it one of the ten best buildings of the decade.

"I was confident of my successor, Mike McCallister. He was a perfect fit for success at Humana, a mix of hard work, preparation, teamwork, taking chances, and serendipity."

With Drs. Allan Lansing and William DeVries, and a Jarvik-7 artificial heart, 1984.

"Louisville was a segregated city when I grew up. Betty and I supported Louis Coleman's Justice Resource Center from its earliest days. His finest hour may have been shaming the Pendennis Club into integrating by staging a lunch right in front." Coleman, left, 1991.

photo: Pat McDonough

Mr. and Mrs. David A. Jones
35 Poplar Hill Road
Louisville, Kentucky 40207

2-26-14

Dear Kevin,

Truly sorry that we missed your Accreditation celebration.

What you've accomplished, with your talented and dedicated team, is remarkable, and so important.

We are so proud of you all!

Most sincerely,
David Sr. + Betty

"I believed in sending concise, handwritten notes to thank people, a kindness I learned from business guru Peter Drucker." Pictured, a note saved by Kevin Cosby, 2014.

With Kevin (second from left) and Laken Cosby. "After reading a story about Rev. Kevin Cosby's work helping St. Stephen youth overcome the myth of black inferiority, I made a significant donation toward his educational efforts."

"My involvement in the public arena included a role in the passage of the Kentucky Education Reform Act and getting the governor to find $50 million to build a runway to keep UPS in Louisville." With Mayor Jerry Abramson (left) and Judge Executive David Armstrong during a legislative debate over health care, 1990.

"Thurman Hutchins Park was a family enterprise. The 'Thurman' was from my mother and the 'Hutchins' from Betty's." Pictured: Four of the six Jones siblings. From left: Clarence, Jean, David, and (far right) Lucy, plus Logan's grandson Andrew and Betty.

I was no stranger to preservation efforts. To lure the national Presbyterian Church to Louisville, I donated two old Belknap warehouse buildings for their headquarters. Then I was given the task of being fundraiser for the renovation, which I was happy to do." 1988.

Romanian Assistance Project, 1990-2006

The humanitarian effort lasted sixteen years and involved hundreds of volunteer American doctors and nurses. "I often said it got off to a good start because of Virginia Kelly Judd (left), who was in her second day on the job when the project fell into her lap."

Hungary

Satu N

Oradea   Zalau

Cluj-

Arad

Mures

Timisoara   Deva

Resita   Torgu

Danube   Drobeta

After President Bush called, "I turned to my old friend Boone Powell for help." The Joneses with Powell and his wife, Peggy.

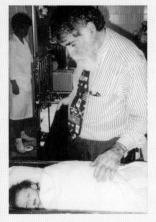

Dr. George Rodgers, the project's chief medical director, made forty-five trips to Romania.

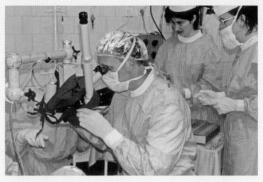

Dr. John Distler training ophthalmologists in Bucharest.

The Humana board gets a progress report in Cluj, 1998.

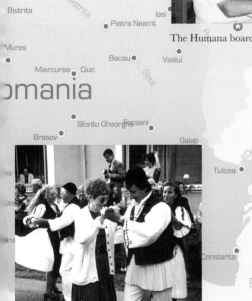

The group had long days—but also times of joy.

GEORGE BUSH

The fall of the Iron Curtain in 1989 brought enormous opportunities for Eastern Europe and its millions of citizens – opportunities to think and act freely that hadn't been enjoyed for two generations. At the same time, it brought daunting challenges. The economies of the former Communist countries had been stagnant since World War II. Enormous progress had to be made, first for these nations to get back on their feet, and second to become competitive with their neighbors to the west.

As president, I knew this would take a great deal of time. I also realized – through experience with such efforts as the Points of Light – that volunteerism could be a powerful vehicle to bring about real change.

In contemplating new ways to accelerate the process, I formed the Citizens Democracy Corps to assist the newly emerging democracies of Eastern Europe in their transition to market economies. I reached out to the American business community and contacted many leaders, including David A. Jones, chairman of the board and chief executive officer of Humana Inc. He agreed to help, and recruited his friend Boone Powell, Jr., president and chief executive officer of the Baylor Health Care System in Dallas. They chose to help in Romania.

In these pages, through the accounts of those who served, you will encounter a remarkable "before" and "after" story. What had been in 1990 a country whose health care system was both dispirited and dispiriting, was by 2006 transformed into a place of achievement, innovation, and hope, due in part to the Romanian Assistance Project. You will also read here of the healthy trans-national relationships built in the course of the last decade and a half. And you will follow the development of a successful public-private partnership model that can be applied in countries elsewhere in Eastern Europe and around the globe.

I salute the many contributors to this volume, whose narratives and photographs create an unforgettable story. It's a story in which all of us – Romanians, Americans, and citizens of the world – can justly take pride.

George Bush

Praise for the project from President Bush.

THE PARKLANDS

The youngest generation breaks ground for a park built for future generations.

"There are places for school retreats and field trips around plants, water, and wildlife, plus the ancient solitude of the Big Beech Woods."

Dan says, "Dad gives me credit for the success of the Parklands, but there is no way I could have done it without him. We became partners and friends."

The Parklands opened in 2016. Now visitors can enjoy twenty-five miles of canoeing and paddling, plus walking, hiking, and biking trails.

"Completing the Parklands would require eighty separate land acquisitions and about $125 million. It would become a very important legacy to me as we restored damaged forests and land, and planted thousands of new trees."

"I consider the Parklands one of the most important things I have ever done. The idea was to find ways present-day Louisville could match the hundred-year impact of Frederick Law Olmsted's work in Louisville parks, and to get ahead of growth while land was available and affordable."

The architectural elements in the Parklands invoke the rural architecture of Kentucky.

FAMILY FIRST

Fiftieth wedding anniversary celebration with, from left: Carol; Dan and Lisa; David and Mary Gwen; and Nancy.

"On weekends, we welcomed babysitting jobs for our eleven grandchildren."

Turning over the role of chairman of the Humana board to son Dave, 2005.

On the slopes with daughter Carol.

"We visited France every year or two because Betty speaks French so well and enjoys it. She makes all the arrangements. I just relax and enjoy." France, 2005.

th son Matt on his wedding day.

Hugging daughter Sue.

In the Parklands with son Dan.

Photo: John Nation

"Betty and I had five children in thirteen years. I'd say the hardest thing in our married life together was raising kids with good values. That was very intentional with us." Celebrating David's 85th birthday, 2016.

Photo: Ted Wathen

As the team worked together to create the Parklands, one of their main goals was "to get it finished quickly enough to allow Betty and me to tour it from one end to the other. They succeeded."

Chapter Twenty-One

MOM AND THE SIX KIDS

"My mom was a character. She was a powerful, powerful woman. I can't carry a tune, but she couldn't either, and she used to love for me to sing to her. She wanted me to sing 'The Old Rugged Cross' and 'Church in the Valley.' I can't sing a note, but I know all the words."

— DAVID JONES

The late 1980s brought the death of my beloved mother, Elsie Thurman Jones, on September 5, 1988, at age seventy-eight. Her death came almost exactly eleven years after my father, Evan Logan Jones, Sr., died on September 4, 1977.

Their six children, born a total of fifteen years apart, have all lived interesting, successful lives. Their extended families would meet often, telling warm and funny stories at reunions as the family grew to more than seventy. I helped them all, particularly in paying tuition for the younger ones as they continued through school and attaining college degrees. As always, those willing to work the hardest got the most help.

Logan, Jr., the eldest sibling in our family, was born on July 7, 1929, and died on October 18, 1982. He was the family leader, competed as a Golden Gloves fighter, and served as a combat infantryman in the Korean War. Logan wanted to begin fighting again after that, but his spleen ruptured, and he stopped. He was a valued employee of Publishers Printing Co. in

Louisville until his death of non-Hodgkin's lymphoma. I flew Logan and his wife to Houston for treatments. He is always remembered for his sense of humor, the tricks he would play on others, and his willingness to help when needed.

Logan and I made the monthly mortgage payments on our parents' home from 1953–1968, except for my three years in law school (1957–1960), when Logan made the payments alone. Logan's son, David Carroll Jones, a Louisville dentist, stayed close to me after his father's death. As a kid, he and his brother Rick would play with my son Dave, and we would all join together for Sundays at their grandparents' house. I later helped David Carroll with college tuition and purchasing his dental practice and home.

David Carroll Jones described our relationship like this: "When I lost my dad at twenty-five, my Uncle Dave reached out to me and asked, 'How can I help you? What can I do? Let's do this.' After sixty-three years of him being my uncle, he, at times, acted more like my dad than he did my uncle."

Another brother, Charles Jones, was born on July 24, 1934, and died on October 16, 2012. He graduated as a civil engineer from the University of Kentucky in 1956. His first job was working on the construction of Louisville's Watterson Expressway, the city's first attempt at modern highway construction.

Charles and I remained close. In the summer of 1957, I was just out of the Navy, working as an accountant and teaching night courses at the University of Louisville. Betty and I lived in an apartment on Glenmary Avenue, just one block from the seventh hole at Cherokee Golf Course.

The temptation was too much. Charles would pick me up at about 6:30 a.m., drive us down near the seventh hole, and park the car. We would slip onto the course and play holes seven, eight, and nine. Each of us would slide a dollar bill under the clubhouse door to cover our greens fees, then play the first six holes on the back nine, thus completing nine holes for our dollar. That's what it cost back then, and you could always find your ball out there because of the dew, but you had to putt twice as hard on the greens to get through it. I'll bet we played that course four times a week for eight or nine weeks.

Charles went to work for Bechtel International Engineering, a large firm in San Francisco. He was later in charge of building a bridge across the Mississippi River at Vicksburg. He then retrained as a nuclear engineer and worked on the construction of two nuclear plants near Vicksburg. He next moved to Anderson, South Carolina, to work at an atomic energy complex, enjoy his grandchildren, and golf at the famed Augusta National Golf Club nearby in Georgia.

Lucy Jones Wisner was born on September 20, 1938, and died on November 30, 2003. She worked as a computer programmer, a pioneer in the field. Her real love was books, and for many years she owned and ran the Once Again Gently Used Books store on Frankfort Avenue, an enterprise her mother could appreciate.

Lucy was an avid reader. She had thousands of books stacked in her store, on shelves, on the floor, and in crowded corners. Her many customers included her sister-in-law Betty Jones, who was always in search of the out-of-print books Lucy found as a pioneer in digital book shopping.

Lucy bought a house only about twenty feet from our mother's house on Fairmeade Road. After Elsie lost her leg in the accident in London, Lucy, along with her sister, Jean, and Jean's stepdaughter Teri, cared for her. Mom never went to a nursing home.

I was a twice-a-week guest at her house. I would sit at the table, drink coffee, and sing to her at her request. She was a character. She was a powerful, powerful woman. I can't carry a tune at all, but she couldn't either, and she used to love for me to sing to her. She wanted me to sing "The Old Rugged Cross" and "The Church in the Wildwood." I can't sing a note, but I know the words.

I read a *Wall Street Journal* report on the hundred highest-rated women investment bankers that brought my mother to mind. One said that while she was growing up, her family had a little red wagon, and the library was a two-mile walk from her house—a journey very similar to those my mother made with us.

Jean Jones Donoho was born on November 28, 1941. While very young, she married a man with a strong scientific bent. In 1957, when the

Russian satellite *Sputnik* had everyone worried, this young man sent up two homemade rockets that frightened the neighborhood and got him arrested.

The young man was brought before the judge with Elsie, his mother-in-law, in attendance. According to a *Courier Journal* story, as the judge pontificated about the rockets-over-Louisville event, Elsie, her Irish background on display, stood up in the courtroom and said of her son-in-law: "Judge, he's just a kid. If you have to put someone in jail, put me."

To which the judge responded, "Mrs. Jones, if you don't sit down and shut up, I'm going to send you both to jail."

That famous family story does not end there. Clarence, the youngest of the Jones children, then thirteen, delivered newspapers. Embarrassed by the story about his family, he carefully cut out the story of the court proceedings from every paper before he delivered them in their Crescent Hill neighborhood that morning.

The *Courier Journal* got calls from everybody in the neighborhood saying, "Somebody's cut a story out of the paper." So, far from keeping people from reading about it, everybody heard about it.

Jean and the young man were later divorced. Jean, after acing the interview examination, joined her mother working for the Census Bureau in Jeffersonville, Indiana, later transferring to the Internal Revenue Service. Jean became one of Louisville's finest bridge players, serving as president of the Louisville Bridge Association. A Life Master, she routinely played in Las Vegas and has played with Microsoft founder Bill Gates.

Clarence Jones, born February 11, 1944, joined the Army and later became Humana's vice president of real estate, where, among other things, he worked on the Florida rescue mission after Hurricane Andrew, eventually retiring to Florida.

My mom's energy and work ethic provided the foundation for our success. She had worked nights to provide for her family when her husband was unemployed. Later on, we easily could have supported her, but she chose to work at the US Census Bureau, where she could use her math and organizational skills instead.

One of her co-workers, Rita Stayton, who was just eighteen at the time, remembers working with Mom to draw maps of specific census districts. At least once, Mom took the Greyhound bus back and forth to Washington, DC, where she worked on a special project for six months. Then, when she got home, she regaled her family and friends with stories of things seen and heard along the way.

She started at the Census Bureau about four years before Wendell and I started what became Humana. According to Stayton, Mom worried about Wendell and me when we began building our nursing homes.

"She was concerned the business would be a failure," Stayton says, "but she was a very proud mama."

Chapter Twenty-Two

EVERY PARENT'S NIGHTMARE

"I didn't say anything to Betty about it the night we watched on television as someone who looked like our son Matt was carried off a Desert Storm battlefield, and she didn't say anything to me.

"Two and a half hours later—at 2:30 a.m.—our doorbell rang. Two Marines in full dress blue uniforms were standing at the door. I had one immediate thought: They only come to see you if your child has been killed."

— DAVID JONES

About midnight on February 24, 1991, Betty and I were home watching CNN as Operation Desert Storm—the massive US-led response to Saddam Hussein's invasion of Kuwait's oil fields—surged into Iraq. We were riveted. Our twenty-four-year-old son, Marine Lt. Matt Jones, was on the leading edge of the battle, serving as a rifle platoon commander with the 3rd Battalion, 9th Marines.

A 1989 Yale graduate with a degree in history, he had recently completed Marine Infantry Officers School in Quantico, Virginia. He graduated in 1990, only a week after Saddam's troops had invaded Kuwait, and was immediately shipped via Twentynine Palms, California, to Saudi Arabia in preparation for Desert Storm.

For six or seven months, we received frequent letters from Matt. We knew he was somewhere in Saudi Arabia. Then the night before the invasion, we received a call, Matt's first while overseas. On the move toward Desert Storm, his forty-man platoon had come across an Army post with a telephone exchange. Following Marine protocol, the enlisted men made their phone calls, and the officers followed.

Matt couldn't give us any details of his situation. He was in a war zone. The next night, Betty and I were watching the often-live CNN coverage of the invasion and saw someone being carried off the battlefield. It looked like Matt.

I didn't say anything to Betty about it, and she didn't say anything to me.

Two and a half hours later—at 2:30 a.m.—our doorbell rang. Two Marines in full dress blue uniforms were standing at the door. I had one thought: "They only come to see you if your child has been killed."

Matt had not been killed. All the two Marines knew was that he had suffered a head wound.

Betty, with her normal, calm presence, asked, "Does the fact you're here in the middle of the night say anything about the severity of the injuries?" The Marines said no; they were following protocols that required that parents be notified of all injuries.

Still, I feared the worst. You don't often survive military head wounds. I thought the two Marines were just letting us down easy.

I also asked questions, but Carol, our youngest daughter, who was home that night, remembers me sitting in my chair with a look of pain on my face, fearing my son was dead. "I'm not sure I've ever seen my dad cry," says Carol, "but I've seen him in really deep pain."

When the Marines left, the three of us huddled together in the front hall for a long time, needing one another. We lived the next twelve hours in anxiety, worry, and fear, desperately seeking information.

Then Matt called home. He told us that after being wounded, he had immediately been taken to the battalion aid station, where the battalion chaplain, a Vietnam veteran and a very fine Catholic priest named Dan Hall, reassured him that all the most critical parts of his anatomy remained attached. He was then flown by helicopter to Fleet Hospital Fifteen, a full-service Navy pre-fab hospital set up in Saudi Arabia.

He had just been through surgery. A piece of shrapnel had struck his left cheekbone and torn a chunk out of his face, almost ripping off his nose. It would leave a scar, but it missed all his facial nerves. He assured us he was going to be fine.

He told us that his platoon had caught heavy fire; in fact, nine of the forty-five Marines wounded in Kuwait were in his platoon. (One Marine, a pilot, was killed.) Matt remembered a mortar shell landing very close, shrapnel peppering his face and legs, and being "knocked out pretty good."

His flak jacket and helmet prevented more serious injury, protecting his organs and his spine. Plastic surgery, conducted by a highly skilled Navy Reserve captain who had left a lucrative Southern California practice to serve his country, would repair his face. Small pieces of shrapnel remain in his body today.

After about ten days in the Navy hospital, and more surgery, Matt was airlifted to Landstuhl, Germany, near Ramstein Air Base. Soon afterward, Betty, Dave, Carol, and I flew to Germany to see him. His first words after greeting his family came from a man wanting to read: "I lost my glasses. It would be great if you could help me get glasses," he said.

The first call to solve that problem was to Dr. Walter Freislederer, the head of the hospital in Augsburg and, at this point, a close family friend—with all five of his children having lived with the Jones family in Louisville and all five Jones children having lived with them in Augsburg. It was a Saturday, he said, and nothing in Germany was open on Saturdays and Sundays. The best solution seemed to be to have a pair of glasses sent over by UPS from Louisville. But before we could make the arrangements, in walked a young sergeant. He saluted Matt and said, "Lieutenant Jones, here is your gas mask, and we found a pair of glasses in the packet."

Matt's next request was for more books by Patrick O'Brian, author of *Master and Commander*, which he had read during the long drive to final attack positions along the Kuwait border. Our family quickly responded.

After recovering in Germany, Matt was sent to the Walter Reed Army Medical Center for a few more weeks of observation. He lived with his brother Dave and Dave's wife, Mary Gwen, in Washington, DC, where he received more visits from his siblings and parents. On his return to Louisville, almost fifty people were at the airport to welcome him home—family, friends, and pilots.

Chapter Twenty-Three

The Dying of the Light

"Once, Wendell and I met with Senator Jay Rockefeller in West Virginia on a business trip. After the meeting, Rockefeller told someone he could hardly keep up with the conversation because Jones would start a sentence, and Cherry would finish it, and then Cherry would begin a sentence, and Jones would finish it."

— DAVID JONES

Around Thanksgiving of 1990, just three months before Matt was wounded in Operation Desert Storm, Wendell, a lifelong heavy smoker, was diagnosed with brain cancer.

Subsequent research indicated his brain cancer had metastasized from lung cancer, slowly stealing his health. He had three operations, all at Humana Hospital-University, where Humana had previously recruited a team of specialists for just such procedures. He got second opinions. He knew he was in a category where maybe he had two or three years to live. As it turned out, he had less time than that.

Wendell seemed to bounce back from each operation and tried to remain active, but in the last few months, he was confined to bed at home. I visited him every day during the final months before he died on July 16, 1991. Those visits and the premature deaths of my close friends Cary Thompson and Allen Duffy, and my brother Logan, put every business problem I would ever face in perspective.

264

Wendell had been a steady, thoughtful presence in my life as we built Humana. We were totally honest with each other. I was the visionary, with Wendell never hesitating to bring reality into the picture. Our partnership made Humana possible.

"It was almost like we were married," I told *Courier Journal* writer Dianne Aprile for a March 23, 1997 profile. "We were sometimes mad at each other, but we also had that loving and respectful relationship."

In some ways, it was an attraction of opposites. I could multitask effortlessly; Wendell focused on one thing at a time. But our minds always seemed to be in the same space; we seemed to know what the other was about to say.

Once, Wendell and I met with Senator Jay Rockefeller in West Virginia on a business trip. After the meeting, Rockefeller told someone he could hardly keep up with the conversation because Jones would start a sentence, and Cherry would finish it, and then Cherry would begin a sentence, and Jones would finish it.

That's how simpatico we were. We were, however, polar opposites in one respect: Wendell's free exercise of profanity to make a point.

My son Dave remembers going on a 1971 spring break business trip in Florida with Wendell and me to check out a hospital. We were greeted by the hospital's top executive. As we walked into the building, Wendell put up his arms, banged on a flimsy door frame, and said, "Dave, this place is a piece of s——. We don't want to buy this."

We all quickly left the building.

"I remember that," David, Jr. said, "because it was like, wow, that was abrupt, and because I don't think I had ever heard a grown-up cuss before. I'd never heard my dad say a cuss word, but Wendell was not that way."

Our partnership had been incredibly successful. In 1989, Humana's revenues had surpassed $4 billion. Its health plan alone had grown into a $1 billion business. The company employed more than 55,000 people and had been chosen by *Forbes* magazine as one of "Twenty Corporations Best Prepared for the 1990s."

So 1990 was the best of years.

It was also the worst.

I don't know how Wendell and I bonded the way we did. I can be on top of ten issues at once. Wendell was like a laser; he did one thing at a time. I loved him. He loved me. He told me, just before he died, that I was the best friend he ever had.

I still miss him terribly. I continued to think about him as I made personal and business decisions long after he had died. But his lasting effect on me was not unique within his personal relationships or in the wider Humana family.

At the request of Wendell's son Andy, many of those friends, neighbors, family members, and Humana employees wrote stories about those relationships. An eighty-eight-page book, *Remembering Wendell Cherry*, was published in his honor.

The book's forty-six remembrances covered all facets of his personality. As Andy wrote in the prologue,

> So much was written about Wendell Cherry during his lifetime, but the accounts tended to focus on Wendell Cherry, the businessman; Wendell Cherry, the civic activist; or Wendell Cherry, the art collector.
>
> His booming laugh and the circumstances that provoked it, his delicious sense of irony and perspective, and his magnificently noble heart are largely unrepresented in the public record. The value of the stories grew for all of us as we realized that they alone—the personal memories of friends and family members—captured the essence of the man. In fact, they were all we really had of him.

Wendell's personal quirks, some softened by nostalgia in the shadow of his death, were legendary. A stepdaughter, Jennifer Morton, wrote of his love of mayonnaise sprinkled with Tabasco sauce and his tendency to eat standing up, with the refrigerator door open.

She remembered a time her mother was very sick and hospitalized.

Wendell cooked the family minute steaks every night for at least a month, with Morton adding the accompanying mustard greens.

"This meal never varied and was never questioned," she wrote. "If Wendell had declared that we were to eat minute steaks and mustard greens for the rest of my life, I wouldn't have objected."

By the time of his diagnosis, Wendell's work with Actors Theatre, the Kentucky Center for the Performing Arts, and the Humana Building had transformed Louisville's cultural landscape.

His sophistication and connections as an art collector enabled him to bring great works to the Humana Building and the arts center for public display. It was a golden age in the civic, arts, and architecture community that has never been equaled in Louisville.

In tribute, a breathtaking exhibit of "The Wendell and Dorothy Cherry Collection" would be showcased at the J. B. Speed Art Museum in 1994. It included works by Modigliani, Maurer, Munch, Degas, Klimt, Soutine, and Sargent—and a combined desk, cabinet, and clock designed by André-Charles Boulle, cabinetmaker for King Louis XIV.

Wendell, the worldly art collector, was never that far from his roots in Horse Cave (population 1,545 when he entered high school). Humana board member Carl Pollard tells of the time he was golfing with Wendell at Harmony Landing Country Club near Louisville. Wendell disappeared for a long time, and they found him over by a fence row thicket, eating wild blackberries, a habit he'd developed as a boy.

Michael Hendricks, who assisted in the construction of the Humana Building, told of the time when the newly opened building sustained a broken water line in December of 1985. The water inundated Cherry's antique-laden office, soaking a Persian rug, damaging an antique secretary, and ruining a patterned hardwood floor.

The office was cleaned out; then fans were brought in to dry the floor. When an enraged Wendell saw the damage, he walked over to the outer wall and kicked the broken water line, thus requiring his wife, Dotti, to take him to the Humana Hospital-Audubon emergency room to get several stitches in his foot.

Before leaving for the hospital, Wendell demanded to see everyone even remotely associated with the construction of the Humana Building at 8 a.m. the next day. About twenty nervous men were on hand as a still-angry Wendell limped into the room. He strongly insisted his office be fully restored by early January when he returned from a vacation. Hendricks wrote,

> After Wendell left, we construction types discussed the sheer impossibility of complying with the schedule. No one volunteered to forward these compelling details to Wendell, so the restoration began.

Louisville architect and friend Jim Walters first had to persuade a very reluctant owner of the hardwood flooring company—who was vacationing in Hawaii—to reopen his plant over the Christmas holidays to supply new flooring, which he did. The floor, walls, rug, and furniture were also refurbished in record time. Hendricks wrote,

> Wendell returned one Monday morning in early January 1986. I happened to ride up the elevator with him. We discussed the article in the current issue of *Time*, which named the Humana Building its "Building of the Year." He was visibly proud. Wendell got off the elevator at the sixth floor and walked without a limp down the corridor to his perfectly restored office.

Some of the more deeply personal stories touched on his attempts to stop smoking, his relationships with his seven children from two marriages, and his occasionally difficult partnership with Dotti Cherry, to whom he was married from 1977 until he died.

Dr. Roger Herzig, Wendell's oncologist, wrote of Wendell's determination to leave a special gift for Dotti, an English Springer spaniel—a breed Herzig's wife bred and raised. Although bedridden and close to death,

Wendell insisted he would pick the puppy. Herzig wrote,

> The puppies were taken to the bedroom. Wendell insisted on having the puppies in bed with him. As they romped in the bed, Wendell made his selection: Cleo.
>
> Wendell had the foresight to know the impact the puppy would have on Dotti. He was determined to make the puppy part of his legacy out of love for Dotti. He made his plans, and despite the unlikelihood that they could be completed per his specifications, he did carry them out.

Dotti Cherry recalled being at her husband's bedside as he died. She said,

> A few days before, Father Jerry Eifler asked Wendell's son Andy and me who was going to give Wendell permission to die.
>
> There was silence. . . . Then I said I had a feeling I should do it. "Well," Father Jerry answered, "I don't believe he will take it from anyone else."

Dotti was alone with Wendell as his breathing faltered. She kept saying, "Wendell, breathe," and he did so for six hours, a time span, she wrote, "that was very difficult for him physically, emotionally, and spiritually."

Wendell's medication was increased, but he never lost consciousness. Dotti described it as six long hours of incomparable grief, gratitude, and heartbreaking finality. As his breathing slowed, her final words came at last: "Wendell, there are no goodbyes for us. Where you are going, there is no time. I'll be with you in a heartbeat."

Then, she wrote, "With his usual sense of timing, Wendell took his last breath."

At his funeral on July 19, 1991, Marsha Norman, the Pulitzer Prize-winning playwright from Louisville, delivered the eulogy. She called Wendell "a man more heroic than his heroes. As wise a judge of life and art as ever lived. As generous a soul as I ever knew. As proud to be a

Kentuckian as if he had marched through the Cumberland Gap and discovered it himself."

Wendell's philosophy of life is posted in my office, where a personal note he scribbled has been framed on the wall. It says:

People before paper

In a memorial tribute held in the arts center on August 29, 1991, I said of my best friend:

> Our Humana building, mirrored so eloquently in the light and graceful walls of this art center, and the remarkable collection of twentieth-century sculpture in both locations, bear witness to his intellect, scholarship, daring, and, once again, passion.
>
> For above all, in everything he undertook in life, Wendell was a passionate man. His passion, coupled with a wry and ready sense of humor, made him a delightful companion, son, husband, and father. Coupled with his energy, intellect, and tenacity, this passion led to a lifetime of remarkable achievements, rare in any time and place, which leave a permanent, positive impact on this community.

I quoted the Italian-born poet, author, and educator Angelo Patri:

> In one sense there is no death. The life of a soul on earth lasts beyond his departure. You will always feel that life touching yours, that voice speaking to you, that spirit looking out of other eyes, talking to you in the familiar things he touched, worked with, loved as familiar friends. He lives on in your life and in the lives of others who knew him.

I also quoted the eighteenth-century Scottish poet Robert Burns on an epitaph Burns had written for a good friend lost:

An honest man here lies at rest,
As e'er God with His image blest:
The friend of man, the friend of truth;
The friend of age, and guide of youth:
Few hearts like his, with virtue warm'd,
Few heads with knowledge so inform'd:
If there's another world, he lives in bliss;
If there is none, he made the best of this.

Chapter Twenty-Four

THE COMPANY SPLITS

"There are a lot of companies that get hardening of the arteries, just like people do. It's really hard for a successful company not to become complacent. It takes real willpower to realize that anything you're doing, somebody's watching. And before you know it, they'll figure out a way to do it a little better."

— DAVID JONES

The year 1991 was tough for me in the most personal ways. I had lost my business partner and best friend, and Betty and I had experienced every parent's nightmare: the possibility of losing a child.

Not long after Wendell died, Humana directors Bill Young and Mike Gellert suggested that I needed help moving the company forward. Wendell's death was devastating on a personal level and could easily have been damaging on a company level, too. Young and Gellert knew that Wendell, as my founding partner, had been consistently willing to challenge me. Having another person like that on the board would be vital as Humana grew in the increasingly complex field it had chosen: running a large hospital chain and a growing health insurance company simultaneously. They wanted to recruit David Jones, Jr. to come home and join the company.

I would never have done that. I didn't want any of my kids working for me. But Young, once Humana's largest stockholder, and Gellert, longtime family friend, chairman of Humana's audit committee, and the New York investment banker who had taken Humana public, believed Dave would be a good counterweight to whatever impulsiveness I might show. So in the summer of 1992, Gellert went to Washington, took Dave to lunch, and shared his sense of need and possible opportunity.

Gellert told Dave, "Look, the company's always been a partnership. Now it's not. The board never really understood the magic of the partnership between Wendell and your dad, but now it's gone. Your family is the company's largest shareholder, and you ought to think about whether there's a role for you."

Humana was in a tough spot in the early 1990s. While Wendell was sick, I was looking more closely at its challenges in integrating health care with health insurance—activities that fit together in some ways but also triggered conflicts of mission and goals. For example, hospitals benefit from filling more beds and serving more patients, while insurers benefit when members stay out of the hospital. The conflicts between the businesses made me think of splitting the company in two.

Health insurance had been a rather sleepy business segment until the passage of the federal Health Maintenance Organization Act of 1973, which was pushed by the Nixon Administration as a response to rising health care costs.

At its core, an HMO pays for care delivered through a defined network of doctors and hospitals, while traditional indemnity insurance reimburses customers for whatever bills they have to pay. HMO premiums are often lower because HMOs contract with specific providers, negotiate lower rates, and then organize such "managed care" features as a primary care doctor for each health plan member to serve as a gatekeeper for that member's care.

I first became aware of HMOs in the early 1980s when a Humana-owned hospital in Phoenix lost a large local HMO contract to a rival hospital group. The Humana hospital had been doing well, but its patient census quickly dropped. When you're in a fixed-cost business, as hospitals are, and you lose a good bit of your revenue, the costs don't go down. I thought HMOs could be the wave of the future, and we had better look into them.

That became more obvious to me when, at about that same time, a local doctor began to organize an HMO at Baptist Hospital in Louisville. Humana decided to compete, and in 1984 we started selling health insurance. Our strategy was to offer lower premiums tied to the use of Humana hospitals—and it worked. After enrolling 50,000 members in 1984, we insured more than 600,000 people in 1986.

I saw that the insurance business was just like the hospital business. Both were old and ready for a change, and I've always believed there's nothing being done that can't be done better. Along with anticipating a better future in the insurance business, I thought it would be exciting to build another business. It was something I enjoyed, and the insurance competition at that point didn't look too strong.

But jumping into a new business we didn't really understand introduced another serious learning curve, both steep and expensive. The first lesson came quickly and was costly: We lost $150 million in 1986 because we had priced our insurance policies too low. We cried a little over it at the time, but in retrospect, that insurance loss was a good wake-up call. It was basically a $150 million investment, and it would be our only investment in what, by 2018, was a company with a $38.8 billion market value. I was certain we could learn the insurance business, as we had previously learned the nursing home and hospital fields.

It took longer to learn that hospitals and health insurance couldn't thrive together in one company. As the insurance division grew, so did the tensions. Blue Cross plans began to whisper in one of our ears that they didn't like the fact that their payments to Humana hospitals were also financing our assault on their own insurance business. Meanwhile, doctors were whispering in our other ear, "Your insurance side can squeeze us by paying us less to treat the patients you insure. But if you're too tough on us, we can move our patients you don't insure to your competitors' hospitals."

In 1991 Humana owned seventy-eight hospitals in the United States and Europe, with 1.7 million members in its health benefit plans. It had a strong cash flow, ample to service the company's debt. So I said to myself, since these two businesses are in conflict, we'll just split the company.

Many companies get hardening of the arteries, just like people do. It's hard for a successful company not to become complacent. It takes willpower to realize that anything you're doing, somebody's watching. And before you know it, they'll figure out a way to do it a little better.

I explained this later in a July 1992 interview with the *Chicago Tribune:* "Humana has reached another of the periodic turning points in history when a strategy, effective in its time, must be abandoned in favor of clearly focused new strategies appropriate for current conditions."

Our company had begun thirty years earlier with nursing homes. It had moved into hospitals, then insurance, and would now spin off its hospitals to shareholders.

It was those issues, along with Wendell's death, that sent Mike Gellert to talk to Dave about coming back to Louisville to help. Dave was then working in the general counsel's office at the US State Department, a job he loved and to which he'd brought extensive international experience and interests: teaching English in China; international banking in Hong Kong, Boston, and New York; and relevant study and writing at Yale Law School. He also had an exciting job offer from his client at State to go to Singapore to become founding executive director of the Asia–Pacific Economic Cooperation forum, which would grow to include twenty-one nations with huge economic interests bordering the Pacific Ocean. He had done legal work on its formation.

Dave had come home years earlier to try to help resurrect Belknap Hardware after I purchased it. As the company moved toward failure, he commuted to Louisville during his first semester of law school to lend help and support—and to see me in some hard circumstances. He had admired my willingness to spend millions to pay off Belknap's many unsecured creditors, something, from a business point of view, I didn't have to do. "But from the moral point of view," said Dave, "he thought it was right, and he's always done what he thought was right." He continued,

> There are many lessons I've learned from my dad. One thing he always says is that when you're in a hole, stop digging—and when Mike Gellert approached me, Humana seemed to be in a hole. Another is from Teddy Roosevelt: It's better to be in the arena because you can't win if you don't play. Dad was enthusiastic about splitting the company, and I thought there was a big opportunity.

Dave talked to Gellert about Humana a few more times, then he and Mary Gwen talked it over with their families for a couple of weeks, weighed the pros and cons of both Singapore and Louisville, and sat down one night over their best bottle of red wine to decide. As Dave recalled, "Mary Gwen was emphatic that our next move had to be to a foreign country. But she said that either Singapore or Kentucky would count."

I was Humana's board chair and CEO when Dave returned from Washington. He first joined the law firm of Hirn Reed & Harper, and then a year later, he started his own business, Chrysalis Ventures, with another young entrepreneur, Doug Cobb. Betty and Doug's mother were lifelong friends. Dave and Doug partnered with and provided risk capital to young and innovative businesses in the Midwest and Southeast, investing more than $400 million in some seventy-five companies by 2018 and working their way through more than 1,200 offers a year.

Dave was our best board member ever, eventually becoming chairman.

It was a learning experience, perhaps mostly for me. Dave never did work for me, and as a board member became one of my bosses. Early on, when I was handing things off to him, he came to me one day and said, "Dad, don't hand me anything else. I've got my own business. You do your business and let me alone." I've always been happy with such sentiments—it's a way for people to grow, and I expect them to.

To separate into two companies, we needed the right people to make it work. Carl Pollard, my longtime friend and business partner, had succeeded Wendell as Humana's number two executive and agreed to go with the hospital company—called Galen Health Care, after the Greek physician and philosopher. Pollard is a gifted and brilliant leader, and I knew he would succeed. Although the hospitals made all the profits, I was convinced the insurance business offered a brighter future, so that's where I stayed. I'd been watching other people in the insurance business and told myself we could do this better. It was a significant move, but I always tend to look ahead, not behind. I don't get emotional about those things.

Pollard called the split "very difficult," and it took about a year to finalize. Decisions had to be made on salaries, benefits, shared services and facilities, and who would stay with Humana and who would go with Galen. I likened the details of the split to "trying to unscramble an egg." Down through all levels of the company, there were real battles going on about who would go and stay where. And I was the ultimate arbiter of that. But all that worked out. In a transaction like that, you just have to do it. And it gets done, and life goes on.

To position both companies for success, we needed to make sure both had sufficient capital—just as when we sold the nursing homes to fund our hospital strategy. In 1992, the insurance portion of the company was not yet profitable, so to provide each company sufficient working capital, Bill Young, the board, and I agreed to cancel the annual one-dollar-per-share dividend on about 160 million shares. That decision prompted a call from an analyst at Fidelity Investments, demanding that we reverse that decision. It would hurt the stock price.

"I'm sorry," I told him. "This is a decision we've made. We had good reasons to make it. We're not going to reverse that decision."

The stock took a hit, but by canceling the dividend, Pollard had adequate capital, and so did we. Humana stock was selling for about $18 a share when the company split. Humana, the insurance company, sold for about $6 a share, with Galen, the hospital company, selling at $12.

The division became effective on March 1, 1993, after the stockholders voted. It separated old friends. Humana board members Bill Young, John Landrum, and David Grissom went with Galen, which was first headquartered in a Main Street building that was later torn down to build the 22,000-seat KFC Yum! Center arena. The boards of the two companies were kept totally separate, with no overlapping directors.

After spinning off its hospitals, Humana was a much smaller and less mature company. Revenues for the insurance business in 1992 had been $2.9 billion, on which we lost $107 million. In 1993 they were $3.1 billion and positive $89 million, respectively—a long way from the profitable juggernaut before the split. But I believed in the future. Before long, I sold all my stock in Galen and reinvested proceeds in the new Humana.

My son Dave never was employed by the company. He saw his role as representing shareholder interests on the board, which he joined in May 1993 after the split was completed. Dave started learning the business by apprenticing himself to our former general counsel, Tom Flynn, who was overseeing the split in an outside law firm. Dave dug deep into our structure and operations under the time pressure imposed by the split, which gave him an intensive introduction to the company. After joining the board, he applied that same intensity to his independent due diligence on the business. He asked executives and market leaders for help learning and made solo visits to our markets, call centers, physician offices, and independent sales agents. He also attended industry conferences to listen to our competitors and analysts.

Tom Flynn, a straightforward, honest Irishman, was our first general counsel. A good general counsel has to be like your conscience, and Flynn was great. He was intense, but he had a strong sense of humor. Not long after he joined us, when I knew he was doing a good job, he came to me and said he'd been offered $60,000 to go to work for Holiday Inn in Memphis. And I said, "Tom, I'm glad you stopped in to see me because I was about to tell you that I've raised your pay to $100,000."

Tom replied, "I don't think I'll go to Memphis."

Galen Health Care didn't last long as an independent company. Pollard merged Galen with Columbia Hospital Corporation in a deal where Galen ended up with about 82 percent of the Columbia stock and control of the board, and Louisville as headquarters. It was like Jonah swallowing the whale. I spoke with Pollard about it, but the final decision was always his.

Pollard became chairman of that board, and Rick Scott, who eventually served two terms as governor of Florida and was elected to the US Senate after that, was president and CEO. Scott was a contentious figure in Louisville because he promised to keep the company headquarters and foundation in town but then moved them to Nashville, taking many executive jobs to Tennessee.

In moving out of town by December 31, 1993, Scott was avoiding Kentucky's onerous intangible property tax on his Columbia stock—a tax later ruled unconstitutional by the US Supreme Court in a North Carolina case. Aware of the deadline, Scott had photographers and accountants document Columbia's departure just before year's end.

The taxes were real. From Scott's standpoint, Kentucky was making it impossible for him to keep his promise to stay in Louisville. So, I don't have any hard feelings for Rick about that. It bothered some, including me, that Nashville was the beneficiary of half the Humana Foundation. In the split,

Galen had gotten half of the money, almost $30 million, which ended up part of the Frist Foundation, controlled by Thomas Frist, Jr., the founder of HCA. We had to rebuild the Humana Foundation, and we did. By 2010, it had grown back to about $100 million, and as the stock boomed and the company made more contributions, it would later grow to $400 million. I stayed on the Humana Foundation board after I retired from the company because I believe in the importance of its work for Louisville.

Pollard retired from Columbia in 1994, moving into the Thoroughbred horse business and becoming chairman of the Churchill Downs board of directors. He had somewhat nervously purchased Hermitage Farm, a large Oldham County operation owned by the late and legendary horseman Warner Jones (also a Churchill chairman, and breeder of Dark Star, who handed Native Dancer his only defeat, in the 1953 Kentucky Derby).

I offered, and Pollard agreed, to go in on half the farm price, with the understanding that for ten years, Pollard could buy me out for what I'd paid. I knew nothing about raising and training Thoroughbreds. But Pollard was a dear friend, and I had confidence he would make the enterprise work, so I offered to join him in that business as well as in owning the farm.

But Pollard had other ideas. He told me, "You've bossed me around for twenty-five years, and you're never going to boss me around again."

So he rejected my offer.

On March 1, 1995, twenty-seven years after Wendell and I bought our first hospital, Humana turned over the management of Humana Hospital-Lexington, its last remaining hospital, to Jewish Hospital HealthCare Services of Lexington, a former competitor.

The Galen-enhanced hospital chain in Nashville did well, but ultimately not nearly as well as the insurance company, Humana.

Part IV

RETIREMENT, RESCUE,
AND REINVENTION

Previous page:
On top of the Silo Lookout at The Parklands of Floyds Fork.

Chapter Twenty-Five

GOING BACK, PUSHING FORWARD

"The board voted unanimously to pass the proposal. Humana would go digital. The financial effect was almost instant—and it wasn't good. As expenses rose to pay the $500 million cost, the stock price fell again, and Wall Street analysts issued worried warnings.

"Wall Street, the smartest people in the world, thought we had lost our minds and were wasting our money. Yet I knew that not launching the new digital program would be even more dangerous. Kodak and Xerox had ignored the digital revolution and failed to thrive."

— DAVID JONES

When I turned sixty-five in 1996, I was ready to turn over the CEO reins—but I needed a successor. An heir apparent with a long record of success in Humana's hospital business left the company that year when weaker-than-expected earnings revealed the company's lack of depth in the health insurance business.

The company turned to Greg Wolf, CEO of a health insurance company Humana had acquired in 1995 based in Green Bay, Wisconsin. Wolf was named COO, and enthusiasm for his leadership ran high. In December 1997, he was named CEO, and I celebrated the occasion by giving Wolf a small replica of my favorite statue: Rodin's *The Thinker*. It symbolized my belief that the CEO's primary job is to think—and then act to lead the company in the right direction.

I continued to chair the board of directors as Wolf ran the company. Growth continued, but performance and profits were erratic, and the stock price fell. Meanwhile, the health insurance sector was consolidating, with many mergers and acquisitions. When United HealthCare came calling in 1998, Wolf was interested and quietly began exploring a possible sale of Humana.

Betty and I were on a Yale alumni cruise on the Rhone River in France in 1998 when I received news that a deal was coming together to sell Humana to the Minneapolis-based United HealthCare, creating the nation's largest HMO. Although I was still chairman of Humana's board, Wolf had not told me that a sale was in the works.

Betty and I were having a good time. We used to visit France every year or two because she speaks French so well and enjoys it. She makes all arrangements, and I just relax and enjoy. We were to visit a region of France she had not seen, so Betty was excited. Then, while the ship was stopped in Lyon, I received the call about Wolf selling Humana. With sadness, we departed, returning to Louisville, where I first joined, then led, our negotiations with United HealthCare.

The sudden talk of a possible sale was shocking to Louisville; one of the city's great employers and benefactors was on the line. The prospect produced a *Courier Journal* story reminding Louisville of Humana's growing reach across the city and well beyond. The monster headline across the front page on May 29, 1998 blared, "Louisville corporate giant bought in $5.5 billion deal."

Headlines on other front-page stories written by six reporters said: "Headquarters to be lost; job impact unknown" and "Sale hurts city's pride, prominence." It all sounded inevitable, save for a little front-page box that said, "What's Next? The deal must be approved by shareholders and federal regulators." It could become final by September—only four months away.

Much more than jobs would be lost. The Humana Foundation had given away $83.5 million since 1981, much of it benefiting Louisville and the state of Kentucky. In both 1995 and 1996, it had given more than $7 million to at least twenty-five groups, with about 51 percent to education, 18 percent for arts and culture, 16 percent for health and human services, and 15 percent for community development. Its 1996 value was estimated at $66.7 million. Although we had learned from Galen's departure five years earlier to keep the Humana Foundation out of the deal, a sale of Humana would mean the loss of thousands of jobs, vacancies in downtown Main Street buildings, and, perhaps more important, a big void in city leadership.

The story mentioned the Jones-Cherry team's leadership in developing Waterfront Park, the arts center, the Humana Building, the old Belknap Hardware complex, the Waterside Building, the Clocktower Building, Witherspoon Garage, and Louisville Slugger Field.

United HealthCare chairman William W. McGuire predicted the merger would save $100 to $250 million yearly, mostly by eliminating administrative costs, merging operations that overlapped, cross-selling service to each other's customers, and lowering payments to hospitals. United HealthCare had about 30,000 employees and Humana about 19,000, with the proposed merger allowing United HealthCare to operate in forty-eight states and Puerto Rico.

With the merger, which the companies hoped to complete very quickly, United HealthCare would assume $850 million in debt. Layoffs were likely. The result would be a health care company with more than 10 million members and projected 1998 revenues of $26.9 billion with a net income of $755 million, or $2.75 a share. United HealthCare would keep its name and Minneapolis headquarters but retain "a significant workforce" in Louisville.

Under the agreement, which was subject to approval by regulators and shareholders of both companies, Humana stockholders would receive one share of United HealthCare for every two Humana shares, which would value Humana shares at $32.06, a 22 percent premium.

The front page of the *Courier Journal* also included a story headlined, "David Jones, ever optimistic, is at peace amid the uproar." It quoted me as saying the sale could create a "painful rupture" in the Humana executive family, as some would have to move to United HealthCare headquarters in Minneapolis.

Talks about how to put the companies together continued through the summer, but the planned merger suddenly failed because of the startling news on August 6 that United had taken a $900 million restructuring charge with job cuts, the sale of various businesses, and the surprise revelation the company was unprofitable.

The situation clearly hadn't been given enough pre-merger investigation. United shares plunged 37 percent, meaning Humana shareholders would have received only $3.1 billion in United stock instead of the promised $5.5 billion. The companies agreed to terminate the merger contract and go forward without the distraction of litigation. Stock prices plunged.

Louisville and its many Humana employees felt a strong wave of relief, but it was hardly universal. The investment bankers who had been leading negotiations before my return were disappointed. They make a lot of money on these deals.

And other merger ideas came along after I retired, like the failed combination with Aetna in 2017.

Humana had grown rapidly between 1993 and 1998, including a $400 million deal to acquire Miami-based Physician Corporation of America. It also won several US Department of Defense contracts to offer health insurance to millions of military families and veterans under a plan called TRICARE. Although Humana was the third largest publicly traded managed-care company in the nation, its income faded as the cost of health care outpaced premiums. In 1996, the company left thirteen unprofitable insurance markets.

A *New York Times* story quoted one analyst as saying, "The industry is offering $1,000 in benefits when it can only afford to provide $750."

I acknowledged the problems: I was slowly gaining knowledge through trial and error—a lot of error. We wanted to grow the company. We began to gain traction. We got better at what we were doing. We tried to bring in people with knowledge and capabilities that we didn't have. Frankly, we had lost a lot of executive talent in the Galen spinoff.

Wolf abruptly left Humana in August 1999 as the *Courier Journal* banner headline declared, "Wolf resigns as CEO of Humana." I returned as interim CEO. The August 4, 1999 story led with: "The rocky twenty-month tenure of Gregory Wolf as chief executive officer of Humana Inc. ended yesterday afternoon when the company announced he had resigned 'to pursue other interests' following two consecutive quarters of earnings setbacks."

Along with the Humana stock drop, Wolf had been buying other unprofitable insurance firms. When asked if Humana's board of directors had asked for Wolf's resignation, all I would say was, "Greg offered his resignation, and we accepted it." I told the *Wall Street Journal*, "When you have been in the business as long as I have, not much surprises you."

On the day before Wolf resigned, Humana stock was down to $10.25 a share from $22 just a few months earlier, a more than 50 percent drop during his twenty-month tenure. Ken Abramowitz, an analyst with Sanford Bernstein who followed the health care industry, said Wolf's departure was probably part of a move by me to put the company back on track quickly.

"Often when companies aren't doing well," Abramowitz said, "retired chairmen roll up their sleeves and come back to turn it around. I suspect that's what's going on here."

Humana's board offered me several hundred thousand shares in stock options as an incentive to return to the company. But as the largest individual shareholder, I didn't need any more incentive to help the company out of the ditch, so instead, I divided the shares among the key members of the team that would lead the company's recovery. In addition, with the stock near record-low prices—at one point, it sank to $4.70 a share—I offered additional stock options to key members.

※

With Humana's stock at a low ebb, there was speculation that the company might become a takeover target for a second time. As I told the *Courier Journal*, "If I were trying to buy somebody, I'd rather buy them at a lower price than a higher one."

But Louisville again dodged the corporate bullet that could have led to the loss of one of the city's biggest benefactors. Soon after moving back into leadership, I appointed what I called a "troika" to help me lead Humana's recovery: Mike McCallister, Jim Murray, and Ken Fasola. With those three superheroes, we did damage control first, then strategy.

Murray was typical of so many successful Humana executives, with a blue-collar background that inspired a sense of family values and loyalty. He grew up in Cleveland, the only child of a father who hung drywall and a mother who worked as a bookkeeper. He worked summers beside his father, with all the attendant taping and dusty sanding. He attended Catholic schools, earned an accounting degree from the University of Dayton, and worked for ten years for Coopers & Lybrand in Cleveland. His wife, Nancy, was one of nine children. They would raise three children.

Murray was transferred to Louisville in 1984 when Coopers & Lybrand wanted to work more closely with Humana. The company was then switching from hospitals into insurance, with its brief fling with the Medfirst "Doc-in-a-Box" business—strip-mall clinics with a small number of doctors and nurses to handle routine medical issues. Though small, the venture had been highly successful, but it alienated many of the physicians who admitted patients to our hospitals, so we sold it.

"I think what David Jones was doing back then was probably about twenty to twenty-five years ahead of its time," said Murray, referring to the medical clinics in retail locations today.

As an accountant, Murray was one of the first people to recognize the serious financial problems facing Humana after Wolf's unwise purchase of other insurance firms.

He remembered having many sleepless nights as he watched the stock drop to $4.70 a share.

"I kept seeing higher and higher levels of losses," he said, "and there were times when I thought Humana would go bankrupt."

Murray's arguments with his colleagues in the late 1990s eventually led him to talk to me, where he shared all his worries about the company. Murray recalled, "I'm assuming that he's going to get pissed off and start yelling at me, and he looks at me and says, 'Jim, the sun will rise tomorrow.' What he was saying to me, was, 'You'll figure this out. I respect you, and you'll figure this out.' He put a lot of faith in me, and that sent a strong message that forced me to deliver the results for him. I owe everything I have to him."

Murray, then Humana's chief financial officer and later chief operating officer, saw me step back a little and allow him, McCallister, and Fasola to lead the company. They got the turnaround started, and McCallister—selected by a board search committee headed by David Jones, Jr.—became the new company CEO on February 1, 2000. I stayed on as non-executive chairman until 2005.

While the troika focused on operations, Dave, then vice chairman of the Humana board, came to me with another suggestion that would lead the company's comeback: Join the digital revolution.

"Dad," he said, "there's something out there called the internet, and if you can't harness that for your business, somebody else is going to take your business away."

We went to an internet conference together and, seeing firsthand the strong interest and possibilities in the digital world, I knew he was right. I immediately named Dave chairman of a net initiatives committee, joined by Bruce Goodman, Humana's chief information officer, and J. Pegues, vice president of strategy.

A valuable consultant during the change was Jacque Sokolov, another of my hires with a fascinating personal history and mindset. He worked with the net initiatives committee as it decided to recommend a $500 million investment in the digital world.

A brilliant student, Sokolov had entered the University of Southern California at sixteen and its medical school at nineteen—without a college degree. He then moved on to the Mayo Graduate School of Medicine, becoming a nuclear cardiology fellow. He spent five years at the University of Texas Southwestern Medical Center in Dallas, where he met his wife, Dr. Mitzi Krockover.

In the 1980s, he became a medical and insurance pioneer in "predictive modeling," a field that would change insurance companies and sophisticated health systems by using historical data and developing mathematical tools to predict costs and improve patient outcomes. "Insurance companies," he said, "had always been pricing their product in the rear-view mirror, as opposed to profiling their patients or their population and analyzing what they think is going to happen. I honestly felt there were very few physicians and clinically oriented people who sat around those large boardroom tables that really understood why certain populations of people cost more money and, at the end of the day, how we could really change the health care system positively by using some business techniques and applications, as well as clinical applications."

As a result, Sokolov, then thirty-two, formed a consulting firm called Advanced Health Plans, later Sokolov Strategic Alliance. Its mission was to work with corporations to promote predictive modeling for their company insurance plans. The goal was to cut costs and improve health care at the same time. Salaried doctors and medical clinics would be part of the plan.

In 1997, when his wife became Humana's vice president of women's health, Sokolov moved from Texas to Louisville. In the late summer of 1999, I called him to suggest we meet for lunch at a Denny's restaurant in Louisville.

We discussed a digital, consumer-driven health plan that would allow patients, insurance companies, and the medical community to transact their business online faster and at much less expense than in the paper- and phone-based present. The plan would allow doctors to check medications, insurance companies to monitor claims, and patients to check their status. Sokolov then became one of the few consultants I would hire in my life.

The internet would change Humana's entire way of doing business, from creating health plans to resolving claims to paying doctors sooner—using tools that most people didn't even know existed. One example I cited: A paper-based medical claim could cost five dollars to process; a digital claim might cost 10 cents. Such savings, multiplied by millions of transactions in Humana's growing Medicare and Medicaid markets, could produce enormous savings with fewer errors.

Over the next four months, the net initiatives committee created a recommendation for me, showing what the company could accomplish with the new system. It was also becoming obvious that it would take years for all parties involved to plug into the network, and the estimated investment cost could be $500 million. Dave believed it would be money well spent.

"If you get everybody online in real time," he told me, "wonderful things will happen."

Sokolov presented a slide show of the new plan's possibilities—and its estimated costs—at an October 1999 board meeting, provoking a discussion that lasted several hours. Many in the room grew impatient. At about 11 p.m., I took over a somewhat worn-out board to ask for a vote on authorizing the money to create the new digital Humana, a concept then basically unknown in much of the medical insurance business.

I went around to each director, acknowledging their histories in hospitals, insurance, pharmaceuticals, and academia, and asking their opinions. Then I added my own. "We've heard from virtually every constituency in the country that relates to health care except one, the shareholders. Being the largest single shareholder, I can tell you what the shareholders are thinking. If we don't go along with this digital proposal, we are going to be out of business. We're going to be bankrupt or acquired in the next few months."

I knew Humana was dealing with serious financial problems because of hospital and market issues and inefficiencies and that the company was ripe for a takeover. I saw the solution, as always, was to simplify by creating a single system that could cover the entire operation.

The board voted unanimously to pass the proposal. Humana would go digital. The financial effect was almost instant—and it wasn't good. As expenses rose to pay the $500 million cost of the digital plan, the stock price fell again, and Wall Street analysts issued worried warnings, even as Humana continued to improve its bottom line.

"Wall Street," I said, "the smartest people in the world, thought we had lost our minds and were wasting our money."

As Humana spent that $500 million over the next few years, I was terrified some other company would buy us at that bargain price. Yet I also knew that, given the company's economic shape, not launching the new digital program would be even more dangerous. Kodak and Xerox had ignored the digital revolution and failed to thrive. I said, "The economy is strewn with companies left behind in the digital revolution. There isn't a business or a company in the world right now that doesn't need to understand how changing technology will impact its business."

Our stock dropped like a rock because, as always, I wrote off the investment as we spent the money. I could have treated the $500 million investment as an asset and written it off over time, reasoning that it would serve us well for ten years, so we write it off over ten years. Many companies would have put that on their balance sheet as an asset.

But I don't believe in that. I never did that at Humana. We never ever had such a "time bomb" on our balance sheet. I believe in telling the truth. That's what it finally comes down to.

We never had an unfunded liability. We never had a defined benefit pension plan. We had a 401(k)-like plan years before anybody had ever heard of a 401(k) pension plan.

To implement the new health plan and build a team, I appointed Gene Shields, a retired Air Force colonel who was Humana's senior vice president for government programs. Then I had Shields and his team move into another downtown building, totally free to innovate.

Shields later said that launching the health plan "was a lot like planning for the Normandy invasion." He said the process required a new look at technical and design issues when the digital revolution was still new. All the medical, business, and government entities had to be connected to the Humana people involved.

"But the Humana team was up to the task," Shields added.

The team decided to test the new concept in the Memphis market, where it was moderately successful. Meanwhile, the whole company was moving online in real time, quite early for the medical insurance business, while McCallister focused the core business on the blocking and tackling of sound pricing for good benefits and service. By the time I retired as chairman in 2005, we could look back on five years of an incline that looked like a financial hockey stick—level for a while and then almost straight up. Revenue rose 36 percent while earnings per share rose 246 percent, more than tripling. The stock closed at $31.72 on the day I retired, well up from that dismal $4.70.

And I was pleased from the outside to see that slope continue. Humana's 2018 insurance revenues reached $57 billion, up from $10 billion in the year I retired. By September 2018, approaching twenty years after the failed attempt to merge, a share would be worth $334, an increase of 7,006 percent. I hope my habit of strategic thinking, followed by all-out support for the next company episode requiring the confidence of total ignorance, will remain part of Humana's DNA.

Chapter Twenty-Six

Walking Away From Death on 9/11

"I went back upstairs and asked everyone to prepare for a walk north. The group then included all twenty-four Humana employees and seven vendors. Some were pulling luggage on rollers, leaving footprints and long thin lines in gray dust. Their trek was described as if they were refugees seeking shelter. A woman's stylish black shoe lay in the middle of the street. A piece of a man's yellow tie lay nearby. There was little conversation. Hundreds of people were crossing the Brooklyn Bridge on foot. Nothing seemed real."

— DAVID JONES

As dawn broke over Louisville on September 11, 2001, I boarded a plane for the ninety-minute trip to LaGuardia Airport in New York. My destination was a high-tech showcase called the Digital Sandbox, at 55 Broad Street in Manhattan, near the World Trade Center towers. Once there, I was scheduled to join Humana colleagues who had arrived a day earlier to prepare for the rollout of the digital system that would revolutionize Humana.

The new system, which we called Emphesys, would bring Humana into the internet age. Almost two years after the Humana board meeting that launched Emphesys—and after thousands of hours of work by company employees to put it together and test it—the plan was ready to go.

After a trial run of Emphesys in Memphis, the national media rollout was scheduled for the Digital Sandbox in lower Manhattan at 10 a.m., only a few blocks from what would become Ground Zero.

Twenty-four Humana employees and executives would be on hand—myself included—along with a half-dozen tech experts from other companies. The night before, many in the Humana group had dinner at the Windows of the World restaurant atop the World Trade Center. They canceled plans to eat breakfast there the morning of 9/11.

Top-shelf executives from Oracle, Reuters, *The Wall Street Journal*, and Cisco Systems had been invited to the rollout. In all, perhaps 150 people would be in the room. Diane Davis, a Humana marketing specialist who had assisted in the production and planning of the New York rollout, later wrote of the gathering:

> Fortune 200 health insurance company Humana Inc. had developed an intelligent online health insurance product that promised to change everything.
>
> And there is no doubt that in a new dawn, it will. To win in the game of high-tech internet functionality, it helps to be first to announce your product to the right people, at the right time, at the right place. September 11 in Lower Manhattan was carefully selected with this goal in mind, and all the cards were falling into place.

Her passage, with its unintended irony, was one of more than twenty essays, poems, and remembrances written for a book I published titled *Stories From 55 Broad Street—September 11, 2001*. I gave the book to all the employees who shared that day.

I had just returned to Louisville on September 10 from a trip to Ireland with Betty. I flew to New York early the next morning, a Tuesday. I wrote in the book's introduction:

> The destruction of the World Trade Center and the deaths of thousands of our fellow citizens have indelibly marked every American. For those in New York's financial district on September 11, 2001, the proximity of the violence produced a

297

unique set of impressions. In hopes that their experiences will help us all come to terms with the meaning and consequences of that horrific day—to hearten the living, even as we honor the dead—these stories are set forth.

One of the Humana tech employees, Sam Garas, wrote of his excitement about being in New York that weekend—a mix of business and pleasure in a city he loved to visit, under the blue skies of autumn.

> We started Emphesys, Humana's new digital health plan, almost two years ago. I joined in May of 2000 with the great hope of using technology to revolutionize the health care industry. Revolutionize may be an overstatement for health insurance, but this was Humana, one of the best companies to work for in Louisville, and I was given a chance to develop something new from scratch that nobody had done before.

On Monday, September 10, Humana executives and technicians spent a long day at the Digital Sandbox rehearsing presentations and coordinating the displays, systems, lights, screens, and web feeds for the event.

The work was exacting, with three rehearsals. Afterward, Humana executives Mike McCallister, Jack Lord, and Bruce Goodman hosted dinner for about thirty people in a private room at the Windows on the World restaurant on the 107th floor of the World Trade Center. It lasted well into the night.

> It was a gorgeous night for taking in the intoxicating view of the city that never sleeps. From the restaurant, you can gaze far below and marvel at the imagination, creativity, talent, and skills that were amassed to create the World Trade Center.
>
> —ANTHONY CHOATE, technology manager

Other Humana employees ate dinner at the China Grill at Fifty-Third Street, then took an informal walking and subway tour. They got off at the World Trade Center and wandered its shops before heading to their hotels, some staying at the Marriott World Trade Center Hotel beside the twin towers and others at the Marriott Financial Center Hotel nearby.

The morning of September 11, those at the World Trade Center Hotel left earlier, but at 8:40 a.m., the group staying at the Financial Center Hotel was riding in a van to the Digital Sandbox. Their driver made a U-turn directly in front of the World Trade Center Hotel. At 8:45, the first terrorist plane struck.

> We had driven two blocks when we all heard a loud explosion. All bodies immediately leaned to the left side of the van. Faces and hands pressed against the windows, trying to look high enough to see what was happening.
>
> A bright orange ball of flame engulfed the upper portion of one of the towers, and a large black plume of smoke was already rising to fill the sky. Millions of pieces of paper began a slow-motion descent toward the streets below. As we watched, we could see shattered pieces of glass glittering in the sunshine. They looked like tiny mirrors rushing past the pieces of paper in a surreal race to be the first to reach the ground.
>
> — ANTHONY CHOATE

Humana colleagues were in various places when the first plane hit. Mike Gellert, a board member since 1967 and founder of Windcrest Partners in New York City, had just come up from the subway when the South Tower collapsed. He was enveloped in a thick cloud of smoke and dust. He tried to outrun it, ducked into a Starbucks for shelter, then moved to a third-floor laundry, where he stayed until the smoke cleared enough to allow him to walk to his office on Forty-Second Street. Others found their way to the

Digital Sandbox on foot or by rented van.

> Some of us were out walking on the street trying to get a bagel
> that morning. . . . We made a choice when we got to the
> World Trade Center not to go in the little shops there. Had we
> done that, we would have been in there when the first plane
> hit. But we had turned right and gone into another store.
>
> I didn't hear the first plane. We were on the street when the
> second plane hit. It was eerie. You saw enormous clouds of
> smoke and all this paper settling down, some of it still burning
> when it got to the sidewalk.
>
> You got the sense that paper was part of people's lives and
> part of civilization. And it was all going up in smoke. It's hard
> to comprehend. People were just standing there with hands
> over their mouths, eyes wide open. It was total shock. We can't
> believe this was happening. We can't believe this is happening
> so close to us.
>
> We were seeing emergency vehicles going in and knowing
> an hour later they were trapped under rubble and weren't
> coming out.

— BRUCE GOODMAN, chief information officer

Humana CEO Mike McCallister sat for a five-minute interview with
Bloomberg Television that morning. He and others with him had just
gotten into their van when the first plane struck the north tower of the
World Trade Center, only five blocks away. Their driver shouted, "It's a
bomb! There's been a bomb! Oh my God."

Traffic stalled into total gridlock. Tiny pieces of steel were falling
from the sky, along with burning debris. People on the sidewalk stopped,
uncertain of what had happened, staring at the smoke and fire. Trapped in
traffic, McCallister decided they should leave the van and walk.

"We're getting out," McCallister said.

"No, you stay," the driver said.

"No," McCallister answered. "We go."

He and the others headed toward the Digital Sandbox. As they walked, the acrid smell of jet fuel hung in the air. How was that possible? McCallister felt the ground shake as one of the towers collapsed. He would tell people he was "the luckiest person they ever met in their lives" for his escape—as well as the escape of the others—and would forever think about the events of 9/11 and the bond created among all those who lived through it.

> When we arrived at 55 Broad Street, we were able to watch CNN. That's when we learned about damage to the Trade Center. We all watched the coverage in disbelief. We were very, very mindful we were just five blocks away.
>
> And then the second plane hit. That's when we knew the first plane wasn't an accident. We canceled our event and continued monitoring the televised news coverage. I asked our team back in Louisville to send out an e-mail message from me letting everyone know it was okay to leave work for the day.
>
> — MIKE MCCALLISTER, CEO

I was drinking a cup of coffee at a Starbucks on the ground floor of the Digital Sandbox when the first plane struck. I watched as people ran in panic from the World Trade Center; then I saw McCallister and his party approaching 55 Broad Street on foot.

Along with all those already in the building, we gathered in a technology center. A news helicopter was broadcasting a live feed. We watched in stunned disbelief on a screen about twenty feet tall and thirty feet wide as the second plane struck the South Tower.

> We all gathered around a television in the Q and A room, and after a few minutes, the South Tower began to fall. It collapsed in a sickening thud that made the lights flicker and turned the

outside from day to night—from clear to black—as a massive wall of dust rolled down Broad Street.

A voice came on the building's intercom and announced that we should all go to the basement. For the first time, immediate peril to our group seemed real. Was lethal dust seeping into the building? If so, why the basement? The basement was somewhere I knew I didn't want to go. It summoned images of a concentration camp—the sudden and final point in a journey of horror that had begun only minutes before.

— TOM NOLAND, senior vice president, corporate communications

The group was herded into a freight elevator, which dropped them down to a bare room with a low ceiling and a few chairs and tables. There was no food and no television—no idea what was happening outside. Someone decided to make a food run up to the fourth floor, where the canceled news event would have been held. Noland went along.

I was seized with panic when I came into a hall and couldn't find any stairs. The elevators weren't working. Someone found the door to the stairs, opened it, and said, "Put a shoe in this so we can get back out if we're trapped."

The door to the fourth floor was open. Within minutes the rest of our team joined us—some hadn't gone to the basement at all. As the dust was settling from the South Tower's collapse, making it possible to vaguely discern the shapes of the buildings out the window, the North Tower came down. Once more, the outside world went black.

— TOM NOLAND

The group fell into a routine of watching television, making calls home from the few phones that worked, munching pieces of kiwi and honeydew melon, and staring through the fourth-floor windows into gray nothing. The intercom announced medical help was available. In time the outside dust settled, revealing the grim, surreal scene.

> Cars, streetlamps, stray boxes, everything was thickly covered with dust. It looked like it had snowed gray. There was the same sense of eerie quiet that comes after a heavy snow. The streets were empty except for a couple of guys peering out from an entryway and an occasional person walking rapidly to the north, mouths covered with cloth. No vehicles moved; the few parked cars looked like abandoned dust sculptures.

> — TOM NOLAND

The Humana visitors in the room were in a mix with people who worked at the Digital Sandbox every day. They lived in New York and had friends who worked in the World Trade Center. The tragedy unfolding before them was more personal. As they watched a replay of the World Trade Center collapse, one young woman doubled over, sobbing, inconsolable.

> Over the next several hours, we watched, listened, and absorbed the news as it came. We had been attacked by terrorists, by the insanely criminal, who took away thousands of lives—workers, police, firemen—buried just a few blocks away.
>
> My first call was to my wife to tell her what had happened. After the second World Trade Tower collapsed, I decided I would call my daughter to tell her I was OK, but also just to connect, to hear her voice. I called her school, identified myself, and said I wanted to get a message to my daughter, who is a teacher.
>
> Before I could say another word, the voice on the other end told me she would go get my daughter because she would

want to speak to me. She put the phone down and walked away. After about a minute, I could hear footsteps returning, then my daughter's voice, shaky and on the verge of tears.

It seems as if the initial message delivered to her was, "Your father is going to be OK" and nothing more. For over an hour she had watched the images on TV and had no idea what "going to be OK" meant. When I told her I was fine, she started crying. That's when I felt things well up in my throat and eyes. As I blocked back my reaction, all I felt was love.

— FRED SMART, senior marketing manager

At about 1:30 p.m., I suggested I go down to street level to check the air quality and the possibility of escape. Joined by Drs. Jacque Sokolov and Jack Lord, I found a police officer who said we could walk north but would first have to walk a couple blocks east to avoid the wreckage.

I went back upstairs and asked everyone to prepare for a walk north. The group then included all twenty-four Humana employees and seven vendors. I had an apartment on Sixty-Ninth Street where they could all stay temporarily, a walk of about five miles. Humana pilot Paul Urbahns had a daughter with an apartment on Twenty-Fifth Street, where some people could stay if they could not make the longer trek to Sixty-Ninth Street. At age seventy, I still played squash and tennis regularly, so I was undaunted by the idea of a five-mile trek.

Some were pulling luggage on rollers, leaving footprints and long thin lines in gray dust. Their trek was described as if they were refugees seeking shelter. A woman's stylish black shoe lay in the middle of the street. A piece of a man's yellow tie lay nearby. There was little conversation. Hundreds of people were crossing the Brooklyn Bridge on foot. Nothing seemed real.

Diane Davis took many photos of the street scenes that would appear in the book, illustrating this dim, gray, silent movie. The narrative continued:

Before our walk, we initiated a "buddy" system, three people to each group, charged with assuring the presence and safety of their buddies. My buddies were Bruce Goodman and Jacque Sokolov.

Several of our colleagues found tablecloths and cut them up and wet them for masks. They were helpful, as passing emergency vehicles stirred up the dense dust that filled the streets. Bruce, our chief information officer and former worker on Wall Street, guided us with remarkable skill, and soon we emerged from the danger zone into beautiful weather but a chaotic scene of dazed, unbelieving people moving northward.

— DAVID JONES

I hoped we could find some still-functioning public transportation along our way to get us out of the city. The group had walked for about twenty-five minutes when, as if by miracle, we came across an empty twenty-eight-seat tour bus parked on a deserted street. The driver, a man named Adam, was working under a raised hood.

I asked him if he would take our party north to drop off some people on Twenty-Fifth Street and proceed farther north to Sixty-Ninth Street. The driver hesitated, saying police roadblocks might stop us. I told the driver I would make it worth his while.

All of us walkers got on board, stowing our luggage below as our saga took another turn. One extra passenger was added, an older woman who also had been walking north. No one got her name, but it turned out she was a 1948 graduate of the University of Louisville's Kent School of Social Work.

Once on board, Mike and Bruce began to broaden the driver's charter, asking whether he could take us all the way to Louisville. When he found out how far it was, he declined, but faced with the superb negotiating skills of our team and the promise "we would make it worth his while," he agreed to take us as far as Philadelphia, where we thought we could charter a bus for the remainder of the trip.

Rosanne Miller and Debbie Alexander (my assistants) in Louisville were working on the bus charter. Bruce was working the phones, Mike led the negotiations, and I sat beside the driver and showed him where to drop various passengers as we made our way slowly north.

As we crossed the George Washington Bridge at 4 p.m., there were twenty-four of us left, twenty-two from Humana, one vendor, Steve Lieber from Chicago, and an invited guest from Washington, Larry Atkins.

— DAVID JONES

Adam eventually agreed to take his busload of strangers to Harrisburg, Pennsylvania, some four hours and 175 miles away. The trip had issues of its own. The bus burned diesel fuel, which would require stopping at three or four gas stations as the needle neared "empty."

A few minutes after the bus crossed into New Jersey, a rear tire blew out. It had dual tires, so the driver continued, with the passengers hearing the thump, thump, thump of blown tire against wheel well. The exit from the expressway into the city of Union provided a little more excitement, as the driver had to suddenly cross a concrete median—and another lane of traffic—to get to the exit, with horns blaring and angry drivers careening around the exiting bus.

Bruce Goodman had lived in New Jersey and knew the turf. He directed the bus to a tire shop. It didn't have the right size tires, so Goodman guided it to another, which did. Meanwhile, the voyagers waited near the first tire shop, where they found some sustenance from vending machines.

Steve Moya stayed with the bus to the second tire stop to protect valuable luggage, and the rest of us descended on a convenient golf driving range, which offered toilets, water, soft drinks, and nibbles since no one had eaten since breakfast.

With a new tire and diesel fuel found by our New Jersey hero, Bruce Goodman, we set out for Pennsylvania. No buses were available in Philadelphia, but Rosanne and Debbie had arranged a Capital Trailways charter in Harrisburg.

At 9 p.m., right on schedule, we rolled into the lovely riverside city of Harrisburg, which had been suggested by the two Pennsylvanians among us, Ken Fasola and Luisa Charbonneau. With Ken's help, we quickly found the Capital Trailways bus depot and a larger, more comfortable bus waiting to take us to Louisville.

— DAVID JONES

Only then did McCallister and I ask the bus driver what his charge would be. He said $150 a passenger, or $3,600 total, a fee that everyone agreed was reasonable given the situation, the tire-and-fuel issues, and the mileage covered. But most of his passengers had credit cards and little cash. I offered to write a check to cover expenses, but the driver refused. He did not take checks. He had no idea if a David Jones check was good.

Mike McCallister began collecting all available cash from the passengers, coming up with about $1,000. Jacque Sokolov, who always carried cash for emergencies, came up with the remaining money. I gave the driver a check for $1,000 as "a gift honoring his selfless act of friendship," and the group headed to Louisville.

After leaving Harrisburg, where we found no restaurants open after 9 p.m., the bus headed toward the Pennsylvania Turnpike. It stopped at an Appalachian Microbrewery, which had stopped serving food, but did provide a cooler of beer. Heidi Margulis shared some vodka she had purchased in New York, and Jack Lord handed out some Tylenol, but sleep was still very difficult for many headed home. Recalling long night watches at sea during my Navy days nearly fifty years before, I went right to sleep without medication.

The bus came across a twenty-four-hour restaurant called Eat'n Park

307

in western Pennsylvania. It was our first full meal. The food and service were excellent, and the restaurant staff gave us a big bag of cookies to snack on after hearing our stories.

Breakfast was at a McDonald's in Florence, Kentucky, just south of Cincinnati and about ninety miles from home. Mike McCallister bought the remaining *USA Today* newspapers, which were filled with stories and photos of 9/11. Not everyone wanted to read them or look at the photos of the World Trade Center dissolving in flames.

The Humana group bonded over the nineteen-hour journey home in ways we couldn't have imagined, with memories about those left behind that still linger. And thoughts of *why not me?*

Beth Bierbower will always wonder if the man who helped her in the deli at the World Trade Center at six o'clock on the morning of 9/11 was still alive. She later learned that two high school classmates, one a longtime friend, were on the flights that crashed into the towers. Dick Brown thought of the innocent children on the same planes.

Heidi Margulis, the daughter of a Holocaust survivor, would write of her mother fleeing a burning school in Germany, her grandfather's perilous path through German concentration camps, and her mother and family arriving safely at Ellis Island in 1941, not far from where the World Trade Center went down.

She wrote about the need to remember but to move on, make a difference, hold family close, and never forget.

Fred Smart had similar thoughts:

> It's interesting how people respond to an experience such as we all shared that morning and how that reaction grows during the day. Some sat without speaking, listening to others share their thoughts. Some laughed and joked their way through their concern. Some who you think would have lots to say, didn't. But each face reflected to the others the collective shock and fatigue that we shared.
>
> The last leg of the bus tour was one of the more memorable

parts for me. I got a chance to spend some time with Mr. Jones, just talking and listening. In the face of enormous success, wealth, and fame, I don't know that I have ever encountered a warmer, more genuine and caring person. He had moved to the very back of the bus and was sitting with Anthony Choate, Luisa Charbonneau, Mary Sellers, and myself. He asked us about ourselves, our jobs at Humana, and our families with genuine interest. He talked about his wife, his children, and his grandchildren with exceptional pride.

I don't believe that everything happens for a reason. I don't believe that some guiding power allows innocent people to die just to teach a lesson or prove a point. I believe we give things a reason so we can bring something of value away from something that makes no sense.

I had stayed at the Marriott Financial Center because the Marriott Trade Center was full. I walked right under the Center Tower at 7:50 a.m. instead of 8:50 a.m. because we had randomly chosen an earlier meeting time. I was safely inside and not on the street because I had decided at the very last instant to leave the hotel early in search of coffee instead of having the hotel's continental breakfast as I had done the morning before.

I am unequipped to sort this out or understand it all. All I know for sure is I was there, and through luck, coincidence, or God's grace, I am still here to share the day and my experience with others.

With a lightning bolt as a prod, I have relearned the overwhelming importance of the basic things in life, no matter how clichéd that may sound. My family, my health, and the sound of my daughter's voice may be all that truly matters on this, that, or any other day.

— FRED SMART

As the first signs for Louisville appeared along Interstate 71 southwest of Cincinnati, some of the passengers clapped; others quietly cried. When we arrived in Louisville at about 9 a.m., the group scattered to their cars to waiting families. Some went home, changed, and went to work the same day, sharing stories with their fellow Humana employees. Keeping a promise to my executive assistant Wanda Ryan's husband, Mike, I played eighteen holes of golf with him that afternoon.

Chapter Twenty-Seven

Betting on People

"Rosanne Miller watched me deal with all issues. She was there when decisions were made on hospital expansion and when work began on the Humana Building and the Kentucky Center for the Performing Arts.

"Her insight into people and memory of all Humana events were legendary. She remembers the day the Humana Building was dedicated. My mother was at the ceremony, and someone asked her how her son was doing.

" 'Which one?' Mom asked."

— DAVID JONES

As I learned from our very first nursing home opening, the secret to success in any company is to find the right people, train them well, trust them, reward them, and let them do their jobs, both among your personal office staff and in the company at large. The same holds true for helping outside community organizations: Do your research and be sure to only place your bets on people or groups willing to help themselves.

At Humana, I had four assistants who worked with me for a total of 156 years, a staff whose work ethic, longevity, loyalty, and knowledge of company history and policies would be very hard to find in any modern corporate structure. Equally important, we all became friends, gathering for lunch over the years.

My office included dozens of photos of family, friends, and co-workers thickly spread across wide shelves and into my outer office. They offered memories of the past and glimpses into the future. One photo taken about fifty years ago shows Wendell and me wearing confident smiles, ready to move ahead on something.

The office family began with Wanda Ryan, who first joined me at the Wyatt, Grafton & Sloss law firm in 1964 after growing up on a 170-acre Kentucky farm in a family of seven kids. She would stay with me on our journey for more than forty-six years, retiring in 2011 but returning as needed. She was the woman mentioned earlier, the first person hired when I began my own law firm and was low on income. She would loan me $20 for lunch as she stayed in the office and ate peanut butter and jelly sandwiches, a generous act I was able to reward later.

Phyllis Meyer, from Jeffersonville, joined me in 1972, retiring in 1989, a busy period of very strong growth for the company. Phyllis was very focused, fearless, and able to take endless pages of shorthand. She also quickly learned that in my writing work, I was forever unable to spell the word "challenge," writing "challange" instead.

Phyllis would play bridge with the office staff at lunch, with Wendell or me occasionally joining them. I thought so much of her abilities that one time, when I was traveling out west with my mother and sister Lucy, somebody asked what to do if we died out there.

I answered, "I'd call Phyllis."

Phyllis would later coach her successor, Rosanne Miller, who had joined the company in 1974 and started working in my office in 1981. Phyllis also selected Rosanne's eventual successor, Debbie Alexander, just before retiring. Rosanne worked for me for thirty-nine years and Debbie for forty-four.

Like Wanda, Rosanne and Debbie had grown up on farms, and they tell me if you grow up on a farm, everything afterward is easier.

Rosanne may be the only executive assistant whose job-seeking resume to a Forbes 500 company included, "I drove the tractor, put up hay, gathered eggs, and got the cows in. I just grew up in Mayberry."

She worked with me as the company grew, divided, fell back, and grew again. She contributed secretarial help, organizational skills, and an amazing memory for company history and details. She also offered business advice—both solicited and not—while serving as gatekeeper for the hundreds of people who wanted to visit the man she always called "Mr. Jones."

She grew up on a farm in Crawford County, Indiana, the third child of Elizabeth and Matthew Totten, their only daughter, their "baby girl." Her grandparents lived on the hill just above their house. Her parents first met in the nearby one-room school. They married in 1938, the Depression and hard times nearly a decade old. Her mother helped with the farm and cared for the children while her father worked the fields, milked cows, and pastored in two small nearby country churches. Rosanne's mom insisted on piano lessons for her daughter.

"She would haul me to the nearby town of English for lessons every Thursday at four o'clock for years," she said.

Their farm would stay in the family for almost 200 years. Rosanne attended nearby Milltown High School, where she was valedictorian among twenty-three students in the class of 1972. To earn money along the way, she worked as a waitress at the Green Acres Grill just down the hill from her parents' house.

With limited options for women then, she thought of becoming a secretary, with no notion of going to college. That changed when she and her boyfriend visited his sister at Indiana State University in Terre Haute.

"We went up to see her," Rosanne recalled, "and I thought, 'Oh, I guess I could go to college.' That thought process moved on to, 'Okay, I'll come here,' and that was literally the extent of my thoughts on that."

After two years, she graduated with a degree in secretarial science. She hoped to work for a big company in downtown Louisville. In May of 1974, about a week after her graduation, an employment agency sent her to Humana for a job interview.

She still remembers the first question she asked her interviewer: "Okay, what do you all do here?"

She also interviewed that day with our director of staff consultants, Dick Schnatter, an uncle of Papa John's Pizza founder John Schnatter, whom I would later counsel as he was growing his worldwide company. She told Dick that her only work experience had been as a waitress at the Green Acres Grill. He saw enough in her to hire her.

She became one of about 250 people working in the headquarters of a company that had just changed its name from Extendicare to Humana and was aggressively pursuing hospitals. She carpooled to work, arriving early to begin sorting mail. Schnatter, a personable man, would greet her facetiously with, "Okay, time for the company song and exercises."

"I started on Thursday, worked Thursday and Friday, and got paid for Monday, Memorial Day," Miller would say of the first days of her long career with Humana. "I thought I was in tall cotton."

In the beginning, in addition to secretarial work, she assisted a colleague and friend, Pat Miller, in developing Humana's quality assurance program. The project included travel to Tampa, Atlanta, and Nashville.

She attended the company's annual dance every November, where I handed out awards for excellence. She and Pat Miller each got one.

Humana was growing at a time when communications technology couldn't keep up. Employees had to get permission to make long-distance calls and then wait their turn. Rosanne was good at shorthand and dictation. She volunteered to work on Saturday mornings—three hours' work with four hours' pay—to take dictation from me, Wendell, Carl Pollard, or Joe Greene, president of hospital operations. In the process, she would learn almost as much about Humana as we knew.

"That's when I got to know all those guys," she said. "And it was stressful at first, transcribing on an old IBM belt machine."

In 1981, she began working for me and my assistant, Phyllis Meyer, while also helping Wendell. In 1989, Phyllis retired, and Rosanne took her place as my assistant.

"That's when I moved into the hot seat, as we called it," she said.

In January 1990, I hired Debbie Alexander to fill the job Rosanne had been doing. The transition was made easier because Phyllis, Rosanne, and Debbie worked well together. They were trusted and had a broad knowledge of company history, personnel, and policies. They were there through tough times when people were fired, the stock dropped, and the future looked difficult.

Rosanne watched me deal with all issues; she learned to adjust to my requirement for short, concise memos and my rapid decision-making. She was there when decisions were made on hospital expansion and when work began on the Humana Building and the Kentucky Center for the Performing Arts.

She was there as countless Louisville civic and political leaders came in asking for advice or money and as dozens of Louisville organizations came looking for support. And she was there for the initial discussions of The Parklands of Floyds Fork.

She also completed college, using the Humana benefits package to earn a business management degree from Indiana University Southeast. Her insight into people and memory of all Humana events were legendary. She remembers the day the Humana Building was dedicated. My mother was at the ceremony, and someone asked her how her son was doing.

"Which one?" Mom asked.

Rosanne went along on one trip to Romania with the company board of directors during the humanitarian assistance program. In Louisville, she set up meetings, helped schedule the company pilots, and made preliminary phone calls.

She had a great sense of humor and always spoke directly. When The Parklands of Floyds Fork was a distant dream, I wanted to speak with heiress Sally Shallenberger Brown, who would become an early substantial donor. Like me, Mrs. Brown got right to the point, in person or on the phone.

"Mrs. Brown, it's Rosanne. Mr. Jones is wondering if it would be convenient if he could come out one day next week?"

"Rosanne, what does he want, money?"

315

"Probably, Mrs. Brown."

"Sure. What day does he want to come?"

Rosanne was my gatekeeper. Our flare-ups were very few and quickly forgotten. I was open to taking company advice from her—and she occasionally felt the need to express it, especially after Wendell died.

Our discussions often took place as I was at "the ledge," a long counter in front of the assistants' desks where I liked to stand while going through my papers and schedules, writing notes, and thinking things over while working. Rosanne explains, "I'm kind of usually one to see where there might be a problem. And I know you can't be successful and have a bunch of 'yes men' around. I learned that from him. So, I'd usually say, 'Mr. Jones, what about this? And if you do that, then what?' I was always saying, 'I don't mean to be negative. I just want you to think about these things.' "

I would reply, "Rosanne, it's okay. I want you to bring out those opinions. If I don't agree with you, that's my prerogative, but I value your opinion and insight into different things you see that I may not see."

When she decided to retire, telling me was one of the most difficult things she ever had to do. She came in with tears in her eyes and explained her love for her job but her need to retire. Her husband, a cancer survivor, had been retired for six years, and he had purchased a winter home in Florida. It was time.

"He couldn't have been nicer," Rosanne said of my reaction, "but he also joked the new company retirement age was eighty-five."

After her retirement, she began playing the piano for the Corydon nursing home, where her mother had been before she died. She also played at the Wesley Chapel United Methodist Church in Floyds Knobs, Indiana, not far from where she had taken her childhood lessons.

Debbie Weathers Alexander—who would work closely with Rosanne and then succeed her as my assistant—was the daughter of tenant farmers living near Carrollton, Kentucky, when she was born.

Her mother, Doris Kamber Weathers, was one of eleven surviving children—two others had died—living in a shotgun house in the Germantown section of Louisville. Her father, Tom, was a World War II veteran who had served in the Army in New Guinea and the Philippines.

Her parents married when her mother was barely a teenager. They had five children, with the youngest and eldest born about twenty years apart. While raising the first three children—Debbie was not born yet—her parents also took in seven of her mother's siblings as that family fell apart. They had nowhere else to go. Twelve people were living in the same house.

As those children moved on, Debbie's family moved to a farm near Salem, Indiana, when she was in the fourth grade. A few years later, her father moved them to another farm not too far away, near New Albany.

On Sundays, her mother would fry chicken, make a roast, and bake a cake as aunts, uncles, and cousins descended from all directions. When she was in the eighth grade, Tom Weathers moved on to factory jobs, and Debbie would then attend Jeffersonville High School, graduating in 1974. She took many college-prep courses, but family finances made college seem impossible.

"It was more like I had to get out and get a job," she says.

She took a job in the Starks Building in downtown Louisville at Insurance Services Office, a company that set fire insurance rates. Her job was to type descriptions of properties that had been inspected—on long rolls of paper.

"So I'm great," she jokes, "at typing the numbers on the top row of the typewriter, and nobody can do that."

She was there for two years. In 1976, a good friend, Renée Patterson, got a job at Humana and told Debbie what a great company it was. She applied, was not hired, but was then called back.

"It was the department that recruited physicians," she remembers. "I worked for a wonderful, wonderful man, John Hollander. I was an administrative assistant in that department for seven years."

The work was great background in keeping up with company reports and growth. Along the way, in 1979, she married her high school sweetheart,

Russell Alexander. She moved on to Humana Hospital-University as an administrative assistant, then to Humana Hospital-Southwest. In December 1989, a friend called her and said there was an opening in David Jones's office: Phyllis Meyer was retiring.

I had never met Debbie. Phyllis conducted the interview after I had been suddenly called away to talk with Mayor Jerry Abramson. Debbie was hired without ever meeting me.

"Phyllis knew him better than anyone," Debbie says. "I don't know who else applied for the job, but I was probably hired because I was so steady."

She began work in the office on January 2, 1990, the year Wendell was diagnosed with cancer. As Rosanne's backup, she answered the phone, routing calls. At that point, personal complaint calls from Humana customers were often funneled through Debbie's office. Somebody might call from south Florida, and she would pass the call on to the right vice president.

Debbie and the others were there through the loss of Wendell and helped me make the sometimes-difficult decisions to move Humana ahead. As others retired, she moved into the role of my administrative assistant, scheduling all my meetings, screening calls, and working with family members and their travel on my plane.

"He has, of course, as everyone does, mellowed over the years," she says. "He's still demanding. If he calls and he wants it, you feel like you owe him that. He's been so generous and fair and good to all of us that you want to do your absolute best."

Debbie was working with me when the company split, a very difficult time for many people as friendships and business interests would be divided into separate entities and then, to some surprise, into two different states as Galen merged with Columbia and moved to Tennessee.

"I remember being sad I didn't go to the hospital side," she says. "What a blessing I didn't. I've had this major guardian angel my whole life."

While a believer in the power of hiring good people and keeping them, I was also willing to hire good people understanding we both could benefit as they earned their leadership stripes at Humana and then moved on to other businesses or community work. A great example is Larry McDonald, who joined the Humana team during its hospital building boom in the early 1980s.

McDonald traces his history to a slave plantation in Tennessee, where his family name was derived from white owners. His father, Charles McDonald, had been named for his father, who, along with his wife, Genevieve McDonald, raised twelve children. The twelve grew up in Louisville's California neighborhood. None of the three boys in the family was able to go to college, but most of his nine sisters did. Three became nurses, and four became school principals.

McDonald's grandfather was a molder at Vulcan-Hart, a kitchen-equipment supplier in the Portland community, the same place his father would work as a molder for thirty-five years. McDonald's mother was a cosmetologist who also worked at General Electric. Neither of his parents finished high school. They raised their five children in the Sheppard Square housing complex, and then in west Louisville.

McDonald wanted to attend the predominantly black Central High School and play on its great basketball teams. His father insisted he go to DuPont Manual—a much more integrated school—where he played basketball and football and was named team captain. In his senior year, Manual upset Male in football 20–6—no small feat in that era—and McDonald had eleven tackles.

Manual required all students to take four semesters of general drafting. McDonald followed those with a semester of architecture courses. The education was lasting.

"Hey, this is what I like," he told himself. "I like the drafting board."

He enrolled at the University of Kentucky in 1970. He dealt with some tough racial experiences at a time when rebel flags could still be found in UK dorm rooms.

Although he decided against walking on to the UK football team, he

319

became a close friend of Wilbur Hackett, a Manual graduate who helped integrate the program. In 1969, Hackett became the first African American captain in any sport in Southeastern Conference history. He eventually refereed college football for twenty-three years.

McDonald initially enrolled as an architecture major. After learning an architecture degree could take six years, he switched to UK's College of Business. It helped that he had a knack for math, and, while also taking courses in Louisville at Jefferson Community College, became one of the first African Americans to graduate from the UK business college.

Because of the racial animosity he experienced there, he decided not to show up for the graduation ceremony. McDonald said, "I cheated my parents because I didn't walk across that stage. Years later I got an MBA at the University of Louisville, and I made sure my mom and dad were there. Maturity teaches you that you do it for your family. You do it for those who sacrificed for you."

After college, he went to work for the non-profit Action Now, where he oversaw housing project property management. He later became a production supervisor in the body shop at Ford Motor Company, supervising spot welders. He worked as a real estate broker before being hired by Humana, which was building hospitals as fast as it could get approval for certificates of need. He felt back at home among blueprints and architects.

McDonald's first job at Humana was helping purchase hospital equipment. He said, "We would go around and meet with hospital administrators and doctors, who always wanted their own brand, their own equipment. But Humana had carved out a unique niche with a national purchasing program that said we're going to get things like CT scanners and hospital beds under national contract for all our hospitals. That way, by economies of scale, when we buy, we get the best price for the best quality."

McDonald worked and traveled with Humana's in-house architects, interior designers, and engineers. "They would design the hospital," he said, "and I would buy everything that went into it, from hospital beds to nurse call systems, and the administrative areas."

He credits his success to the drafting courses he took in high school and then being able to work with Louisville-area architects such as Jim Walters, Wayne Estopinal, and Steve Wiser.

"In life," he said, "you never know when you go through an education process that what you've learned, what you're trained on, is going to come back into play."

His personal mentor was Jonah Hughes, another African American in the corporate office. In 1985, Hughes helped guide McDonald into integrating the Humana management training program. McDonald said that led to "becoming part of the due diligence team. Humana went through ten to fifteen mergers and acquisitions. That was fun for me because I would go as part of the team of people who would evaluate the potential of a company to be acquired.

"I became very comfortable. After I proved I could play at that level, people didn't look at me as black first. They looked at me as somebody who really knew the business."

While at Humana, McDonald became very involved in the company's community efforts. They included the YMCA Black Achievers Program, the Leadership Louisville Foundation, Metro United Way, the Fund for the Arts, the Home of the Innocents, the Boy Scouts, and dozens of other organizations and trusts. In that way, he became a role model for me.

His work led to his becoming president of the Lincoln Foundation. Established by Berea College in 1910, it provides year-round, specific, non-traditional education programs in schools and colleges, often through the Whitney M. Young Scholars Program in Kentucky and Indiana.

Betty and I were its largest donors, along with the Humana Foundation. It has always been my belief we have to educate every child. You can't patronize people or make them dependent and expect good things to happen.

✳

It was also my belief that we must provide low-income families a good chance to finally live the American dream of owning their own home. To that end, Ben Richmond, then CEO of the Louisville Urban League, worked with me to build forty-seven new houses for those families, a cause that would have a continuing impact in the city's poorer areas for years afterward. Richmond was another who knew where I was coming from: He'd been there, too.

"I was raised well," Richmond said. "We were poor as you know what, but I never knew we were poor because my parents made sure everything we needed to have was there."

His father was a self-made man, an itinerant small-church African Methodist Episcopal (AME) Zion minister without a high school diploma who would nonetheless lead many successful churches. His mother, who had had some college classes and insisted all her children earn degrees, became a music teacher and singer who opened kindergartens for black children long before Head Start.

Moving from church to church, the Richmond family lived in North Carolina, Arkansas, and Mississippi. Along the way, Ben's mother started what were essentially private kindergartens to raise a little extra money— and teach needy children the alphabet and nursery rhymes. Years later, Richmond would frequently meet people who told him what a difference that start had made in their lives.

Richmond's father preached, worked in a Ford Motor Company facility, and washed windows at the nearby Kroger market, with his children helping him. He settled in Canton, Mississippi, and then Jackson, where his son attended segregated schools before going to Tougaloo College, a historically black school founded in 1869 by Christian missionaries to educate freed slaves.

Like his father, Richmond fought for civil rights while living in the segregated South of the 1960s. Like his mother, he was a singer: He received his BS degree in music education, expecting to become a high school or college choral director.

He taught music at a junior college and was encouraged to go to graduate school. Barred by race from graduate schools in Mississippi, he earned his master's degree at the University of Wisconsin by attending eight weeks of summer school for three years. That led to a fellowship at the Northwest German Music Academy in Detmold, Germany, where he taught English, sang in the choirs, traveled, and learned German in intense, immersive classes.

In 1979, at age thirty-five, he returned to the United States. He was hired by the Urban League in Madison, Wisconsin, as a counselor and found he enjoyed helping others, many of them young ex-offenders needing direction. His life changed when one of the young men he helped find work—and a new life—called him down to the Urban League lobby for a "thank you" and a big bear hug.

"It made me feel like I had never felt before," said Richmond. "I just stood there and said, 'Wow, I'd like to have that feeling happen over and over again.' "

He moved to Battle Creek, Michigan in 1982 to run an Urban League center. Five years later, he was hired by the Louisville Urban League. While he was introducing himself to city leaders, we had coffee and breakfast at the Holiday Inn at Second Street and Broadway, the first of our many conversations.

We talked backgrounds, finding similarities and shared interests. He had lived, taught, and traveled in Germany. I was then taking German classes at the University of Louisville, trying out foreign language study. In 1990, I would spend a month in Berlin studying intensive German while Betty lived in France.

We discussed Louisville's needs, the fact that I had grown up in a section of the city that needed an economic boost, more jobs, and better housing. Richmond mentioned the Urban League's housing counseling program. I said I had an idea to build houses for low-income families in the inner city.

The result was a partnership that the Louisville Urban League called REBOUND—Rebuilding Our Urban Neighborhood Dwellings. Working with Mayor Jerry Abramson, Main Street Realty's Ken Payne, and architect Jim Walters while I contacted a network of local bankers for accessible loans, the partnership built forty-seven new homes in Louisville's Russell neighborhood from 1991 through 1994. REBOUND also helped remodel a drug store at Eighteenth Street and Muhammad Ali, not far from where I had grown up.

The city sold REBOUND the ready-to-go lots for one dollar. The 1,200-square-foot homes—priced at $60,000—had three bedrooms, one-and-a-half baths, and air conditioning, a blessing in Louisville's steamy summers. I gave each family $5,000 to help with the down payment, and they had to demonstrate they could pay off their mortgage loans, some up to thirty years.

I also funded the design-and-build phases of the project, estimated by Richmond to be $3 to $4 million, with much of the money paid back as homes were sold. Then I would drive by the project regularly to check its progress and continued to be a regular contributor to the Louisville Urban League.

"REBOUND," said Richmond, "demonstrated that you could come into an area like this. We were the first to build a house here—a brand new house—in fifty years."

Inspired by that success, other agencies and contractors became involved in building and refurbishing homes in the neighborhood. Sixty additional homes would soon be built, with tens of millions more in local and federal dollars invested over the next fifteen years by ongoing partnerships, creating more than 100 new homes for people living in Louisville's low-income and West End neighborhoods, helping to stabilize them. Streetscape improvements were also included.

Not all such shared efforts were as successful. In April 1994, acting on economic development research showing that black entrepreneurs faced significant barriers in their access to capital, I joined fifteen other Louisville executives and corporations in creating the African-American Venture Capital Fund to invest in black-owned businesses with the potential to grow and create jobs. The fund raised and invested about $8 million; Humana and I each contributed $1 million, and I recruited other corporate leaders to get involved.

"What we need is the wisdom and experience of many of you out there to spot the people who can use the money wisely," I said in a news release.

An April 21, 1994 *Courier Journal* story told of an initial venture fund press conference at Burns Enterprises on South Fifteenth Street, an African-American-owned business led by Tommie Burns, Jr. One speaker at the conference, Charlie Johnson of Active Transportation Inc., said, "This fund says a lot about this community. It restores my faith in humanity . . . my faith in groups being able to work together."

The fund made investments in the stock of its companies, rather than making grants or loans. It backed entrepreneurs with business plans that were well-researched and specific. When the fund acquired equity in a company, it put representatives on the company's board, thus having a role in overseeing decisions and progress. Burns and Johnson were original directors of the fund, along with Bruce Lunsford, chairman of Vencor Inc., and me.

One startup company was a television station temporarily using the call letters WYCS-TV for "We're Your Community Station." Its programming was primarily geared toward the market's black and Hispanic communities.

Ultimately, the fund's results were disappointing. None of the companies it invested in grew as hoped, and sales of the equity resulted in the loss of most of the fund's capital when it was wound down in 2017. The liquidating distribution, however, was donated to the Louisville Urban League.

Chapter Twenty-Eight

WIDENING THE PATH

"I'm trying to hold my composure. Tears are in my eyes. My father's a rock; he's old school, but when we got back to the car, there were tears in his eyes. No one had ever done anything like that for us in our lives. It was a game-changer for our church. A big game-changer. It was the first time in my life I ever saw my father cry."

— The Reverend KEVIN COSBY

W hen I turned fifty in 1981, I was a wealthy man, having moved from west Louisville to tobacco markets to the University of Louisville, from the Navy to Yale Law School to international business success. I'd been able to buy my parents the first home they ever owned and a new car. Betty and I had built our dream home on thirty acres of meadow and woods.

But beneath all that, I was still a pugnacious guy from west Louisville who could ask himself: "How does a wealthy man drilled since birth to 'Do unto others as you would have them do unto you' use his wealth for good?"

My goal became to widen that path to social, educational, and economic opportunity. My first instincts drew me back to west Louisville. When Betty and I returned to town in 1960, we saw a West End hollowing out as white citizens left for new suburban neighborhoods. We understood that housing segregation was blocking black citizens' access to new neighborhoods, and we participated in open housing demonstrations in the early '60s.

White flight would reduce the West End's population dramatically, in astonishing proportions. In 1950, the area was home to nearly 148,000 people, 73 percent of them white. By the 1960s, the West End had 60,000 people, with minorities accounting for 82 percent of the population. The white population, once over 100,000, was less than 11,000.

Louisville was very much a segregated city when I grew up; its racial, social, and economic boundaries were obvious to me as Logan and I traveled downtown and in our classes in school. Betty and I experienced an even harsher segregation in the South in the 1950s, me while working tobacco markets in Georgia in 1950 after high school graduation, and Betty in Norfolk, Virginia, where she taught at a junior high school in 1956 and 1957 while I was in the Navy. The next school year, that school closed rather than integrate, joining Virginia's "massive resistance" to the Supreme Court's *Brown v. Board of Education* ruling, which declared racial segregation in public schools unconstitutional. These experiences further sensitized us to the damage that racism and poverty could do.

My civic work in west Louisville would be framed around relationships with people whose passion for education, moral order, and—often—for the organized combat of competitive sports lined up with my own.

From 1960 through 1972, I would regularly take the short walk—first from my law office, eventually from Humana—to the downtown YMCA. The attraction: the regular lunch hour pickup basketball games with anyone who showed up. The players included Louis Coleman, an imposing African American man with an unlikely nickname for a preacher: "Buster."

The gym was small, with a running track above the court, preventing jump shots from deep in the corners. The games were always intensely competitive. The losing team had to sit and wait for the next opening—and nobody liked to sit and wait. Coleman and I enjoyed the jostling and banging that came with winning and staying on the court.

I liked him because he was able to do what most, but not all the players, were able to do: He could absorb a few bumps without getting excited. He became a good friend. We played racquetball, and Coleman won, so I took him to the squash court, where I won. We were both competitive and got to know each other well.

Coleman grew up in Louisville's historically black Smoketown and was a Central High School graduate. He earned a master's degree in community development from the University of Louisville and a Master of Divinity degree from Louisville Presbyterian Theological Seminary.

When we met, he was leading the Shelbyville Congregational Methodist Church in Shelbyville, Kentucky—about thirty miles away—where he then lived. He also led the First Congregational Methodist Church at Thirty-Ninth Street and Garland in Louisville—the same street where I had grown up—and managed the Presbyterian Community Center in Smoketown. And because even a preacher with three jobs could use the extra income, Coleman refereed high school football games, too.

Coleman became Louisville's most important political activist of his generation against segregation, racism, violence, drugs, pollution, and economic disparities. To advance those goals, he founded the non-profit Justice Resource Center and, with bullhorn in hand, became a fixture on the streets of Louisville and across Kentucky for thirty years. Aggressive but not belligerent, he became adept at attracting media coverage, with radio, television, and newspapers all willing to oblige. He was mentioned in more than one thousand stories in Louisville's *Courier Journal* in the 1990s alone.

"We are going to agitate and agitate and agitate until justice falls down from the heavens," Coleman once said.

Fearless in his church work, Coleman would lead members of his Louisville congregation to protest outside a neighborhood crack house at midnight—and thus bring in police presence. He carried food, clothing, and concern in his well-traveled van, including multiple trips to New Orleans after Hurricane Katrina devastated that city in 2005.

I admired Buster, whose calm, even temperament when carrying his ever-present bullhorn at community rallies reflected the nature I had seen on the basketball court. I also admired his dedication and effectiveness in promoting change. His finest hour may have been shaming Louisville's

Pendennis Club, a white upper-class enclave downtown, into integrating in March 1991.

He did it by setting up a couple of card tables right in front of the Pendennis Club. There were white tablecloths, silverware, and two white waitresses serving him on the sidewalk since he wasn't welcome to eat inside—in front of all the television stations in town. The club integrated instantly. It was a brilliant move.

Betty and I supported Coleman's work from the Justice Resource Center's early days. We donated money to build community gymnasiums in Louisville and Shelbyville. We purchased a new van for Coleman every few years as his old one wore out.

I thought of him as "The Conscience of the Community." I took his advice on civic issues and admired his tenacity and courage. In my view, our bond was grounded in blue-collar backgrounds, hardscrabble neighborhoods, and competitive dispositions. We shared those experiences and attitudes with many Humana executives and employees who went on to help others achieve. They all connected me, in a way, to my past.

My interest in helping west Louisville also led me to the Reverend Kevin Cosby, the moving force behind Louisville's largest and most influential black church. A generation younger than Coleman, Cosby also grew up in the West End but came back to it with skills, experience, and perspective born of different challenges and achievement.

His father, Laken Cosby, Jr., was born into poverty, the son of a sharecropper in north Alabama who moved his family to Louisville during World War II. The life the Cosbys left behind in Alabama recalls the lives of eastern Kentucky coal miners sung about by Tennessee Ernie Ford:

> *You load sixteen tons, and what do you get?*
> *Another day older and deeper in debt*
> *Saint Peter, don't you call me 'cause I can't go*
> *I owe my soul to the company store.*

"I've got pictures of the family coming off the train," says Kevin Cosby. "My grandfather said he could never get ahead because after he paid for his tools, the supplies, everything he had to pay, he was in debt. He owed the owner of the farm so much he could never get ahead."

Alabama would not pay for the education of black people past the eighth grade. There were no public high schools for them. So, when Cosby's father graduated from Louisville's Central High School in 1950 at age twenty, he was the first Cosby to graduate from high school.

Once in Louisville, Laken Cosby, Sr. had learned to pour concrete at construction sites, doing small jobs at odd hours. His big break came when, after being cursed by a white man for an admittedly poorly done job, he ripped out his old work, stayed all night, and fixed it. That led to a good recommendation and more work. He eventually became the largest African American contractor in Louisville. His Cosby Concrete Company poured the floor at Ballard High School and the downtown Galleria.

The family work ethic was passed on to Kevin's father. A determined man with a soft-spoken manner, Laken, Jr. served in the US Air Force, developed a successful real estate company, and became president of the Louisville chapter of the NAACP. In the 1970s, he fought for school integration and later served three terms on the Kentucky State Board of Education. In 1988, he became the first black chairman of the Jefferson County Board of Education.

Kevin Cosby's mother's roots were in Kentucky. His maternal grandfather, Benjamin James Miller, moved from Peytontown, Kentucky, in Madison County, to Louisville to attend Simmons College in the 1920s. In 1951, he became one of the first black graduates of Louisville's Southern Baptist Theological Seminary. He had to do it despite sitting in the hallways during some classes: Kentucky's Day Law of 1904, then still in force, prevented blacks and whites from being in the same classroom. (Some professors defied the law and allowed Miller to sit in their classrooms.)

Miller organized St. Stephen Church in 1926 and served as its pastor for more than forty years while teaching Greek, math, and the New Testament at Simmons. His work and education deeply influenced his grandson: "I wanted to be a clergyman like my grandfather," Cosby said. "He was my idol. I adored him."

Kevin Cosby's mother died of cancer when he was eleven. His father remarried, and when Kevin was in seventh grade, his family moved from 4631 Westchester Avenue, in a once upscale white section of west Louisville, to the Mallgate apartments in St. Matthews, an east Louisville suburb.

Before the move, Cosby's classmates had all been black. After the move, he was the only black kid in his school. In the ninth grade, his family moved further east, to Barbourmeade, where he attended racially mixed but socially segregated Ballard High School.

That entire high school experience—with its direct and indirect harassment—gave him an early look at racism. He went from not understanding the economic and social problems in the black community to examining their root causes—racism and segregation. His family history—the migration from debt slavery in Alabama, the strong work ethic, the barrier-breaking grandfather who started a church while also teaching—added motivation. Kevin Cosby wanted to—*needed to*—do something about racial injustice.

He earned his Bachelor of Science degree at Eastern Kentucky University. He would earn a Master of Divinity at the Southern Baptist Theological Seminary in Louisville and then his Doctor of Ministry at United Theological Seminary in Dayton.

In November 1979, at age twenty—even before graduating from Eastern Kentucky University—he became pastor of the St. Stephen Church, where B. J. Miller had been pastor. When Cosby became minister, St. Stephen had about 150 members, a chapel, and a small educational building in a poor and declining neighborhood.

Under his leadership and inspired by his preaching, some forty-one years later, St. Stephen had more than 15,000 members with satellite churches in Hardin County, Kentucky, and Jeffersonville, Indiana. The churches hold six weekend services for black and some white parishioners, with white staff members helping. Cosby credits much of that growth to people willing to come back to their old west Louisville neighborhood physically, psychologically, and financially.

"One of those persons who came back," he told a journalist, growing very emotional as he spoke, "was a man named David A. Jones, Sr."

I met Cosby after reading a *Courier Journal* story in the 1980s about his work helping St. Stephen youth overcome the myth of black inferiority by stressing the importance of education.

"When you don't apply yourself academically," Cosby would preach, "you are just reinforcing that myth."

I asked Cosby to join me for breakfast. Cosby called his father—who insisted on coming along. At the meeting, the Cosbys told the St. Stephen story, emphasizing its already rapid growth. We talked about our experiences, especially our mothers, and a shared outlook accomplished only through education.

I promised the Cosbys I would buy St. Stephen a bus to bring children to those education classes and would donate $100,000 a year for the next three years to help fund them.

Kevin Cosby, remembering the moment years later, said, "I'm trying to hold my composure. Tears are in my eyes. My father's a rock. He's old school, but when we got back to the car, there were tears in his eyes. No one had ever done anything like that for us in our lives. It was a game-changer for our church. A big game-changer. It was the first time in my life I ever saw my father cry."

The money for St. Stephen came with no strings attached. All I asked was that Cosby do what needed doing. We grew close after that first meeting. Betty and I invited Cosby and his wife, Barnetta, to our house for social occasions. I helped with the building fund that financed a full-fledged Family Life Center at St. Stephen. Our foundation made a second mortgage loan to St. Stephen to build a new, larger sanctuary in the early '90s, when no bank would extend that much credit—and was repaid early as the church, and member donations, grew as Cosby had projected.

Cosby became president of the 126-year-old Simmons Bible College in 2005 when it was about to close because of low enrollment, poor facilities, and lack of funding. Cosby knew Simmons's history as one of the first colleges founded by newly freed slaves after the Civil War. He envisioned a rebirth as a historically black institution educating not just preachers but African Americans from west Louisville and beyond.

He shared this vision, and Betty and I immediately donated $1 million to launch it. We added $50,000 a year afterward as family bonds deepened, with David Jones, Jr. becoming a member of the Simmons board and a regular at St. Stephen Church.

In building the new Simmons College, Cosby has refused to accept the $70,000-a-year salary as president. He saw the school win back accreditation, form partnerships with the University of Louisville and Jefferson Community College, and earn federal recognition (and funding) as a Historically Black College or University. He acquired land and buildings, moved the college back to the original campus site on Seventh Street, added two other sites near St. Stephen Church, and started to provide student housing. He has given Betty and me credit for making that possible.

Our belief in the positive influence of strong churches and civically engaged ministers led me beyond west Louisville as we also helped in the rise of the Canaan Missionary Baptist Church and its leader, the Reverend Walter Malone, Jr.

Malone, a Fisk University graduate, had started the church on March 16, 1983, at the Little Flock Baptist Church building on Hancock Street. Malone quickly built the church into Canaan Missionary Baptist Church, big enough to purchase a $1 million facility with a parsonage and gymnasium at 2203 Dixie Highway.

In March 1992, the Canaan church broke ground on a $1.2 million expansion with a new sanctuary, library, music room, and office suite. With Malone as its intense, inspirational leader, the church soon needed an even larger facility. That led to the opportunity to purchase the former Southeast

Christian Church on twenty-two acres of Hikes Lane property—well away from Louisville's western edge—with an auditorium seating about 2,500 people.

I had known Malone through civil rights work. The Jones family's C.E.&S. Foundation extended a second mortgage loan that enabled Canaan Baptist to acquire the Hikes Lane property, which was renamed Canaan Christian Church. As with the second mortgage loan to St. Stephen, no bank would lend this much to Canaan—and as with St. Stephen, the church paid off the loan early as its growth met and exceeded projections.

The Hikes Lane complex grew to include a youth ministry, a sports ministry, a men's ministry, a prayer partner program, and a non-profit community development corporation. Its mantra is "empowerment and commitment." Church members are expected to give 10 percent of their income and personal time to build the community, to give back—to pull the wagon.

Chapter Twenty-Nine

LEADERSHIP LESSONS LEARNED

"Profit is never a mission, vision, or an end, nor is it a dirty word. Rather, profit is an absolute requirement. Enterprises that fail to cover all costs, including the cost of capital, soon perish, along with their goals, jobs, and pensions."

— DAVID JONES

As a dedicated advocate of summary reports and get-to-the-point conversations, I have, over the years, put together a few short summaries of some of my lessons learned. I penciled out *Accounting 101* for Dave when he returned from China and jumped into a banking training program, and *Investing 101* when relatives, widowed friends, and suddenly wealthy acquaintances seemed at risk from professional advisors' self-interested advice. I have shared both documents with many along the way and have included them in the Appendix at the end of this book.

When health care reform heated up in Washington, I put my thoughts on how to fix our broken health care system down on two pages of paper and shared them with anyone who asked my opinion. I have included them in the Appendix, too. Health care is complicated, but my strategy for fixing it is not.

335

Both before and after I retired, I taught often, usually at the invitation of a professor or teacher to talk to their class, and generally in response to some variation of the question, "How did you do it?" The discussions that ensued and the pleasure I took in them led me to put together a concise list titled "Leadership Lessons Learned."

Gathered over time, and then written in barely an hour, I learned and followed these lessons for my forty-four years of building Humana. They proved useful in all facets of developing company businesses. They also helped when I was dealing with people seeking community favors or donations, and in creating the charitable foundations that were important for me to share our profits with people, churches, and organizations in need.

I believe those Leadership Lessons Learned will work for any company or enterprise. Here they are, just thirteen simple points:

1. Family is first. Do your job, but enjoy your family and other interests. Have a life!
2. Always be honest! Integrity is the most vital character trait.
3. Be optimistic and confident. A leader must inspire confidence.
4. As a leader, you must have clear and sufficient authority to accomplish assigned tasks. As your responsibilities expand, always insist upon receiving requisite authority.
5. A leader must have strength of will.
6. Focus! Have a clear idea of the goal you plan to accomplish.
7. Next, you must determine what's critical. You must think that through.
   a. This is where we want to go.
   b. These are the things that, if we don't do them all, we won't get there.
   c. These mission-critical elements, especially outcomes, must be measured!
8. Next, build a team that can do these things and have a continuous two-way conversation with them, enabling each team member to understand and appreciate how their individual effort contributes

to achieving the goal. Their honest feedback will often refine and improve your ideas and may identify some that simply won't work.

9. Remember always to thank your colleagues for their effective efforts! Earned recognition is a powerful motivator.

10. Always try to create conditions that allow your colleagues to do their best work. Not easy, but possible with constant thought and attention.

11. Make decisions quickly once you have the facts. Nothing kills morale and momentum like bureaucratic lassitude! We promised our hospital leaders that all properly documented requests would be decided within one week. We stuck to that promise, and it was enormously helpful and appreciated.

12. Profit is never a mission, vision, or an end, nor is it a dirty word. Rather, profit is an absolute requirement. Enterprises that fail to cover all costs, including the cost of capital, soon perish, along with their goals, jobs, and pensions.

13. Complete today's work today. Don't procrastinate.

In sum, inspirational leadership requires:

Integrity
Optimism
Confidence
Authority
Strength of will
Clarity of vision/mission
Clear, continuous two-way communication
Earned recognition
Measurement of each element critical to success
Creating conditions that allow colleagues to do their best work
Rapid decision making
No procrastination

Heidi Margulis took those lessons seriously in her more than thirty-year career with Humana, much of it working directly with me. Her take on my approach: "He had his sayings, like, 'You don't have a clear idea unless it fits on the back of a business card.' And, 'We are in a business that is incredibly complex. It's scan and review. Long articles, 500-page books—three points.' "

She is the daughter of a Holocaust survivor; her mother was fourteen when the Nazis burned her school, forcing her to flee in the flames. The Nazis seized her grandfather, but he and her grandmother survived. In 1941, after a journey that included one German concentration camp, one French prison camp, two escapes, and two French hideaways, the family found its way to Ellis Island and freedom.

Later, her mother's family moved to Louisville, settling into the Highlands. Her father, a pharmacist, was from St. Louis. He bought a Schneider Drugs pharmacy at Eighteenth and Oak Streets, not far from where I grew up. His wife, Heidi's mother, was his bookkeeper.

Margulis was competitive as a swimmer at Lakeside Swim Club and as gymnast at a gym that was a precursor to Turners. A motivated student, she was pushed by her father who, when she brought home a very good report card, said, "Well, it's nice you got an A. Don't they give A-plusses?"

She won a full academic scholarship to the University of Louisville, where she majored in international studies, graduating with honors. Along the way, she did a summer internship in Quito, Ecuador. While there, she taught English, then traveled the Amazon.

She eventually found her way into government. In 1974, she worked as an intern for US Senator Dee Huddleston, then went on to become a staff assistant for US Senator Wendell Ford. She worked with Louisville Mayor Harvey Sloane, ran Sylvia Watson's successful campaign for county commissioner, and then helped build a development program for women, Skill Makers, and another called Models and Mentors.

Her first connection to Humana—and later to me—came when she was hired as a licensure analyst in our new group health division as the company moved into health insurance.

"I started on November 11, 1985," she said. "That was right when the Humana Building opened." Her job was to help obtain licenses for all the new insurance and health plan companies. I had wanted them all licensed in six months. With Margulis's background and Humana's push to grow, she and I often teamed up to explain and sell our new product to federal and state regulators.

Margulis eventually became Humana's senior vice president of government relations and contact with the federal government's massive Medicare program. At one very high-level congressional meeting in Washington, I gave her the affectionate nickname "Pit Bull." The meeting concerned a reimbursement issue for Medicare HMO coverage and the possibility of Humana's payment being cut because of a new methodology.

Participants included Senate Majority Leader Bob Dole of Kansas and Sheila Burke, his chief of staff, who was so powerful she was often called the "101st senator." Also there were Republican senators Arlen Specter of Pennsylvania and Alfonse D'Amato, from New York. We sat on a balcony outside Dole's office overlooking many of Washington's monuments and the White House.

Burke was a nurse by profession. I wanted the meeting to ask Dole to reconsider a reimbursement proposal she had devised. Dole handed the meeting over to Burke, who insisted the proposal would not be changed. Margulis noticed my anger rising over the lack of any real conversation on the issue.

Margulis believed a good staff member's responsibility is to take bullets while other people cut ribbons. She feared I would impulsively say something to damage our case. She put up her hand, saying, "Mr. Leader, with all due respect to Sheila, we disagree for the following reasons," which she then outlined as damaging to beneficiaries.

Dole, D'Amato, and Specter still agreed with Burke. The new methodology would be phased in eventually, with changes that satisfied all parties. As we walked to the elevator, I—who never did get to have my say—thanked my "pit bull," a name that stuck.

At a subsequent Healthcare Leadership Council meeting in Washington, Margulis and I disagreed on a position for some Medicare public policy legislation. Before the meeting, we argued. She told me all the reasons she believed I was wrong. I went into the meeting. Margulis flew back to Louisville, believing she would be fired.

When I got back to Louisville, I called her to my office. I told her, "I know we disagreed. And I voted the way I wanted to vote, but I respect you for voicing your opinion, and I want you always to continue to do that. I hire people to think and not dig in the weeds."

Our public policy work took on some sacred cows. I pushed to have all Humana hospitals declared smoke-free. As a result, Louisville tobacco companies Philip Morris and Brown & Williamson took their medical insurance business to other companies.

I required the new Humana Building to be smoke-free. We also created a $2 million program through the Humana Foundation called Teens Against Tobacco Use. It recruited company volunteers who donated 50,000 hours, placing mentors in schools to discourage teens from smoking. In states that allowed it, we required new employees who smoked to attend a smoking-cessation program.

Margulis saw me angry just once. A story on the back page of the *Wall Street Journal* correctly described how Humana was not dealing with certain member complaints accurately or in a timely fashion. I brought the article into a management committee meeting, threw it on the table, and demanded changes.

Margulis tells another revealing story about me. During President Bill Clinton's first administration, Betty and I were invited to the White House, with three other couples, for dinner with the president. Betty had a family conflict; we sent regrets.

In 2018, Margulis wrote me a letter saying she was retiring. "There are no adequate words to describe my admiration and respect for you, the deep gratitude I feel for your years of mentoring, and surrogate fathering," she wrote.

She thanked me for creating a work environment in which company leaders could be motivated to reach summits they never knew they could achieve: "You truly gave me the opportunity of a lifetime to ultimately drive changes in public health policy in an investor-owned company that through its transformations has made and continues to make a difference in people's lives."

She signed the letter, "Fondly, Your Pit Bull."

***

At age eighty-seven and retired from Humana for fifteen years, I continue to push for progress and improvement in Louisville and Kentucky. My method remains good communication, approaching each problem with focus, clarity, and brevity. I sum up that philosophy with a pointed message: "If you can't write your idea on the back of my business card, you don't have a clear idea."

My focus now is on education—primarily for children and young adults in need, those who have the intelligence, ambition, and tenacity to get an education but are stymied by financial problems or poor government policy choices. We feel good when we do something that truly makes a difference in the lives of kids.

Working with Democrats and Republicans over the years, I am aware that people tend to attach political labels to my words and actions, depending on the issue and their personal beliefs. I ignore all that in search of consistent overall improvements.

I don't care what political persuasion people think I am. I'm a results person. There's probably not a more liberal person in Louisville when it comes to human suffering or disadvantage. I've lived that life. I grew up poor, but it wasn't "poor me." We never thought of ourselves as poor because we had a happy family life. We had plenty of books. We had a church we went to four times on Sunday.

I'm involved in many, many things that have to do with helping others. But the foundation of my belief is that people—individuals—are ultimately accountable for themselves.

To that point, and with more than sixty years of experience in creating success across all political, community, and business lines, I also set down some concise thoughts on how to ease unemployment, enhance the American work ethic, and rebuild the country's decaying infrastructure without new taxes. I always saw myself as a person of action, so this venture into political philosophy may stray too far, like the mobile home parks—but I've given it a lot of thought.

Here's a short version:

In the Depression of the 1930s, President Franklin Delano Roosevelt noted our nation had many varied infrastructure needs and a lot of unemployed citizens. He created the Works Progress Administration (WPA) and the Civilian Conservation Corps (CCC), which employed millions of people who then built much-needed infrastructure, including refurbishing many of our national and state parks. This work was crucial to breaking the Depression's grip, not just on the American economy, but on the wounded American psyche.

We should reuse the FDR model, with states playing a key role. States would identify their infrastructure needs and hire private contractors to organize and produce measurable results. The money for this would come from such government programs as welfare, food stamps, Medicaid, and unemployment compensation in the form of block grants.

Able-bodied non-workers who now receive benefits should be required to work in exchange for them. A large majority of the unemployed truly wish to work, a habit deeply ingrained in our history and culture that we don't want to lose. Yet when it's financially advantageous to abandon work for government benefits, many naturally choose that route, which may lead to dependency and loss of self-respect.

This suggested approach was used successfully by President Bill Clinton in the late 1990s when he moved federal welfare programs to the states through block grants. It can work again. It must.

*

In a way, creating a successful enterprise is as simple as A-B-C-D. It begins with clarity of thought combined with a clear mission. You've got to have a clear mission.

The second task is determining what's critical. You have to think that through: "This is where we want to go. These are the things that, if we don't do them all, we won't get there."

The third thing is building a team that can do those things and having a two-way conversation about it. You make sure everybody on the team understands the goal and is free to make suggestions about better ways to reach that goal, because nobody's smart enough to figure out all the things that need to be done. You need a team to do that.

And the fourth thing is to say, "Thank you." Earned recognition is powerful.

That's basically all there is to it. You can read all the books you want, but I have a lot of experience and know it works. And it worked in everything that I did.

Chapter Thirty

CHANGE OF COMMAND

"I never feared change, nor did my team. Change is constant and is a blessing in that it blunts the deadly sin of complacency, which saps the growth of so many successful ventures."

— DAVID JONES

Humana had long required directors to retire at seventy-three, so there was never any drama about when I'd step down. I was confident in my successors: Mike McCallister had taken over in 2000 and was doing a great job, and the board named David Jones, Jr. to succeed me as chairman on April 26, 2005, at Humana's annual meeting. The company was in good shape, with consolidated revenues in 2004 of $13.1 billion and a net income of $280 million. The company's market capitalization was over $5 billion, leaving me feeling good about the initial $2,000 investment Wendell and I had started with in 1961.

As Humana's first employee, I guided the company through what became amazing growth. When Humana was in both the hospital and insurance businesses, it had 105 hospitals and about 75,000 employees, with about 70,000 of them working in the hospitals we spun out in 1993. The number of insurance employees grew from about 5,000 that year to almost 20,000 in 2005, while the number of people we insured grew to more than 7 million, including nearly 600,000 seniors in Medicare Advantage plans. Beyond that, I would be credited for the many health care-related companies started by former Humana employees, many of whom stayed in the Louisville area.

I left Humana with no regrets. It was time to go. I didn't cry when we left the nursing home business or the hospital business. I'm always focused on what's ahead, not behind. Plus, I have been to several change-of-command ceremonies with Matt, our son in the Marines. The ceremonies are instructive. The Marines march around the new and old leaders, who salute each other, and the outgoing leader walks away. One minute one is in charge; the next minute, the other. There's no ambiguity about it.

Courier Journal business reporter Patrick Howington covered that 2005 annual meeting, at which I formally retired. A few days earlier, he had interviewed me for a front-page perspective on my life and had commented on how he was surprised to see I was wearing an inexpensive analog Timex watch identical to his. The explanation for my preference for Timex came later, at the annual meeting retirement party. Mike McAllister mentioned that the company had given me a watch with "Humana" inscribed in gold letters on its face.

"I know it's a little bit corny," McAllister said of giving me the watch, "but he normally wears a $10 Timex."

"It's a nice watch," I said of his gift, "but it doesn't glow in the dark like my Timex."

Mike McCallister was a perfect fit for success at Humana, a mix of hard work, preparation, teamwork, taking chances, and serendipity. He had grown up in Indianapolis, the son of two employees of Western Electric, which evolved as part of AT&T. His parents had transferred to Shreveport, Louisiana, where Mike went to high school and worked summers as a roofer. He went to college at Louisiana Tech, majoring in accounting, worked year-round as a picture framer, and became an excellent golfer.

In the spring of his senior year in college, Extendicare was well on its way to becoming Humana. Our policy was to hire new employees to work in hospitals near their hometowns since they were familiar with the area, people, and culture. A college graduate's degree mattered less than intelligence, enthusiasm, work ethic, and willingness to eventually lead.

Mike was hired in 1974 as a financial trainee for a small hospital in Springfield, Louisiana—population about 3,000. By age twenty-five, he was running a hospital.

As I learned in the Navy, CEOs who had received a command of any sort at a young age are less risk-averse and more successful than those whose first command came later in life. We rarely hired an experienced manager to lead our hospitals. Rather, we hired college and MBA grads, about half female and half male, trained and mentored them internally, and promoted many at young ages to executive director of a small hospital, always with a regional supervisor available. Humana training was often a two-year program in which new employees spent six months in four different areas of expertise.

McCallister had a great ability to get along with people but, at the same time, hold them accountable. When the company was floundering in 1999, I brought him to Louisville permanently to join my troika of problem-solvers.

The best predictor of future success is past success. McCallister's first move as CEO was to bring the net initiative team back into the company fold as it moved ahead with Emphesys, thus mixing the old traditional health care company with the push to bring Humana into the digital age. At a time when 70 percent of the nation's economy was consumer-driven, very little of the health care industry was—consumers got whatever benefits the government or their employer paid for, administered by whatever plan the sponsor chose. McCallister and Humana were preparing for a new day when there would be more consumer choice.

That came about in 2003 when Congress passed the Medicare Modernization Act, which offered new opportunities for seniors to choose private health plans—Medicare Advantage plans instead of original

Medicare, or Prescription Drug Plans if they wanted to stay with original Medicare. It is astonishing that Medicare didn't cover prescription drugs before 2003. Adding that benefit was huge for seniors and created another new opportunity for Humana. With our work building Emphesys, we already had a head start. We were ready for the retail environment, where seniors could choose for themselves.

McCallister has fond memories of the day in 2005 when I went into his office, sat down, and told him I was retiring.

"Well, you know I'm stepping down."

"Yes," McCallister said.

"You got it. It's your job. You got it."

"Okay, good."

"You know where I am if you need anything, but I will never call you."

"I'll call you," McCallister answered. "I'm pretty self-reliant, but I'll call you if I need anything."

We remained close friends. McCallister did call me about business a few times, as would Bruce Broussard, who succeeded McCallister as CEO in 2011 and created even more success. I called McCallister once, not to provide advice but to seek a donation for The Parklands of Floyds Fork. His response was very generous.

My transition into retirement—such as it was—didn't take long. I had a lot of other things I wanted to do. Two of the most central—The Parklands of Floyds Fork and Main Street Realty—were already underway in 2005. Dan was digging deep into the idea that would become the Parklands, while Main Street Realty had grown from the passive holding company for the old Belknap buildings to an active developer. And, of course, I would continue to be involved in Louisville's civic and political leadership, too.

I also began thinking seriously about writing a book about my life and Humana, including stories from friends and co-workers. I started working with Bob Hill and collected a few short summaries of what I'd learned along my own path.

My philosophy was consistent. Team members change, but the need for integrity, clarity of thought, and laser-like focus on the mission never changes. I never feared change, nor did my team. Change is constant and a blessing in that it blunts the deadly sin of complacency, which saps the growth of so many successful ventures.

As I said so many years ago in Humana's 1981 annual report, the world is always turning, the system is evolving, and those who do tomorrow what they did yesterday are likely to be caught short.

Chapter Thirty-One

RETIREMENT, BUT NOT REST

"Losing Walmart was somewhat reminiscent of two earlier community battles: the booming Reynolds Metal Company's leaving town in the 1950s as suburban Anchorage residents fought plans for a research park in their neighborhood, and the long fight that had delayed a new East End bridge over the Ohio River. Again, I saw that self-interested groups with no real sense of the community need tried to stop important projects—and often succeeded."

— DAVID JONES

When I left Humana, I took a great team with me. Rosanne Miller and Debbie Alexander brought institutional and people knowledge across all my activities, and Wanda Ryan added record-keeping of every penny spent and commitment made. Ken Payne and Bryan Johnson were working on a variety of real estate projects, supporting the nascent Parklands effort, building a strong development team, and more. Our family foundation had grown and was helping us support important education initiatives and other work in Louisville and beyond. And I kept my plane in Humana's hangar under a cost-sharing arrangement that benefited both sides, which meant contact with my pilot friends didn't change a bit.

I'd vacated my CEO office on Humana's sixth floor in 1997, in our unsuccessful first attempt at succession, moving to a more secluded spot on the second floor where I was near the Humana Foundation (on whose board I continued to serve) and could use the stairs instead of the elevator to come and go. In 2006, after my second retirement, I moved my offices to the American Life Building, just across Main Street, co-locating with the new Parklands office.

Staffing this new phase of my life reflected lessons learned in all that had come before: Work with great people, set bold and clear goals, and empower them to do their best work through trust and earned praise. My role, as always, was to think about what mattered and drive decisive action.

During this period, Main Street Realty continued to grow, quietly becoming a successful real estate development company with more than a billion dollars of commercial, industrial, residential, and community properties in the Louisville area and Florida. By 2015, its business projects totaled more than two thousand single-family lots, four million square feet of distribution centers, and two million square feet of commercial development at the intersection of Louisville's Gene Snyder Freeway and KY 22. Louisville projects included The Summit (now the Paddock Shops), Mockingbird Gardens, Old Brownsboro Crossing, Abbott Glen, Longwood, the Louisville Metro Commerce Center, Settlers Point, Cedar Grove, and Woodbridge. In Florida, we developed Galleon Bay.

I'd always loved real estate, and my competitive nature savored this business success. But my deepest passions were working to improve my hometown through a range of civic projects, philanthropy, and the focused effort to create The Parklands of Floyds Fork.

A lot of my newfound time and interest was taken up by a proposed new interstate bridge over the Ohio River connecting the East End of Louisville with southern Indiana near Utica. It had been discussed for about fifty years before I got involved and led a team to pull the project along and get it built.

"Every workday afternoon," I said of those years of delay, "thousands of vehicles are backed up on our interstate highways, all filling the air with fumes as they inch toward the Kennedy Bridge bottleneck. This daily traffic disaster also creates perhaps the region's largest source of air pollution."

The bridge had originally been proposed as part of President Eisenhower's Federal Highway Act of 1956, although no specific site had been mentioned. In that time frame, a federally supported highway loop (I-265) had been completed around Louisville—except for about a seven-mile link to Indiana at the East End of Louisville.

By 2010, it was the last section of interstate highway in the country that had not been started. The prime opponent was a group called River Fields, an organization involved in some minor environmental work in its wealthier area of town, but whose real agenda, many suspected, was closer to NIMBY—not in my backyard. The bridge issue languished for decades, partly because of ongoing lawsuits by River Fields, citing environmental concerns. One suit involved the Drumanard Estate, an old house and fifty-five acres that had been declared a National Historic Home. Bridge opponents based part of that suit on the claim—later disproved—that a garden on the estate had been built by the firm of Frederick Law Olmsted.

Another reason for the delay: Some Louisville civic and political leaders didn't push the bridge for fear of alienating powerful people and political donors who were involved with River Fields.

Over time, the idea of building one new bridge had evolved into building two new bridges—one in the east and another downtown. One of the early cost estimates for the bridges was $4.1 billion, a figure later reduced to $2.3 billion, but still enough to make tolls necessary.

The bridge discussion moved ahead when, after a meeting of Louisville leaders and an outside planner, the planner came back and said Louisville was a perfect mismatch. It wanted all the high-tech, high-education, clean industries that would bring in lots of high-paying jobs, but it didn't have the infrastructure or education system to create them. I suggested we start with two new Ohio River bridges and got unanimous support.

Fifth Third Bank CEO Jim Gaunt and I were chosen to meet with southern Indiana leaders to discuss the possibilities. Those leaders included

Ned Pfau, an industrial and community leader; Kent Lanum, president of the Ogle Foundation; and Dale Orem, former mayor of Jeffersonville (right across the river from Louisville) and longtime bridge proponent. We all agreed two bridges would be better than one, and tolls—although unpopular—would be absolutely necessary.

It was a very good meeting, and the Indiana folks told us as far as they could remember, we were the only people who had ever crossed the bridge in their direction. The eventual outcome was the formation of a group called the Louisville and Southern Indiana Bridges Authority. At first, I tried to negotiate quietly with the River Fields opponents to move the project forward. That got no results, so I began to go more public with my efforts. I led the first truly organized, well-funded push for the new bridges.

I created a group called Kentuckians for Progress. I enlisted, in particular, the help of three community leaders: David Nicklies of Nicklies Development, Sandra Frazier of Tandem Public Relations, and Rebecca Jackson, who had filled several important local government and civic roles.

Nicklies's history was very much Louisville. His grandparents immigrated from Germany and Lebanon. His father, Charles, served in World War II, then settled in Germantown, working as a contractor and commercial plasterer. His mother, Mary, was from a family that owned two restaurants—one that the family lived above, with a family-owned liquor store next door.

Nicklies had worked on construction jobs with his father, and he eventually started his own development company with shopping centers and subdivisions. His company also created Kids First Louisville, a group working to improve education for local children. We had a lot in common and got along very well. He pushed to be on the executive committee of Kentuckians for Progress, then agreed to chair it. We hired lobbyists in Frankfort and Indianapolis to push legislation to allow bridge tolls.

"We're one community," he said. "Southern Indiana is a part of that, too. Mr. Jones and I have talked about it many times. Then there's this one group of folks who have held this city back forever."

Nicklies developed a broad plan to take on River Fields, legally and with publicity, including ads, appearances, and billboards along I-71. His proposed budget was $350,000. I volunteered to give $100,000. Nicklies came back and said he couldn't get the rest of the money from anyone else. The opposition power structure was too strong and too interconnected. Would I be willing to fund the entire effort? I thought it over for about ten seconds and said, "Yes."

The second person working with me was Sandra Frazier, the great-great-great granddaughter of the founder of the Brown-Forman distillery. After working for advertising and public relations firms in Boston and Louisville for many years, she founded Tandem Public Relations in Louisville in 2005. Its clients would include Fortune 500 corporations, non-profit organizations, public institutions, small businesses, and public-affairs campaigns. She had worked with Dan Jones on Nature Conservancy activities, served on the Filson Historical Society board, and later joined the 21st Century Parks board, where she served as co-chair of the capital campaign that raised more than $125 million for the Parklands. Her connections, business savvy, and community involvement made her another good fit to work on the bridges project.

Rebecca Jackson, our third main voice in the bridges debate, also had a long history of personal, political, and civic involvement. Her father had been a tenant farmer from Short Creek, Kentucky, and her mother was a cartographer at the Army Map Service in Louisville.

Jackson had a long career as a special-education teacher and learning specialist. Then, running a grassroots campaign in 1989, she was elected Jefferson County clerk, becoming the only female office-holder—and Republican—in county government. In 1999, she was elected judge-executive—akin to mayor of the county—then became CEO of the WHAS Crusade for Children, a beloved community fundraiser that raises several million dollars every year at the grassroots level. After retiring from the Crusade, she joined our bridges project as our radio and TV spokesperson.

"I talked to people" said Jackson. "I connected the dots between River Fields and why we didn't have a bridge. We got a lot of people on board. Our immediate goal was to get it started, to turn a shovel of dirt on this thing."

Meanwhile, US Representative Anne Northup of Louisville, a Republican member of the House Appropriations Committee, got the funding to start the construction of two bridges at the same time.

I began going more public. In July 2011, I hit back on the River Fields lawsuits, emphasizing to a reporter the irony that the "pro-environmental" group's opposition to the East End bridge was causing ever more pollution as the traffic on overcrowded roads spewed fumes into the air.

That same month, I joined about one hundred Louisville business, community, and government leaders at the Galt House, a downtown hotel, for a press conference to demand that River Fields drop its Drumanard Estate lawsuit. My message to River Fields was to end the litigation, return to its praiseworthy environmental roots, and allow the bridge projects to begin. In September 2011, I offered a $10 million loan to jump-start the project, with other community leaders also ready to pledge.

I also funded legal research that proved the Frederick Law Olmsted firm had designed the Drumanard garden, but it had never been built. In July 2013, US District Judge John Heyburn II dismissed the final River Fields environmental lawsuit, saying bridge opponents "failed to raise a single factual issue to support their allegations."

Meanwhile, $338 million had been budgeted and was being spent to build twin tunnels under the Drumanard estate to get the project moving. To begin the process again would have taken more years of public hearings, study, and cost.

"I don't know if they knew it was true or not," I said of the proponents' claim of an Olmsted garden on the Drumanard estate, "but it was definitely untrue." And it had cost taxpayers hundreds of millions of dollars.

What would be called the Lewis and Clark Bridge in honor of the two explorers whose partnership was formed in Louisville opened on December 18, 2016, about fifteen years after I first became involved. The downtown bridge, named for Abraham Lincoln, who spent his early years in Kentucky and Indiana, had opened earlier.

The immediate beneficiary of the Lewis and Clark Bridge was the six thousand-acre River Ridge Commerce Center in Indiana, a few miles from the new bridge. The business park would grow to include more than sixty companies and 10,500 workers while paying about $42 million annually in local and state taxes with an estimated $2.4 billion overall impact in the Southern Indiana/Louisville region.

※

Given my life in Louisville, there were some events within its business community I would take very personally. One occurred in October 2016, when after years of hope, planning, meetings, and lawsuits, Walmart canceled plans to invest $30 million in a new store at Eighteenth Street and Broadway, the site of a Philip Morris cigarette factory that had closed fourteen years earlier. The store would have employed about three hundred people and been about five blocks from where I grew up, an area badly in need of an economic boost. But it was blocked by narrow-minded, obstructive preservationists who used restrictive zoning rules and meritless litigation to overcome larger neighborhood needs.

Walmart cited business factors as reasons for the cancelation: online shopping that hurt many big-box stores and "project delays." Those last two words seemed to refer to the fact that the project had been delayed by self-styled preservationists and local residents who had filed a lawsuit saying the proposed store violated the city's development code.

Their complaint: The code requires buildings to be built out to the sidewalk along Broadway, a main street running through downtown. As planned, the Walmart would have been far from the street to accommodate a large parking lot, just as the abandoned Philip Morris factory was.

The Louisville Board of Zoning Adjustment had unanimously approved Walmart's design. The preservationists' suit was dismissed by a Jefferson Circuit Court judge but was then appealed to the Kentucky Court of Appeals, delaying any construction. Three years after the Walmart was proposed—and on the same day the appeals court dismissed the appeal— Walmart announced it was dropping plans for the store anyway.

Through Main Street Realty, I had personally been involved in developing two Walmart stores and knew how they could create a vibrant neighborhood. Losing Walmart angered and energized me. It was somewhat reminiscent of two earlier battles: the booming Reynolds Metal Company leaving town in the 1950s as suburban Anchorage residents fought plans for a research park in their area and the long fight that had delayed the new East End bridge over the Ohio River.

Again, I saw that self-interested groups with no real sense of the community need tried to stop important projects—and often succeeded. The Walmart pull-out had been another blow to a neighborhood badly in need of jobs, stability, pride, and a retail outlet. The media focus on the area had become drug use and the increased murder rate, including a seven-year-old child killed by a stray bullet while sitting at the kitchen table eating cake.

Pushing into an area I call "windmill-tilting," I wrote a letter to all the Louisville Metro Council members in September 2017. I asked them to correct the "flawed policy choices which empowered the Walmart travesty." No stranger to Louisville preservation efforts, I listed the projects I had led or partnered in, involving "a capable team of passionate members with a clear idea" relying on common sense, not litigation or coercion.

My preservation credentials included the Belknap buildings that became the home of Presbyterian Church USA headquarters, Gardencourt mansion, the site of Vincenzo's restaurant, and the Actors Theatre building and parking garage. Also listed were several cast-iron building fronts on Main Street that became the face of an expanded Humana Building, historic buildings in the Parklands, Simmons College, and the expansion of St. Stephen Church.

"In killing Walmart," I wrote, "needy and deserving residents were denied affordable goods, including fresh food, three hundred jobs, and, most important, HOPE! What possible satisfaction can legislators who crafted this weapon, and officious interlopers who wielded it, obtain from this result?"

If any good came of the Walmart fiasco, it's that it became a catalyst for change, the tipping point to create a much-needed focus on a neighborhood in decline and Louisville's overall need for self-examination. I directed my energy to forming a new revitalization group that would take a good look at all of Louisville's needs. My partner in assembling that group of business CEOs and religious, civic, and political leaders was Chuck Denny, CEO of PNC Bank's Kentucky and Tennessee markets and another Louisvillian with roots in the West End neighborhood—a man I had mentored and whom I consider to be tops among the next generation of Louisville leaders.

The Louisville project had its roots in Nashville. Denny's work there had led him to join a committee of about seventy-five community leaders, each a company CEO or civic leader, to prioritize Nashville's needs. No substitutes were allowed; only CEOs could attend meetings.

We believed Louisville needed a similar committee. It was first labeled Agenda for Action, with members coming from every facet of leadership in Louisville and Southern Indiana. The leader of the Nashville group was also invited to explain how their group worked and what it had accomplished. No one turned down the invitation. About fifteen leaders attended the first meeting, and thirty the second. Everyone agreed to support the group's first undertaking: improving public K–12 schools.

Denny and I sent a letter to everyone who had attended our meetings, asking each of them to compile a list of five things they thought most important to Louisville's future. No politics were involved. Two weeks later, we had responses from twenty people. The top five Louisville issues mentioned were:

1. Public school education
2. Crime
3. Air service
4. Economic development
5. Tax and pension reform

We thanked those who had responded and said we would look for a leader for each issue, adding those were "tough, vital issues that must and can be improved, as Nashville's experience shows."

Progress was soon apparent. A front-page July 28, 2017 *Courier Journal* story said a private push to increase non-stop flights from the Louisville airport had gained the financial backing of Louisville's Metro government and "various civic partners" totaling $2.6 million. Another $4 million were to be raised from investors and private companies as incentives to airlines to increase non-stop flights. Los Angeles and Boston were the target cities.

As the group moved forward in other areas, its name became the Steering Committee for the Advancement of the Louisville Agenda (SCALA), with Sandra Frazier, a leader with me on the bridges project, joining me as co-chair.

Our founding members included Louisville Mayor Greg Fischer, Roman Catholic Archbishop Joseph Kurtz, Bellarmine University President Susan Donovan, Volunteers of America CEO Jennifer Hancock, and Spalding University President Tori Murden McClure, whose credentials included being the first woman and American to row solo across the Atlantic Ocean. Others included St. Stephen Church Senior Pastor Kevin Cosby, Catholic Education Foundation President Richard Lechleiter, Metro United Way President Theresa Reno-Weber, and Southeast Christian Church Senior Pastor Dave Stone.

Despite that broad-based membership, one SCALA opponent—a group named "Dear JCPS," JCPS being an acronym for Jefferson County Public Schools—complained in the *Courier Journal* that SCALA was an "elite business group" with "closed membership" being given "power and privilege" in an attempt to take over the schools.

I later described that notion as "uninformed." The names and occupations of all of its members were released to the public. I had gone to public schools for sixteen years and knew education was the city's top priority.

"SCALA is not the problem," I said. "A major problem is that too few JCPS students have learned to read at a job- or college-ready level! A travesty that must be fixed!"

Four members of SCALA—including Reverend Kevin Cosby—

wrote a February 1, 2018 op-ed piece in the *Courier Journal* outlining the "indisputable facts" about JCPS and the reasons the group sought strong outside leadership to correct them. The list included Jefferson County Public Schools' poor proficiency rates on state assessments, the performance gaps between white and black students, and the low rates of JCPS students prepared for college.

I took a long look at that history and decided to act. As a guy who grew up in a union family, a former member of the hod carrier's union with a son and a daughter who had been union members, I gave money to SCALA and certain politicians because we needed change.

All of us who had built these successful companies started with a little bit of hunger and a little bit of grit, and a little bit of wanting to better our situation. Our only purpose in forming this group was to make Louisville a better place to live, work, and bring up children.

In a February 8, 2018 opinion piece in the *Courier Journal*, I mentioned a recent story about a possible state takeover of Louisville's public schools if an ongoing audit recommended that approach. I said I favored any approach that would produce positive results.

That led to a wave of media criticism that a bunch of old, wealthy, white guys wanted to take over the schools. That was wrong. I'm the beneficiary of seven years of government-paid higher education on top of twelve years of public school education in Louisville. That was the foundation of my career. Education is our most vital infrastructure.

I'm totally passionate about wanting all kids, especially the disadvantaged, to receive a good education, as I did. Sadly, many are not. The status quo must change.

The SCALA organization would later change its name to "Impetus." It would have about sixty members, including David Jones, Jr., with Sandra Frazier as chair.

Betty and I had always tithed, but by the 1980s, I realized our resources had grown to the point where we should be more organized in our giving. The same was true with Humana. So I started two charitable foundations, the Humana Foundation in 1981 and our family's C.E.&S. Foundation in 1984. After stepping down as chair of Humana Inc., I stayed on the foundation's board. I also worked closely with family members on C.E.&S.

Wendell and I may have officially created the Humana Foundation as a 501(c)(3) in 1981, but the records show the company had been making contributions since the 1970s. In the early years, I basically ran it out of my pocket, but in 1992, I realized it needed a leader. Virginia Kelly Judd worked closely with me on the Romania Assistance Project, and I admired the work she was doing and her ability to make decisions and deal with people. So one day, as she and I were getting on the elevator together, I asked if she would also help with the Humana Foundation. Her job would be to go out into the community, meet people, learn about their projects, and then come to me to talk about them. I had investment specialists to handle the financial matters. She eventually became the foundation's first executive director.

The foundation's outreach would grow to include cities and schools across the country, many with a Humana presence, although that was not a prerequisite. The foundation grew with the company. A Humana report showed the company and foundation had donated $273 million from 1975 to 2016 while funding more than two hundred grants. About 60 percent were in health and wellness, 22 percent civic and cultural, and 16 percent in education, although in the latter years, the focus was much more on education. I believe in volunteerism, so every Humana employee receives one paid day a year to volunteer in the community.

The hiring of Bruce Maza to head our family's private C.E.&S. Foundation included another dose of good luck, adaptability, and serendipity. In 1997, Maza, who had a long record in foundation work, received a call from a friend at the Lilly Endowment in Indianapolis, letting him know a Louisville family was looking for a "values-based person" to become the first executive director of a family foundation.

Bruce is a very thoughtful and articulate man. His initial interview was with Dave and Mary Gwen, and he always remembered that during the meeting, their daughter, Becky, came in and crawled up on her father's lap, making the point that family mattered to all of us.

His interview with Betty and me also went very well. We discussed the role of education in forming an individual's ability to succeed and that philanthropy had to play a vital role in that. He was also excited that all our children could participate in the grant process to pass it on to the next generation. And I explained to him our first rule of philanthropic success was, "Betty and I have always tried to give at the intersection of passion and competence."

He did a great job, staying with us for seventeen years. The 2019 annual report listed the family foundation's assets at $74 million and noted that it had awarded nearly $100 million in grants since inception. Its goal was to identify, fund, and nurture projects in education and global competency and to improve the urban environment. Its focus became education, with a particular emphasis on Louisville, where public education continually lags behind.

The family foundation did things like donate money to triple the number of children at a kindergarten readiness camp. The always carefully measured results showed readiness jumped 80 percent in some schools. That was important to me. Reading readiness is an economic issue.

I don't care what children's backgrounds are or if they're red, black, yellow, or white. Learn how to read comprehensively, write coherently, and understand basic math, and they have a good chance to have a good life.

The emotional rewards that come with helping other people and organizations always make the efforts worthwhile. Betty and I received many letters from people we helped along the way. One came from Robert C. Post, Dean of the Yale School of Law. He thanked me for our contributions to the Twentieth Anniversary Global Constitutionalism Seminar, which brought in twenty-eight justices of constitutional and transnational courts from around the world.

"The entire school is forever grateful for your assistance in establishing what has become the preeminent international program at Yale Law

School," Post wrote.

This was just one example of our work at Yale, where we liked to seed good ideas and then let the law school or the university raise a big endowment after the concept was proven, often from someone who wanted their name on it. We didn't. This partnership helped Yale innovate and sustain not only the Global Constitutionalism Seminar but the China Law Center, the Career Opportunities Assistance Program, and others. I also recently gave a start-up gift to the new law school dean to fundamentally restructure legal education at Yale, which I hope will have an impact on preparing graduates for leadership—in the law and beyond. That dean, Heather Gerken, is herself a great leader.

Closer to home was a letter from Gabriele "Gaby" Bosley, executive director of Bellarmine University's foreign language and international cultures program, supported by the Jones family and our C.E.&S. Foundation. In a recent office move, she had gone through thirty years of files and documents "testifying to the enormous impact your longtime funding of the international programs at Bellarmine has had on our students and faculty," she wrote.

"Many, many hundreds of students were able to study, intern, student-teach, or do clinicals abroad because of your scholarships, and many thousands of students were impacted by the broad programming we were able to develop around the globe over these several decades."

In response, we sent a note:

"Dear Gaby,

"Your long and loving recitation of our support for your amazingly frugal yet totally effective programs brings a song to our hearts. We helped a bit, but you made it happen."

Chapter Thirty-Two

Seeing the Forest, for the Future

"During the creation of the Parklands, we really became partners and friends. One of the things he said to me that made me very proud was we had a great partnership. And I never heard him refer to anyone other than Wendell Cherry as his partner.

"But more important was the fact that we became friends. There was nothing wrong with the father/son relationship—that continued the whole way. But to have that friendship was, for me, very special."

— DAN JONES

To expand the education of our family, Betty and I would occasionally take the children to Bernheim Forest, south of Louisville, a 16,000-acre mix of native trees, meadows, lakes, art, arboretum with hundreds of rare plants, and a welcome center.

And when we lived on Village Drive, all our kids would walk over to nearby Cherokee Park and play in Beargrass Creek. These experiences ignited Dan's interest in the diverse Louisville Metro Parks system, much of it created by Frederick Law Olmsted. Years later, Dan would conceive—and lead the development—of the four thousand-acre Parklands of Floyds Fork, based on the work of Frederick Law Olmsted.

After Dan and Lisa returned to Louisville, he taught history at U of L, started Different Strokes, a chain of golf centers with different partners, and began working with Louisville Metro Parks on its projects. He helped fund Metro Parks's purchase of Fairmont Falls on Thixton Lane, a remote, nearly eight-acre site with lovely, tumbling waterfalls closely tied to local history.

He followed that by leading the planning and construction of the eighty-eight-acre Thurman Hutchins Park, near the Ohio River, another family enterprise. David Jones, Jr. donated the land. Betty and I paid for improvements, which included biking, hiking, baseball and soccer fields, a playground, and a picnic shelter. It was a green oasis along a much-traveled River Road flanking the Ohio River.

The "Thurman" was from my mother, and the "Hutchins" was from Betty's mother. I did not want the Jones name on it. That long-held idea was reinforced in a biography I had just read about General Ulysses S. Grant, a most humble person. If you actually do things, you don't have to tell people about them. So what if they know or don't know.

The initial inspiration for the Parklands came when Metro Parks director Brigid Sullivan and Bill Juckett, chairman of our local Olmsted Parks Conservancy, asked for a meeting with me to discuss ways present-day Louisville could match the 100-year impact of Frederick Law Olmsted's work in Louisville parks. Knowing Dan's passion for parks, I asked him to join us. The invitation would change Dan's life—and the Louisville landscape—but it took a little while for that to happen.

"It was an interesting meeting," Dan would say later, "and at first I didn't think much about it. I like parks. I knew the story of Olmsted. And I began to think we should do the same thing, and we should prepare a plan to get ahead of growth while land was available and affordable."

Dan was ready for a change. He became excited about the possibility of building a new park system in his hometown to honor the man behind Louisville's original park system. He hired Dan Church, a Louisville architectural and urban planning consultant, for $35,000 to come up with a preliminary plan for the last major undeveloped part of Louisville.

There were three possible sites for a new park, including meandering Floyds Fork on the city's eastern edge, an area still remote yet vulnerable to development. The planners came up with the idea for a connected park system spanning about twenty miles along Floyds Fork and encompassing almost four thousand acres, almost all of it then in private hands.

Dan brought the plan to me.

"What do you think?" he asked.

"I think it's doable," I replied. "Go for it."

In preparation to build the park, Dan returned to Yale in 2004, with his wife and four children, to earn a master's degree. He became class valedictorian in a two-year program in its School of Forestry and Environmental Studies.

He returned to Louisville, where he founded a non-profit entity, 21st Century Parks, and began the creation of The Parklands of Floyds Fork. The Parklands would come to include four major distinct parks and a connecting strand within a contiguous 19.4 miles along the river. All of it would be lined by walking and bicycle paths, with much of it also accessible by car—Olmstedian in concept, design, and final product.

The Parklands were welded together over ten years in a very complex mix funded by $125 million in local, state, federal, and private money—including Humana and our family foundation. They connect more than eighty separate parcels of land along Floyds Fork. I chaired our fundraising capital campaign steering committee, which was co-chaired by six other very active people: Jim Bloem, Chuck Denny, Sandra Frazier, Phil McHugh, Joe Pusateri, and David Wood. Our amazing outside helper and drill sergeant was Louisville's legendary fundraising guru Christen Boone.

I became very involved in the process. Main Street Realty handled all the contracts and bids for 21st Century Parks, absorbing all overhead costs during construction. As always, I insisted everything done at the Parklands be measured to reach the desired goal.

I consider the Parklands one of the most important things I have ever done. It had its beginning when former Jefferson County Commissioner Steve Henry had begun acquiring land along Floyds Fork for a Future Fund project, a land trust, not a public park. Henry, an orthopedic surgeon and former lieutenant governor of Kentucky, is the husband of Heather

French Henry, a Kentuckian who was Miss America in 2000.

Betty and I had put up a half-million dollars, and Sallie Bingham put up $250,000 to enable Steve to buy several parcels for about $2,000 an acre. The average price for acquisitions went to $10,000 an acre, and when sewers arrived in the neighborhood, the price went to about $30,000 to $40,000 an acre.

The plan received a huge boost in September 2005 in a 10 p.m. phone call to me at home from US Senator Mitch McConnell, also a Louisvillian, while I was working out in my basement. Earlier, I had talked to McConnell about the possibility of $10 million in federal funding for roads and bridges in the still-hoped-for park. McConnell said, "Dave, I've looked at all the proposed projects for the Commonwealth, and yours is the best. I know that you and Dan will cause it to happen. It's not going to be $10 million. It's going to be $38 million."

Fresh from my workout, I was unsure exactly what McConnell had said, and answered, "I'm out of breath. May I sit down? Would you please say that again."

"It's $38 million," McConnell repeated, "for roads and bridges."

With that money in the pipeline, the Parklands went from long-term dream to near reality. It was designed by the architectural firm of Wallace Roberts & Todd (WRT) of Philadelphia, assisted locally by Jim Walters's firm, Bravura.

Dan had a lot of praise for Walters, who he said eventually became much more hands-on involved in the Parklands than WRT. The Louisville Parks Department, Louisville city government, Kentucky government, and Future Fund were also heavily involved in the park's creation.

Another key person in creating the Parklands was Chuck Denny, regional president of PNC Bank and on the 21st Century Parks board. He and I, along with Dan, would lead the fundraising early on.

Denny came by his love of parks naturally. He grew up in Louisville's far West End. On Sundays, he would walk up to Shawnee Park to play golf, a sport at which he excelled.

Working days, he earned a business degree at night school at the

University of Louisville and went to work for Liberty National Bank and Trust. In 1980, he joined First National Bank, where I was a director. We bonded instantly. Two years later, I asked him to handle the bank's relations with Humana. Denny said of me, "I always thought he looked like some big Norwegian Viking. He was this really big guy with a shock of blond hair and piercing blue eyes, just a larger-than-life type of guy."

Decades later, Denny and I were working on fundraising for the Parklands. We were talking about a possible donor, and while Denny was walking out the door, I asked: "How much are you going to ask for?"

"David, I don't know. How about maybe half a million dollars."

"Make it a million."

The donor ended up giving $500,000, but the larger message had been delivered: Reach for the stars.

"It was never about him," Denny said of me. "It was always about everybody. Team first."

Completing the Parklands would eventually require eighty separate land acquisitions. There was no government condemnation; each purchase had to be separately negotiated with the landowners, most of them by a low-key native Texan and former assistant director of football operations at the University of Louisville, Kevin Beck.

Completed in August 2016, the park's mantra is, "Safe, clean, fun, and beautiful 365 days a year from dawn to dusk for free." With an original and uncertain goal of a few hundred thousand visitors, more than three million people would visit the park four years later. Dan's future goal is to get more of Louisville's underserved and minority populations to visit.

The cost for land, construction, and amenities was about $125 million. Of that, $38 million came from the federal government, $10 million from the state, and $1.5 million from the city of Louisville. The balance was donated by individuals, foundations, and corporations.

An additional $40 million has been raised as an endowment fund to help ensure the parks are clean, safe, and well-maintained in perpetuity. By design, the Parklands became a working environmental laboratory in Louisville's ever-diminishing backyard, and an instant hit with Kentucky and southern Indiana residents. Invasive shrubs were cleaned out, and thousands of new trees and shrubs were planted, all with an eye toward the next century. Its attractions include children's playgrounds, picnic areas at both ends, a dog park, and ornamental bridges.

Visitors can enjoy twenty-five miles of canoeing and paddling, walking, hiking, and biking. There are places for school retreats and field trips around plants, water, and wildlife, plus the ancient solitude of the Big Beech Woods. A more recent addition is the Moss Gibbs Woodland Garden, with more than 47,000 plants and trees along an uphill path.

In 2010, the Parklands won a national honor, the Place Maker award, from the Foundation for Landscape Studies, headed by Betsy Barlow Rodgers, founder and longtime head of New York's Central Park Conservancy. An ever-expanding mountain bike trail opened in the park in 2017.

The Parklands would become very important to me, a legacy that could reach back one hundred years as we restored damaged forests and land and two hundred years into the future as we planted thousands of new trees. I wore my blue Parklands shirt to work almost every day, and people joked among themselves about burying me in it.

The Parklands will shape the development of Louisville's southeast region, just as the Olmsted Parks did when built on the city's outskirts in the 1890s. Lovely neighborhoods will arise, filled with healthy people enjoying the many miles of trails for walking and the twenty-five miles of stream for paddling and much more.

Dan is the visionary, creator, operator, and caretaker for the Parklands. But he sees me as an active and vital partner—and more. Dan said,

> He always gives me credit for the success of the Parklands, but there is no way I could have done it without him. We really became partners and friends. One of the things he said to me

that made me very proud was we had a great partnership. And I never heard him refer to anyone other than Wendell Cherry as his partner.

But more important was the fact that we really became friends. There was nothing wrong with the father/son relationship—that continued the whole way. But to have that friendship was, for me, very special.

Epilogue

by Bob Hill

"We've just been sitting here singing old hymns."

— DAVID and BETTY JONES at the hospital

After sixty-five years of marriage, the funerals for Betty and David Jones were held in the soft and gentle light of the Highland Presbyterian Church only one month and three days apart. Survivors included five children, three daughters-in-law, and eleven grandchildren.

The emotional, heartfelt words delivered by Reverend Cynthia Campbell and Jones family members in both services—and the needed laughter that occasionally came with them—brought into perfect focus all the good the couple had done for Louisville, the nation, and the world, and the mostly quiet, determined and careful ways they went about it.

Campbell had often visited David Jones at the Nazareth Home near the end of his life. It was her sense that after Betty died, the separation had been very hard on David. Her closeness to both made her feel comfortable in offering final words. Her memories included visiting them when David was hospitalized at Baptist Hospital East. Both David and Betty were holding old Baptist hymnals when she arrived.

"We've just been sitting here singing old hymns," David explained.

✳

Betty Lee Ashbury Jones died on August 16, 2019, after a gradual decline that seemed to have started a couple years earlier with complications from a fracture in her back. Her obituary said,

> She passed away at home just as the sun was setting, peacefully and painlessly, surrounded by her husband, children, and grandchildren, her youngest grandchild holding her hand, all singing the lovely ballads she had sung to them when they were young. Gentle and generous, her beautiful, mighty, luminous spirit remained intact until the end.

Campbell spoke directly to Jones family members of that love at a private church service on August 21, 2019:

> She gave you the very best of herself and loved doing it. Her pride in you was enormous. Her hopes for you were always high. Her joy in being with you was beyond measure.
>
> The things she taught you—explicitly and by example. The joy and fun she created even in the midst of challenging times. Songs learned by one generation and passed on to the next. The way in which she made a home—a good and loving place—for you all.

Carol Jones, the youngest child, spoke of that love in more basic familial terms:

> Thank you for tea times and book clubs, beautiful thank you notes, and always a good title to share. Thank you for the Popsicles and chicken fingers in the freezer, for letting frogs in the house and dogs spend the night, for letting us play Risk and sleep on the pool table and throw Pop Its in the driveway.

Thank you for keeping the cookie jar and basement refrigerator full and keeping the kitchen permanently stocked with chicken salad, coffee cake, Doritos, and chicken tetrazzini.

Thank you for keeping a stash of extra clothes in the back hall closet so our children could play hard and not strew the mess throughout the house (and thank you for laughing it off when they did strew the mess throughout the house).

Thank you for playing in the leaves and the sand and the pond with our children. It makes me happy to know that my children share a family history and culture with their cousins and aunts and uncles through the books you read to us and the songs you sang to us.

Thank you for listening to me, for loving me, for challenging me, defending me, accepting me, for laughing with me, and crying with me. Thank you for reminding me that things look better in the morning and most things come out in the wash.

David Jones, Jr., the eldest, said he was filled with sorrow over the loss of their mother but not sadness. He said,

The gratitude I feel leaves no room in my heart for sadness. Gratitude to my mom for all of who she was and stood for. Gratitude for the miracle of having such a mother and for the gift of time together to know how much she loved me, and my children, and my wife, Mary Gwen, and that she knew how much we loved her.

As the service ended, Carol took the lead when family gathered around the flower-draped casket to say a blessing for Betty—the same blessing Betty led when she and David joined Carol for Friday Shabbat with her family: "May the Lord bless and keep you; the Lord make His face shine upon you; the Lord lift up the light of His countenance upon you and give you peace."

Burial was in Cave Hill Cemetery, the historic Louisville cemetery of rolling sculptural beauty, with its 120,000 gravesites dating back to the 1840s. Its graves are occupied by some of Kentucky's most famous, including Muhammad Ali, George Rogers Clark, Colonel Harland Sanders, and sculptor Enid Yandell.

Its arboretum-like landscape is filled with trees huge and ornamental; its feel is peaceful, sacred, and reverent. After final words were spoken at the grave site, those gathered sang "I'll Fly Away" to bid Betty Lee Ashbury Jones a farewell.

> *Some glad morning when this life is over*
> *I'll fly away*
> *To a home on God's celestial shore*
> *I'll fly away.*

David Jones's funeral at Highland Presbyterian Church was on September 21, 2019, exactly a month after Betty's. The mourners first rose to sing "Amazing Grace," its sweet sound filling the church.

Reverend Campbell praised Jones for his ability to see potential in others, often before they could see it in themselves. She offered perspective for his death as presented in Ecclesiastes 3:

> *To everything there is a reason,*
> *and a time to every purpose under the heavens:*
> *A time to be born, and a time to die,*
> *a time to plant, and a time to pluck up*
> *what has been planted.*

The familiar words of Psalm 23 followed, after which David, Jr.'s wife and children offered comfort in the Maya Angelou poem "When Great Trees Fall."

And when great souls die,
After a period peace blooms,
slowly and always
irregularly. Spaces fill
with a kind of
soothing electric vibration.
Our senses, restored, never
to be the same, whisper to us.
They existed. They existed.
We can be. Be and be
better. For they existed.

Dave then spoke of his father's final days. He said he had been admitted to the hospital more than five months earlier with what proved to be multiple myeloma, how his back had collapsed, and he lost fifty pounds as radiation burned and chemotherapy poisoned his body.

Yet, he told family and friends, dwelling on that would be wrong:

> Dad never, ever stopped being the man he was. As he weakened and mobility, energy—even the fearsome grip of his handshake—fell away, the essential light of his being shone brighter than ever.
>
> This essence was joyful and overflowing with gratitude. Dad took his joy from people whose names and stories he remembered and loved learning till the end. He loved his family and basked in his grandchildren's calm caring and stories of new learning or adventures.
>
> His last communication was a smile, earned recognition for a song well sung.

Carol, as she had done with her mother, eulogized her father in playful but sincere love:

Thank you for playing golf with me and teaching me how to use my left hand, for playing football in the backyard, watching *The Dukes of Hazzard* and singing John Denver, for reading to my children and taking them swimming, for the duct tape and Saturday morning doughnuts.

Thank you for paying the phone bill at the German hotel when we went to see Matt so many years ago—I still don't know how much that cost.

Thank you for teaching me how to laugh at myself and for trying to teach me—by example and even in your final days— to accept reality and move on when the time comes. We're seeing now how well that lesson has been learned.

Dan began his thoughts with a comment his daughter had made: how very sad and yet astonishingly beautiful it was that his father had passed just a short time after his mother, and how his father had often said—and proven in his lifetime—how much he loved all his children equally and without reservation.

Dan again marveled at the example his father had set, always with clear words when necessary, and how in their fifteen years together building The Parklands of Floyds Fork, "he had continued to be my father, but he also became my partner and my friend. At that moment in the journey, I also took time to look up at a new road. He understood that new road, and he left me well prepared . . . he was a singularly remarkable man."

Matt was the last of the Jones children to speak, reading a Robert Burns poem that had been a favorite of both of his parents, "Epitaph on a Friend." It was the same poem, Matt and his siblings later found out, his father had read at Wendell Cherry's funeral.

> *An honest man here lies at rest,*
> *As e'er God with His image blest:*
> *The friend of man, the friend of truth;*

The friend of age, and guide of youth:
Few hearts like his, with virtue warm'd,
Few heads with knowledge so inform'd:
If there's another world, he lives in bliss;
If there is none, he made the best of this.

As the service ended, the Jones family, accompanied by piano music echoing through the soft light, sang "When the Saints Go Marching In." It was soon followed by another family chorus of "I'll Fly Away" at Cave Hill Cemetery.

I'll fly away, oh, Glory
I'll fly away
When I die, Hallelujah, by and by
I'll fly away.

David was buried beside Betty, their names carved in solid granite. Their large, unpretentious gravestone rests in a broad cemetery plot facing an elegant bench where mourners and admirers can sit. Above them, as in the days of their youth, are the broad, spreading limbs of a sugar maple tree.

Afterword

by David Jones, Jr.

It's been four years since Dad passed away, and he's still very much with me. His gratitude to the people who cared for him, his constant joy at their competence and precision; his sense of humor till the very end, and the pleasure he took from his grandchildren; his intentionality in saying goodbye to each of his kids, leaving at least me with unambiguous guidance; my sense that he was at peace as he faced first Mom's death a month earlier, then his own.

Dad was going strong until spring 2019. On April 3, Mom woke me with an early call: "Can you meet your dad at the hospital? He woke up with a bad nosebleed, and an ambulance is taking him to the ER." I did, and the nosebleed proved to be nothing. But he went from there to a scheduled appointment with a neurologist, to whom he'd been referred for back pain. Not long after, I got another call: "Your father has been admitted to the hospital for testing. We suspect cancer."

Twenty years ago, multiple myeloma was a death sentence. Now, thanks to treatments defined over the past five years or so, the doctors describe it as "a disease you die with, not from." Maybe, but the treatment—radiation and chemotherapy—sapped strength from the aging fighter's body, and the cancer ate away at spinal bone before it was killed off. He knew pain in the first months after diagnosis, and seeing this tore Mom up and wore her out.

He went home from the hospital, but integrated care of the bodily systems upended by cancer treatment, and of two frail old people at home, proved elusive.

What a life. Dad loved talking to Bob Hill, loved Bob's gift for storytelling, and hoped to leave his own life story as a tale of more than business success. As I read Dad's words in this book, new themes of his life appear.

- Dad was optimistic and energetic, despite big losses along the way. All of his best male friends died early, of dread diseases: his best college friend, Carey Thompson, of leukemia in 1963; his older brother, Logan, his ally in fighting for and supporting the family through the tough Depression and war years, and whose willingness to carry those burdens alone freed Dad to go to Yale Law School, of non-Hodgkin's Lymphoma in 1982; Allen Duffy, his closest law school friend, of leukemia in 1986; and Wendell Cherry, his partner in every way in building and repeatedly reinventing Humana, of cancer in 1991. His mother lost her leg in 1970 and never walked again—just at the point when Dad's financial success would have opened up the world to this curious, combative, and ferociously well-read woman.

- He talked often about the "confidence of total ignorance." Often in error, never in doubt, perhaps—but he and Wendell were never ignorant. They were just inexperienced and very early in the steep learning climbs that Dad loved, and from which he never shirked. He did indeed try to calm my mother (without success) by joking that the banks from which Humana had borrowed the money that he and Wendell personally guaranteed were the ones really at risk in the deal. But as I read Dad's words, I always see, beneath the humor and the bluster, the little boy who pulled a wagonload of books home from the Parkland library with his mom every week. He and Wendell were voracious, consuming, aggressively physical readers. They devoured books and magazines, newspapers, and case studies. My dad also talked, and *listened,* to everyone he met—because he expected to learn.

• He hated pretension, condescension, and prejudice. The scruffy Louisville boys laughed and laughed at the New York marketing elite who gagged at Carl Pollard's snappy sportscoat—but they learned fast, and they were relentless in choosing and trusting people who could get things done, not just talk about them. The company that Dad built, just like the Parklands he helped Dan build and the city he loved, grew on the practical capacity of people who grew as they learned, more than on expert credentials.

• He was proud, more than anything, of the hundreds of thousands of good jobs that his entrepreneurship created and the tens of thousands of families whose world changed because of those jobs. He loved the fact that he'd given so many people the opportunity to do their best work.

• Dad was skeptical of inherited wealth. He and Mom worked hard to raise unspoiled kids as they grew wealthy, and they acted on their values in estate planning. But what they mostly did was give away their money while they were alive: joyfully, and mostly anonymously. Dad related little of this in his memoir, sharing almost random examples of their philanthropy. And although I worked closely with Dad on so much, including the family and Humana foundations, on education giving and more, I have been astonished to learn the scale of their giving, which has become clearer now that they're gone. Even as I write this, I'm still learning. For example, the president of Middlebury College recently shared a "summary presentation" of my parents' support, putting the total at over $36 million. "Their vision, leadership, and generosity," she writes, "quite simply have changed Middlebury forever."

• Dad could be impatient, and he had a temper. But he was better at thanking people than anyone I've ever met: thanking them for their specific contribution, remembering their names and personal circumstances, joining their story to his own. Seeing his love for people in action over his last six months, every day through pain and confusion, was his last gift to me.

• He loved my mom, and she loved him. Their sixty-five years together set an example that I treasure. But they were clear-eyed and transparent that staying together was a choice, that love was a discipline that one honed through care, attention, and effort. When Mom set off for grad school in her fifties, leaving Dad at home each summer with one or two kids, she needed space and freedom to grow. He adapted, supported, and their adventure was enriched.

After Mom passed away, I thought Dad was rebounding. When we took him to the funeral home for Mom's visitation, we'd agreed he'd stay for an hour, but he stayed for three, talking to every person who waited in the long line before the doors closed. Later he seemed lifted up by the friends and family who came to his house for her wake. He worked at physical therapy and expressed determination to walk again. He encouraged me to go to India on a study tour of new, technology-enabled models for home care.

But adrenaline and toughness masked the emptiness of his physical reserves. He called me to come home early because he knew he was dying. When I arrived, his mind, love, and sense of humor were intact, but his body was shutting down. Thirty-six hours before he died, at the Nazareth Home near Bellarmine University, he was dozing in a recliner with a granddaughter leaning over on either side of him and two of his children in the room. He opened his eyes, looked at everyone, and said, "A watched pot never boils."

Said it with his mischievous grin.

Appendix

Some Thoughts on Health Care System Reform

by David A. Jones

January 2018

I offer a clear and simple health care reform proposal that will move us toward the honorable goal of providing truly universal coverage. By requiring consumer engagement, it will lower the unsustainable growth in health care costs.

I.   How Health Care is Paid for in America

In America, the elderly and the poor receive subsidized health care through Medicare and Medicaid. Our nonelderly near-poor are provided for by hidden subsidies.

When health care providers provide free or below-cost services, they add the costs of such uncompensated care to the charges of those who can pay—namely, the privately insured, a.k.a. the American worker.

This cost shift, according to the Washington, DC-based Urban Institute, paid for $62.1 billion of services to the uninsured in 2009, a substantial part of the estimated cost of insuring that group. For its helpful role as the necessary conduit in this system, the health insurance industry has been unfairly criticized.

II. Universal coverage is the needed bedrock of an honorable, functional, and affordable American health care system. We all, including the young and healthy, need to be in the same boat together—no exceptions.

Universal coverage renders moot the controversy over pre-existing conditions and further moots the frivolous notion that we can wait until we're ill or injured to purchase insurance.

Here is my version of necessary and generally easy-to-understand health care reforms. Most require little or no federal funding. They will slow the growth in health care costs. This will lessen subsidies needed to reach the honorable goal of universal coverage.

1. Increase competition and lower costs by allowing individuals and small employers to purchase insurance across state lines.

2. Insured individuals and small employers should be granted parity with ERISA-enabled self-insured employers, and relieved of the requirement to purchase state-mandated products and services, often of dubious value. Such mandates add 20 to 30 percent to the cost of their insurance.

3. Portability—"Evergreen Cobra"—allows individuals to maintain with their ex-employer an affordable level of insurance, such as a high-deductible plan, when they leave a job, so long as they pay the full premium.

4. Allow paid buy-in, at local insurance rates, to Medicare or Medicaid for consumers who are denied coverage

because of pre-existing conditions.

5. Lawsuit (tort) reform. Fear of litigation leads to "defensive medicine," legitimizing expensive, unneeded medical tests and services.

6. Require all providers in federal programs, by a date certain, perhaps in five years, to connect electronically and use standard forms. They can and will figure out how to comply. This will aid transparency and provide robust real-time information, allowing consumers to assume greater personal responsibility for their health care and its costs.

7. Tax Reform—We pay for truly vital needs, such as food and water, with after-tax income. Employee health costs are largely paid with pre-tax income. This has created a huge accidental, never legislated tax subsidy. Using US budget forecasts for 2011–2015, the Washington, DC-based Center for American Progress estimates that this subsidy will exceed $1 trillion for those five years. This subsidy should be phased out over a five- to ten-year period, increasing consumers' "skin in the game" and providing enormous resources for subsidies needed to achieve universal coverage.

8. Medicare—It will soon be bankrupt and must be reformed. Here's how: For five years, current beneficiaries should be grandfathered. Baby-boomers, already familiar and largely satisfied with private insurance, should be allowed to choose to retain it when they become Medicare eligible. After five years, all new Medicare beneficiaries should be required to maintain private insurance.

Privately insured Medicare members should receive a voucher equal to perhaps 75 percent of the age and location-adjusted national average cost of traditional Medicare, to spend as they wish in a robust, competitive marketplace. This will allow them to acquire the plan that best meets their individual needs, paying any balance personally. Subsidies, varying by income, must be provided to enable low-income seniors to purchase an average-cost plan, although each person should pay some portion of the premium.

This reform should lower costs significantly while maintaining the personal responsibility and engagement to which these new beneficiaries are accustomed. Importantly, it will save our vital, well-loved, but soon-to-be-bankrupt Medicare program.

Medicare (and Social Security) eligibility age should rise as life expectancy rises.

9. Rapid, unsustainable spending growth in Medicaid, disability, and other federally mandated programs is overwhelming state budgets. In turn, this is devastating public school, university, and infrastructure appropriations.

   Federal appropriations for these programs should be converted to block grants to the states. This will cap out-of-control federal expenditures, and allow states freedom to innovate and achieve the massive productivity improvements needed to maintain these worthy programs.

   This is a proven strategy used by President Clinton in 1996 to moderate out-of-control welfare costs while maintaining program integrity.

10. Universal coverage requires a solid mandate with no exceptions. The young and healthy may not like it, but as

they age, they will wish to be included in the insured pool. Both fairness and affordability require that they join now, along with all citizens. Subsidies, varying by income, must be provided to those unable to purchase an average-cost plan, but each person should pay something.

In addition to the ten issues for which I suggest solutions, there is a massive cultural issue that must be addressed.

An estimated 70 percent of all health care costs in America result from self-inflicted causes, chiefly obesity, smoking, and alcohol/drug abuse. This is among the most difficult and worrisome of all health issues. A healthy population is a vital national interest, so incentives, negative as well as positive, must be crafted to alter such destructive behavior.

CONCLUSION

These suggested reforms are clear, simple, and build upon existing strengths. They are more easily understandable than the complex Affordable Care Act, and many are likely to be broadly accepted.

Investing 101

by David A. Jones

August 7, 2012

The first and critical step is to decide how much risk you wish to accept. If you're young and just beginning your career, saving a bit of money each month and investing it all in stocks makes sense. As you age and your family and responsibilities grow, it makes sense to become a bit more conservative and add some fixed-income securities (bonds) to your portfolio. Again, where possible, invest an equal amount of money each month rather than a large sum all at once. This way, you will purchase more shares when prices are low and fewer shares when prices are high. While you might get lucky and invest all when the market is low, you could just as easily do so when prices are high. Don't try to guess where the market is. There is absolutely no way to know.

Stocks can go up or down, but they represent real people producing products and services and always striving to succeed. That's why I like stocks.

When a company isn't doing well, there are real people who will try to change and turn things around.

Bonds pay a fixed rate of interest and a return of principal at maturity.

The risks in bonds are that interest rates generally may rise, and that will cause the value of your bond to decline, as potential buyers will purchase bonds with the new, higher rates. They will only purchase your bonds if you lower the price to the point where the rate of interest earned equals that on the new bonds.

Further, if there is any inflation during the period between bond purchase and maturity, your purchasing power will erode. That is, you will receive the face value of the bond at maturity, but the goods and services that the sum will then purchase will be less than at the date of purchase. Governments almost always debase their currency by allowing or creating inflation. For this reason, I would NEVER purchase a bond with a maturity longer than one year.

Still, when stock prices fall, as they did by about 50 percent in 2008, the value of having a portion of your assets in bonds becomes clear. They tend to hold their value and cushion the fall.

So, at our present point in life, I like an asset allocation of about 60 percent in stocks and 40 percent in very short-term, high-grade corporate bonds. Short-term US Treasury bonds are safe but pay almost no interest at this time.

My discussion today deals with liquid wealth or savings. We also have real estate investments through Main Street Realty and venture capital investments through Chrysalis, so our entire portfolio is quite diversified.

I divide the 60 percent stock portion of liquid wealth so that two-thirds are invested in US stocks through a low-cost Vanguard Total Stock Index Fund.

The other one-third is invested in a low-cost Vanguard Total International Stock Index Fund.

These stock index funds provide great diversity, as they include small, medium, and large companies in the US and throughout the world.

I believe Vanguard offers the lowest fees, clear reporting, and takes little time, thereby allowing an investor to have a life. It has worked for me and freed me to spend my time on activities of my choosing.

I hope this is helpful!

Love!
Dave/Dad

Accounting 101

Some Thoughts on the Balance Sheet,

Income Statement, and Cash Flow

by David A. Jones

1983, updated 2012

BALANCE SHEET

I. CURRENT ASSETS

    A. CASH − encumbered in any way? If so, it should be reclassified as noncurrent.

    B. ACCOUNTS RECEIVABLE − one of the two most important and trickiest assets in terms of possible danger (i.e., hidden time bombs—or potential troubles)

        1. Size in relation to revenues will show how fast receivables are being collected.

        2. Receivables should be aged, i.e., ranked by days outstanding, to see if some are growing old, a sure sign that they will be hard to collect.

        3. Basically, are they worth their stated amount?

    C. INVENTORY − the second danger area

        1. Size vs. revenue

        2. Any old, obsolete, or damaged goods included?

        3. Is it actually present and owned by the company? (Same comment re: accounts receivable.) Auditors independently confirm receivables with debtors

and observe the taking of physical inventory. These steps are mandatory if either asset is material (i.e. significant).

D.   Prepaid revenues and/or expenses must be analyzed to assure assignment to the proper period.

II.   PROPERTY AND EQUIPMENT

A.   Is it there, owned by the company, and actually in use?

B.   Are repairs and maintenance expenses added to the asset account rather than charged as an expense? This hypes earnings (which may help a manager earn a bonus) but creates a worthless asset, which will have to be written off (possibly) as depreciation expense over a long period. It also lowers tax deductions and increases taxes, which lowers cash flow and weakens the company.

C.   Is the depreciation policy realistic? Short lives increase tax deduction and cash flow and strengthen the company by returning cash sooner, when it's worth more (always consider the time value of money!!), but lower earnings and possibly current bonuses. Thus, some short-term thinkers will lengthen depreciable lives. (Humana, since 1973, has used a twenty-two-year life for new hospitals vs. forty-five years for HCA. Last year, we dropped to fifteen years, as allowed by the new tax law.)

III.   OTHER

A.   Probably goodwill, mainly. Check to be sure that it's written off over a realistic period. All issues same as property/ depreciation, so its write-off hits hard and most managers will use longest possible period (forty years, I believe).

B. Assets not used in the business (i.e., long-term notes received for the sale of assets). Are they present, owned, and worth stated value?

ON ASSET SIDE – Major issue is always: Are assets actually present, owned by the company, and worth stated value?

Canadair, a Canadian government-owned company, just incurred a write-off in excess of one billion dollars because it had been capitalizing expenses (i.e., adding them to asset accounts rather than treating them as expenses of the period in which they were incurred). Their stated and wildly optimistic intent was to charge such expenses against revenue to be generated by future airplane sales. Expenses included research and development costs, depreciation, and even administrative salaries. However, no bank would lend against such a worthless asset, so the company ran out of cash and had to confess that its profits reported over the prior five years were all false and its losses were actually staggering. The management was fired, and a political crisis was created for the Prime Minister.

LIABILITIES – Most issues concern classification, as current vs. long term. You must be sure that all liabilities are recorded, however, and there are some serious areas:

1. You need to be sure that all assets have been paid for (by reduction of some other asset or creation of liability— accounts payable, etc.), especially inventory which has arrived but has not been paid for, as where thirty or sixty days are allowed for payment.

2. Pension liabilities (related ones include accrued or accruable salaries, bonuses, vacation, and sick pay; any contractual liability to continue employment in the future, etc.). Many companies have promised (often formalized in union contracts) to pay for life, a pension whose amount is unknown because it's based on the last three to

five years' salary, or the highest salary. Also, occasionally the pension is indexed to the Consumer Price Index after retirement. This CPI provision is standard in federal pensions and prevalent in state and local government pensions (our public servants have raided the treasury and mortgaged the future, usually done either secretly or quietly), but this is rare in tax-paying entities.

These unfunded pension liabilities are estimated to exceed those of the Social Security system. It is distressingly common for management of publicly owned companies to underestimate the size of the liability, which often shows up only in a footnote.

This underestimation occurs because the liability is a function of several variables, each of which may be manipulated by the exercise of judgment. They include employee turnover rate, inflation in the future/compound rate of salary increase until retirement date, and compound rate of investment earnings on pension fund assets.

The pension plan described is called "defined benefit/final pay." When present, you must be extremely cynical as you analyze this liability, which will be understated more often than not.

Well-managed companies use either a "defined benefit/career average pay" (where the company takes no inflation/salary increase risk) or (as we now do at HUM) a "defined contribution plan" where an annual payment is made to each participant's personal account.

At retirement, the participant receives the account, including investment income, gains, and losses, and whatever income or annuity the sum generates.

"Defined benefit/final pay" plans, in effect, bet the company on unknown future events (similar to the government, they are almost always installed by managements who own little stock) and constitute one of the largest single areas of balance sheet risk (except in rare cases where management has reduced current earnings enough to cover those uncertain future costs).

The October 21, 2004 *New York Times* reported that General Motors had an unfunded health care liability, similar to "defined benefit" plans described above, of $63.4 billion, based on estimated future annual increases of 8.5 percent in health care costs. If such costs increase at 10 percent, the liability rises to $74.3 billion, and to $90 billion if the annual increase is 12 percent. This is a current example of a singularly unwise decision to bet the company on unknowable future events.

3. Other contingent liabilities, which may not be recorded – guaranties, open-ended obligations of any sort (such as Westinghouse's agreement to supply uranium to utilities at a fixed price while owning no supplies and being forced to purchase at a market price greatly above sales price). A short sale of stock is another example. A stock's price can drop to zero, limiting potential profit to the current price, but it can rise to infinity. Currency and commodity speculation, etc., are additional examples. Written assurances from management and inside and outside attorneys are helpful but don't stop fraud.

INCOME STATEMENT

These issues are just the other side of the balance sheet. Management will seek to inflate accounts receivable and inventory (i.e., turn expenses into bogus assets), minimize or omit expenses (which would otherwise show up as liabilities), minimize depreciation and amortization (of goodwill), and generally try to shove today's problems into the future to be dealt with by successor management. Analogies are federal entitlement programs such as Social Security and Medicare, which create benefits without passing an equal, concurrent tax increase to pay for them. The burden is simply pushed forward to the next generation.

Be constantly vigilant for optimism in all accounts, balance sheet and income statement, which are really two sides of the same coin.

Two additional areas of concern have surfaced in the time since these thoughts were first written. They are closely related and are actually just new approaches to placing revenues/expenses in appropriate periods.

First, The Big Bath: CEOs, especially new ones, sometimes clean up a balance sheet by taking a large charge on the income statement of the period (The Big Bath) for assets deemed to be worth less than their book value. Then, in subsequent accounting periods, the asset values miraculously improve, creating instant earnings for a chosen future period, probably one for which the executive receives a bonus. Such manufactured earnings should be excluded from any bonus arrangements, and boards and their compensation committees must be vigilant in providing oversight.

Second, Acquisition Accounting: In acquisitions, the selling company management and shareholders are primarily interested in the purchase price. If they receive cash, they are largely indifferent to acquisition accounting. If they receive stock in the surviving entity, they may become willing accomplices in major write-downs of their assets at the time of acquisition.

This is just another form of The Big Bath, allowing the surviving company to "discover" significant value in written-down assets, producing bogus earnings in a convenient future period. This ploy also requires strong board oversight.

CASH FLOW

Analyzing cash flow is necessary to determine the quality of reported net income. Since bogus profits can be generated by

1.   Inflating accounts receivable and inventory
2.   Listing expenses as assets
3.   Minimizing depreciation and amortization

it's important to follow the cash.

Cash can come from operations, borrowing, sale of assets, or issuance of new shares. These are all legitimate sources of cash, but only cash from operations should be used to verify the legitimacy of reported earnings.

If cash from operations is less than reported income, the culprit is likely to be one of the three bogus profit sources listed above.

Trust, but verify!

A final thought—a balance sheet is a still picture of an enterprise in motion. At life's end, accounting for an enterprise is easy because all revenues and costs are known. Along the way, many problems and uncertainties arise in seeking to assign revenues and matching expenses to the proper time segment, which is arbitrary (a month or year, normally). So, opportunities exist (or can be created) to accelerate or delay both revenues and expenses, so be alert!

Points of Interest

A Timeline

1931   Elsie Jones gives birth to her second child, David, in Louisville, on August 7. David is born into difficult circumstances. The Depression will eventually leave his father, Evan Logan Jones, jobless for four years. Elsie works nights at a laundry to support the family. Fortunes improve when Logan lands a job across the river in Indiana, building boats for World War II.

1949   David joins his older brother and role model, Logan Jones, Jr., in Golden Gloves boxing. They are trained by Joe Martin, the Louisville police officer who later trains Cassius Clay, a.k.a. Muhammad Ali.

1949-1950   A straight-A student, Jones graduates from Male High School with the motivation, but not the means, to go to college. He works for a year in tobacco markets in the South.

1950-1954   Jones attends the University of Louisville on a Navy ROTC scholarship, supplementing his income by working at gas stations, the post office, a flower shop, and the W. T. Grant variety store. He also works for an accountant, Irv Wasserman. He is named Outstanding Senior at U of L. David meets Betty Ashbury, a U of L freshman and the daughter of a pharmacist and a teacher. She is named the school's Outstanding Freshman Woman.

1954-57   After graduating with an accounting degree, Jones commissions into the Navy. Ensign Jones gets a forty-eight-hour pass to travel from his duty station in Athens, Georgia, to marry Betty in Louisville on July 24, 1954. Betty promptly enrolls at the University of Georgia, studying, among other things, bacteriology. In November Jones passes the CPA exam.

Jones is promoted to lieutenant junior grade, handling supplies, navigation duties, and currency exchange in foreign ports. His tours include the Mediterranean, the Caribbean, the Middle East, Africa, India, and Guantanamo Bay, Cuba. Stateside, he serves in Athens; Norfolk, Virginia; and Key West, Florida.

1957–60   Jones attends and graduates from Yale Law School. He supplements his monthly GI Bill stipend of $110 by teaching accounting and working for Irv Lasky, CPA. Betty works, too, running a nursery for the children of graduate students.

1960   The Joneses—now with two children, David, Jr. and Susan—return to Louisville. David takes a job with the law firm of Wyatt Grafton & Sloss for $425 a month and becomes friends with another young lawyer in the firm, Wendell Cherry. Jones teaches nights at U of L.

1961   The Joneses' third child, Dan, is born. Jones and Cherry borrow $1,000 each and recruit four other investors to build a nursing home. Their company, incorporated on

August 18 as Wendav and quickly renamed Heritage House, will evolve into Humana.

1967   The Joneses' fourth child, Matthew, is born. Heritage House is renamed Extendicare.

1968   Extendicare completes its initial public offering in January.

1969   Jones, Cherry, and three other young Louisvillians buy the Kentucky Colonels of the American Basketball Association for $500,000. They sell the team five years later for $2.5 million. Their nursing home company has become the largest in the nation.

1971   The Joneses' fifth child, Carol, is born.

1972   Jones and Cherry sell the nursing homes to concentrate on hospitals.

1982   Jones joins the board of Abbott Laboratories, serving until 2003, when he retires as lead director.

1985   Humana's 417-foot-tall headquarters opens. Jones says, "For the first time in the history of the company, Humana is taken seriously in its hometown, not because of all the things we had done that were truly helpful, but because of our new building. There's something about architecture, the solidity of it." *Time* magazine will later name the Humana tower one of the ten best buildings of the 1980s.

1986   David and Betty are co-founders of the Joy Luck Book Club, a convivial, contentious gathering that meets eight times a year. David eventually earns the dubious and enduring honor of having recommended the worst book in the club's thirty-two-year history: Leon Uris's *Mitla Pass.*

1988   Elsie Thurman Jones, Jones's revered mother, dies on September 5, at age seventy-eight.

1990   President George Herbert Walker Bush calls Jones and asks him to help rebuild the health care systems of poor and despairing Eastern European nations just freed from the Iron Curtain. Jones agrees and leads a group of ten health care colleagues to Bucharest, Romania, launching the sixteen-year Romania Assistance Project, which sends hundreds of volunteer US clinicians to train and support Romanian counterparts.

1991   At 2:30 a.m. on February 25, two Marines in full dress uniform knock on the Jones family's door. Son Matt, a Marine lieutenant, has been wounded during Operation Desert Storm. David and Betty visit him as he recuperates from his wounds in Germany and Washington, DC.

1991   Wendell Cherry dies of lung cancer on July 16. He is fifty-five.

1993   Humana splits into two separate, publicly traded companies: a stable, profitable hospital company and a small but growing insurance company that has not yet earned a profit. Jones chooses to lead the insurance business, believing it has an exciting future. The insurance company retains the Humana name.

2001   On September 11, Jones and twenty-three Humana colleagues are just down the street when terrorists crash two passenger jets into New York's World Trade Center, felling two towers and killing nearly three thousand people. Jones, seventy, leads his team to safety and manages its safe return to Louisville on buses.

2004   Jones becomes founding chairman of Hospira (NYSE HSP), a new Illinois-based company created by Abbott Laboratories. Hospira focuses on generic injectable drugs and biosimilars, drugs made from a human cell.

2004-19   Jones joins son Dan in creating the almost four thousand-acre Parklands of Floyds Fork, a hymn to nature on Louisville's eastern edge. They work together for more than fifteen years, with Dan leading the effort and Jones pitching in to help raise $125 million for land acquisition and construction.

2005   Jones retires—without fanfare—from Humana, one of the nation's most successful and admired companies.

2019   David and Betty mark their sixty-fifth wedding anniversary on July 24. On August 16, Betty dies, at age eighty-six. David dies thirty-three days later, on September 18, at eighty-eight.

Acknowledgements

T his book is my father's story. His voice is loud and clear, as if he were still here and speaking to us. But that voice could not have come through without Bob Hill's skill as both storyteller and story-collector, which he applied to help Dad voice his story and to encourage the many friends and family members Bob interviewed to share theirs. Dad loved sharing his stories with Bob and hearing Bob's stories in return, and I'll be forever grateful to Bob for sparking so much joy. They had a great partnership, which from my vantage point also looked like a lot of fun.

My own partner in this effort has been Jill Johnson Keeney, editor extraordinaire but so much more. Before Dad died, he asked me to see his draft through to publication, with a focus on sharing the book with family and friends – whether anyone else was interested or not. It took a good while before I could start this process, and while Jill didn't exactly take me by the scruff of the neck and shake me, there was something like that. She knew Dad professionally from her days at the *Courier Journal*, Louisville's newspaper, when they'd sparred a bit, and then from years at Humana helping to tell the company's story. She also knew both my parents personally, as she and her husband, Doug, were in their wonderful book club for a number of years. Jill knew the context, but to it brought unstinting focus on clarity and the details that made publication possible.

I'm also grateful to Julia Comer, who designed the book. She did a beautiful job as a professional, but also took on this project with special intensity as a Romanian immigrant to Louisville who had met Dad and knew my parents' passion for their work in Romania. Dad always tried to work at the intersection of passion and competence, and Julia poured both into this book.

This book's design also benefited from the fine work of several Louisville photographers. Thank you to Bob Hower and Ted Wathen of Quadrant Photography, to John Nation, and to a number of former *Courier Journal* photographers whose work we were able to access through the Barry Bingham, Jr. Collection at the University of Louisville Archives and Special Collections.

Special thanks to the team at Main Street Realty, both during the publishing process and before Dad passed. Debbie Alexander, Rosanne Miller, Wanda Ryan, Bryan Johnson, and others brought caring, intensity in getting things done, institutional memory, and great record-keeping to this project, as they had to so many others before.

Early on in the process, when Dad and Bob had completed their first draft, Dad asked a few people who knew him and also knew about writing and publishing to read and critique the book. They were me, my brother Dan, Tom Noland, and Doug Keeney. Doug also provided publishing advice along the way.

Sadly, Tom was diagnosed with a rare cancer and died while we were editing this book. I missed the contributions he no doubt would have made. Mom always said Tom was the only person she trusted to speak for Dad.

C. Ray Hall, one of Bob's longtime colleagues at the *Courier Journal,* was also an important part of the process, helping Bob turn the interviews into transcripts and the ideas into drafts.

Dad always said there was nothing done in other places that couldn't be done in Louisville as well. This book shows that is true with publishing. Thank you to Old Stone Press for leading me through the publishing process, with all its details, deadlines, and unexpected twists and turns.

Finally, Dad did not include in his narrative all the people who were part of the story. He died before the give and take of the process got to, "Who's missing?" But there's one omission I'm certain he would have rectified. This falls in the sphere of home life, where his concern for the privacy of his family was intense. The hardest issues I heard discussed around my parents' kitchen table involved his strongly extroverted drive to act as publicly as necessary to change what he thought needed changing, and other family members' equally strong desire to live their own lives, some of them quieter.

Had Dad been alive to write these acknowledgments, he certainly would have thanked the colleagues who worked in his house. On his behalf I acknowledge with deep gratitude my parents' domestic team, who contributed so much to their lives and to their children's: Nelontine Williamson, Susie and Richard Allen, Mary and Paul Beamus, Kim Delaney, Ken Mayberry, and Tony Williams. Their stability, kindness and hard work gave my parents time to parent and to live their value of putting family first.

And, of course, special thanks to my colleague Debbie Hammer, whose unbreakable calm, ceaseless attention to detail, and prodding sense of humor helped all of this come together. And to my wife, Mary Gwen Wheeler, for wise, patient counsel on this project, and for the great adventure we're sharing.

DAVID A. JONES, JR.

June 2023

INDEX